IMAGES
of America

OAKLAND

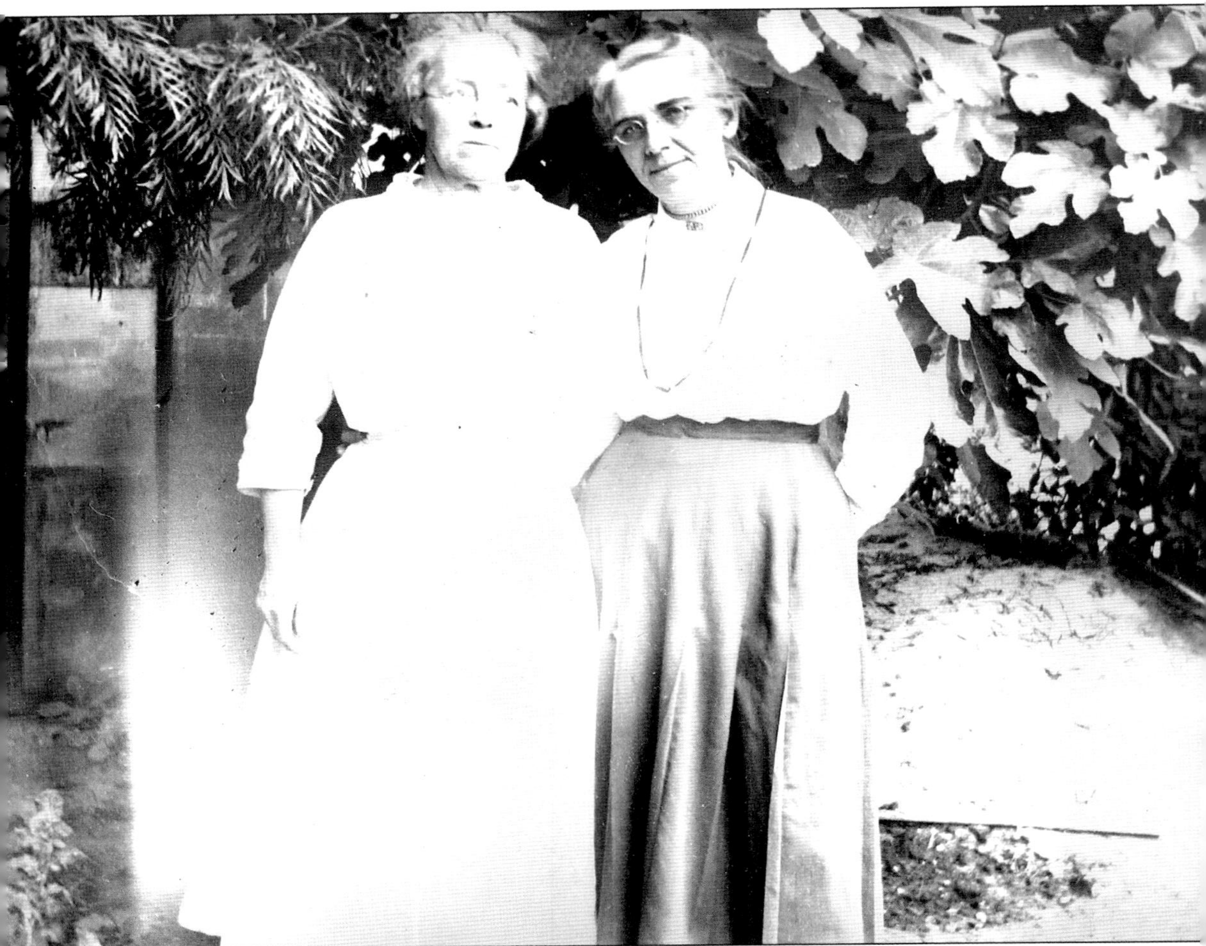

Alice Ann Manter was a professional photographer who chronicled life in Oakland in the early years of the 20th century. Without her photographs, many of which were made into postcards, this book would have been less complete. Manter is shown on the right wearing glasses. The woman on the left is her cousin Annie Van Huesin of Sacramento, California.

IMAGES
of America

OAKLAND

Oakland Area Historical Society

ARCADIA
PUBLISHING

ISBN 978-0-7385-3582-1

Published by Arcadia Publishing,
Charleston, South Carolina

Printed in the United States of America

Library of Congress Catalog Card Number: 2004101909

For all general information, contact Arcadia Publishing:
Telephone 843-853-2070
Fax 843-853-0044
E-mail sales@arcadiapublishing.com
For customer service and orders:
Toll-free 1-888-313-2665

Visit us on the Internet at www.arcadiapublishing.com

To the memories of Alice Manter and Lucile Small and to the passionate work of Ruth (Wheeler) Wood and Alberta Porter.

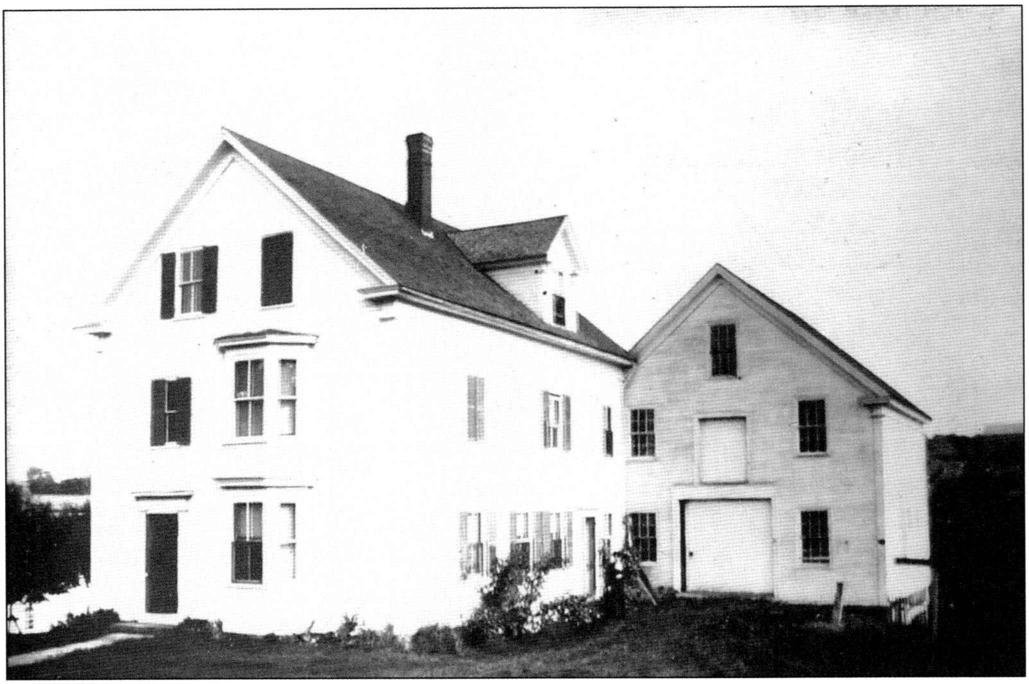

This was the home of local photographer Alice Manter. The house, which no longer exists, was located on Water Street. It was later occupied by Sargie Warren.

CONTENTS

ACKNOWLEDGMENTS

Although I have written the text and organized the photographs here, this book would not have been possible if four people in particular had not been so involved and committed to the history of the town. The first is local photographer Alice Ann Manter. The second person is Lucile Small, a descendant of many early settlers, an avid and competent genealogist, and a donor of many photographs to the Oakland Area Historical Society. Lucile died on March 22, 2004, and her passing will be a sore loss for all who care about this town. The third person is a lifelong friend of Lucile, Ruth (Wheeler) Wood, who is the curator of our museum and is, as Lucile was, a true treasure to the town of Oakland. Finally, Alberta Porter, president of the historical society, was the driving force behind getting these pages into print. She is an active contributor for a new generation of Oakland citizens. These women, who are so important to the history of the town, have contributed so much to this book.

—Michael J. Denis
Vice President, Oakland Area Historical Society
April 2004

Introduction

The casual traveler driving today through the town of Oakland could hardly guess what the town was like 100 years ago. Many towns have kept their original purposes, either as farming communities, manufacturing centers, or commercial areas, but Oakland has shed several skins in its more than 200 years of settled life.

Beginning in the late 1700s as a small farming community that was part of the large town of Winslow, Lincoln County, Massachusetts, the town remained mostly farmland and woods for half a century. There were the usual small mills—gristmills, sawmills, and the like—but the town primarily produced food for its residents, sometimes with a small surplus for local markets.

The mid-1800s brought change. The first real factory was built in this area c. 1842; by then, Oakland was part of the town of Waterville, which had separated from Winslow in 1802. The factory in question was the first to produce edge tools—cutting tools for the farmer and lumberman, such as axes, scythes, sickles, and other sharp instruments. Several other edge-tool factories soon followed. Portions of the town's main watercourse, Messalonskee Stream (sometimes called Emerson's Stream), were dammed, producing abundant waterpower for many more small factories. It was said that Messalonskee Stream, though significantly smaller than the nearby Kennebec River, produced nearly as much waterpower because of its waterfalls. Of particular importance was the Cascade, a 100-foot waterfall located just outside the downtown area.

With the arrival of the railroad in 1849, the village's products could now be sent east toward Bangor and south toward Portland and Boston. Industry boomed. Axe factories were joined by woolen mills, and by the 1870s, there were nearly as many people working in the industries as there were on the farms. Oakland had just shed its first skin.

At the time, Waterville was divided into two villages. The village by the Kennebec (known today as Waterville) was the quiet, residential area, while the western village (known today as Oakland) was the industrial part of town. Differences in interests between the two villages caused them to separate in 1873, and the west village became West Waterville. The name was changed to Oakland in 1883, and the new town started out on its own with little visible connection to its parent town.

From the early 1900s through the period just after World War II, Oakland produced more axes, scythes, and other edge tools than any town on earth. The constant sound of the trip hammers pounding hot metal into axe heads could be heard, and the hundreds of workers grinding edges, painting handles, stoking coal or charcoal furnaces, and boxing and labeling the final product made Oakland a bustling industrial community. Waterpower also made the production of electricity possible, and a small electric company was formed in Oakland. By 1902, that company became Central Maine Power Company (CMP), which today is the largest electric utility in Maine.

In the meantime, the recreational assets of the town were just being realized. More people had leisure time and the money to enjoy it. The creation of the Somerset Railroad c. 1870 and, later, the extension of the electric street railway by CMP from Waterville into Oakland, made it easy for people "from away" to come to Oakland, either to enjoy the lakes in the area or to use Oakland as a jumping-off point for the resort area of Moosehead Lake, where the Somerset Railway eventually ran.

With the end of World War II, demand for the high-quality tools that Oakland workers produced fell, and competition from cheaper foreign tools spelled the end for all of Oakland's axe factories. One by one, they shut their doors; the trip hammers went silent, and the mill whistle no longer called workers. The woolen mills also disappeared, the final straw being the closing of the Cascade Woolen Mill in the 1990s. It was time for Oakland to shed another skin, its industrial skin, in favor of a new recreational and commercial one.

Today, Oakland is a quiet suburban town for most of the year. Its downtown, although it is undergoing renovation and restoration, does not draw the shoppers it once did. Its factories, now numbered on one hand, hire only tens of workers instead of hundreds. Its farms, now also able to be counted on one hand, supply only a tiny fraction of the food they once produced. Yet despite all the changes that have taken place over the past 200 years, today Oakland is a community that is rebuilding itself. It is transforming itself again for the 21st century and preparing for what this new century will bring.

In an age when most women were subservient to their husbands, fathers, brothers, or sons, Alice Ann Manter was a standout. Manter was born on March 30, 1857; she died in 1917. She was a music teacher, an artist, and a professional photographer. Her photographs, many of which were made into postcards, were taken mostly from 1906 to 1917, although some were dated as early as 1898. The postcards themselves are readily identifiable due to the white space on the right side of the photograph and the gold inscriptions.

Manter and her family, including her father, Daniel E. Manter (1824–1901), her mother, Sophronia F. (Bailey) Manter, (1828–1917), and an older brother, George Washington Manter, lived in Sidney, Maine, before moving to Oakland in 1887. According to her great-niece, Ruby Manter Easton of Andover, Massachusetts, Alice Manter attended what is now the University of Maine at Farmington and was a teacher for a time. As a professional, she photographed much of Maine, turning many of her works into the postcards used in this book. She never married, though there is speculation about a romantic interest. The town of Oakland is indebted to this intrepid photographer for her chronicling of the everyday life of the town. It is with genuine respect that the Oakland Area Historical Society shares many of the Manter photographs.

—Michael J Denis
Vice President, Oakland Area Historical Society
April 2004

One

THE AXE AND SCYTHE INDUSTRY

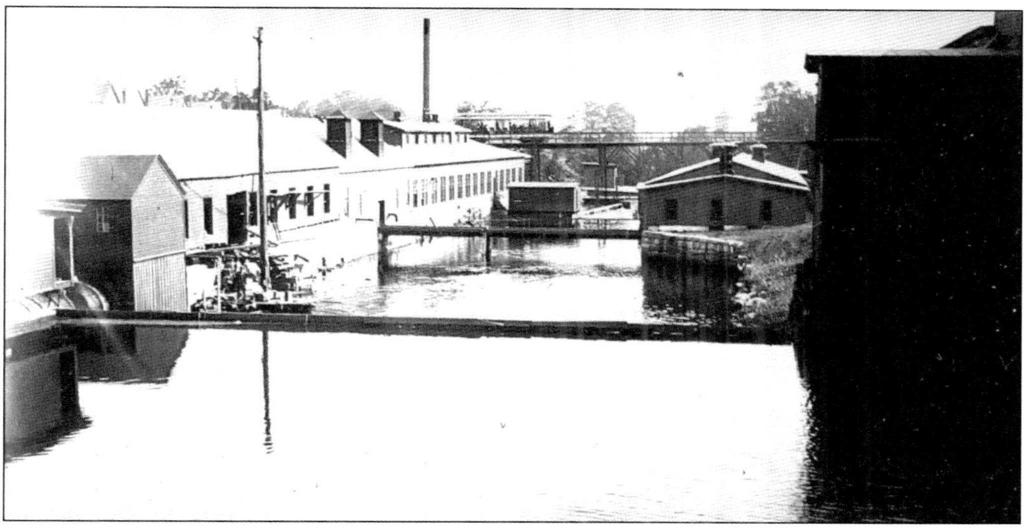

This card shows the Dunn Edge Tool Company, looking north from the present-day Kennedy Memorial Drive Bridge. A Waterville, Fairfield & Oakland streetcar crosses on the trestle over the stream (top center of the photograph). Incorporated in 1857, the Dunn Edge Tool Company (DET) was established and organized by Reuben B. Dunn. It manufactured axes, scythes, hay knives, and grass hooks. The improved Cyclone knife made by DET in 1889 was the most efficient tool of its kind. DET continued to operate until 1920, and in 1921, it was sold to Seymour Manufacturing Company. Seymour, in turn, sold in 1923 to North Wayne Tool Company, which stayed in business until 1967.

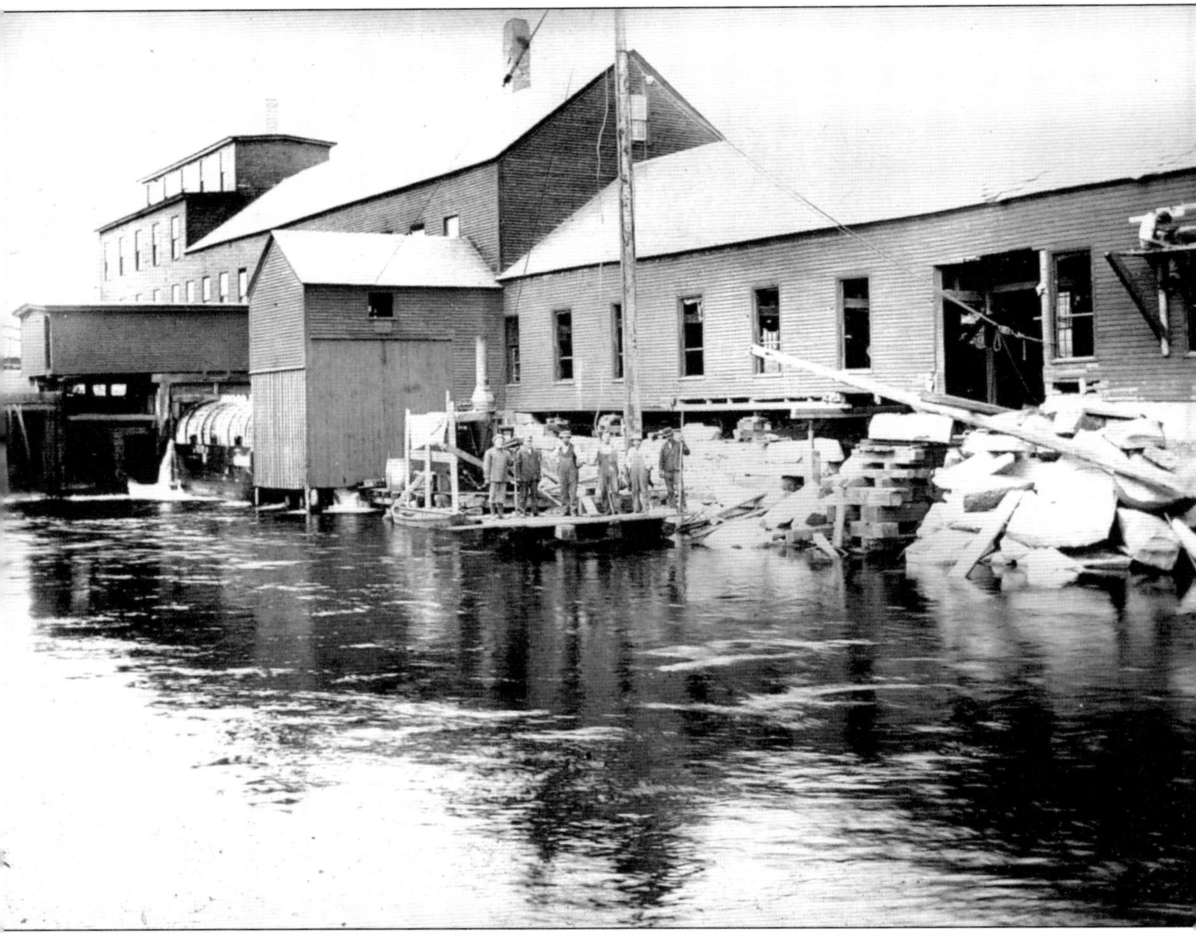

This photograph shows the Scythe Shop, looking upstream toward the southwest. Until the years after World War II, Oakland produced more scythes, axes, and other edge tools than any other place on earth.

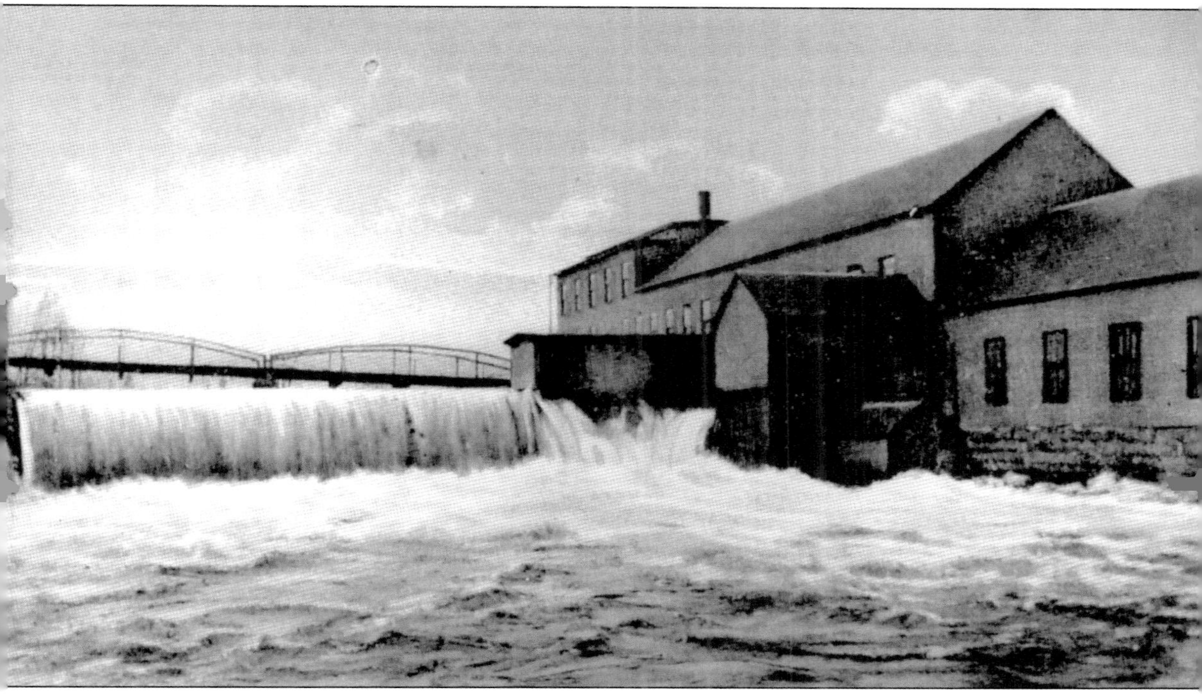

This view is of the west side of Messalonskee Stream, looking southwest.

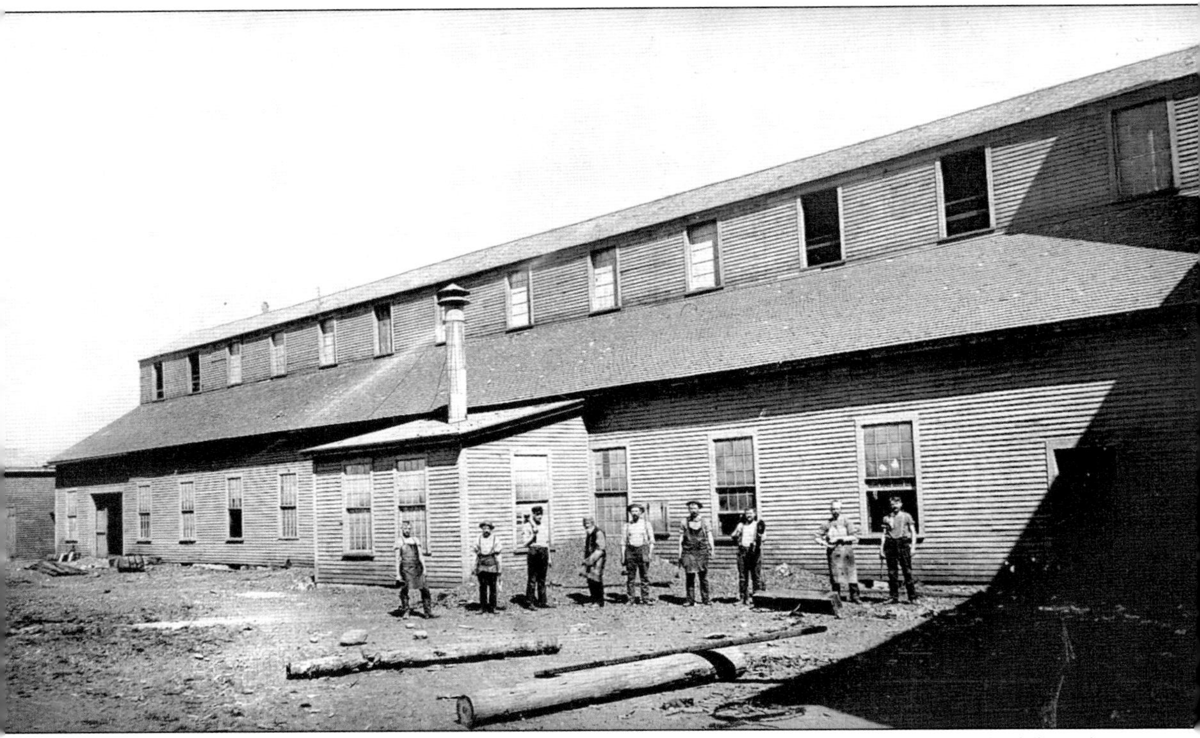

None of the Dunn Edge Tool Company buildings is left today, attesting to the end of the edge-tool industry in the town.

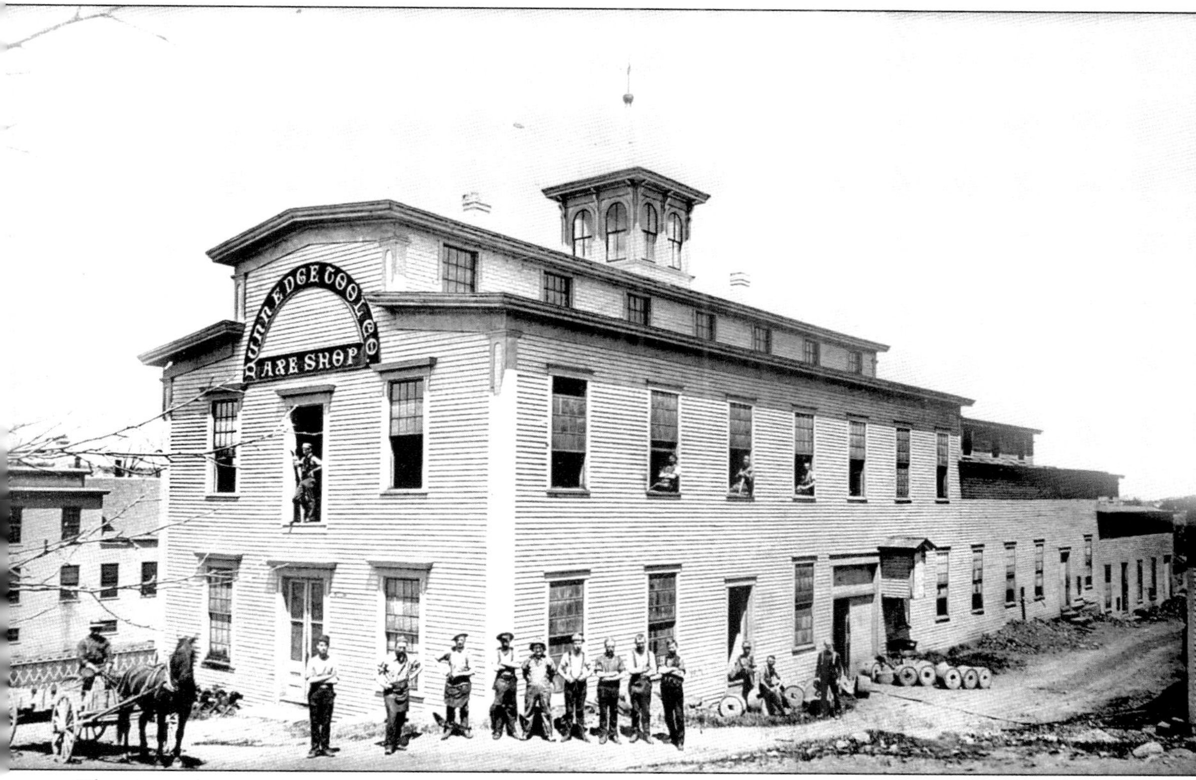

The Axe Shop at the Dunn Edge Tool Company was located on the east side of Messalonskee Stream. The Dunn Edge Tool Company became the North Wayne Tool Company c. 1922 and was effectively out of business by the 1960s, when the last of the buildings burned. The Axe Shop was owned by the King Axe and Tool Company in 1926 and was located on the Cornforth Dam.

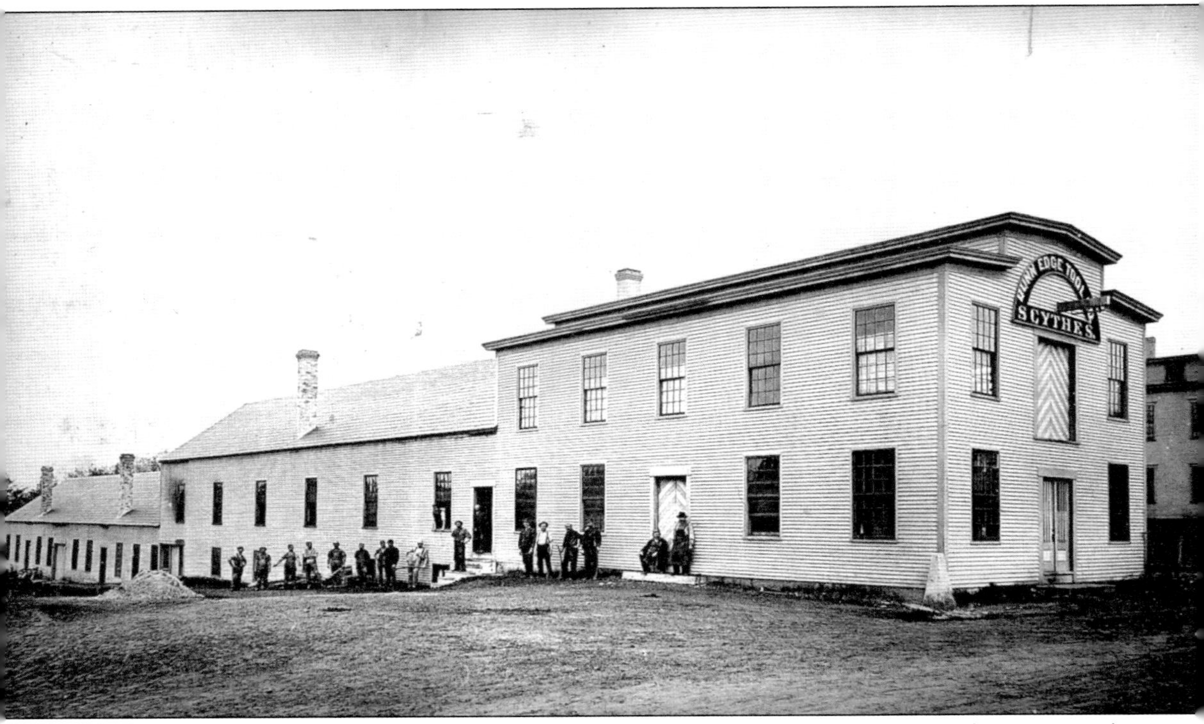

This photograph shows the Scythe Shop at the Dunn Edge Tool Company. Scythes were made in Oakland beginning in the 1840s, when the town was still part of Waterville. The length of the fall of water on Messalonskee Stream was greater in Oakland than the fall on the Kennebec River at Waterville, although the volume of water was less.

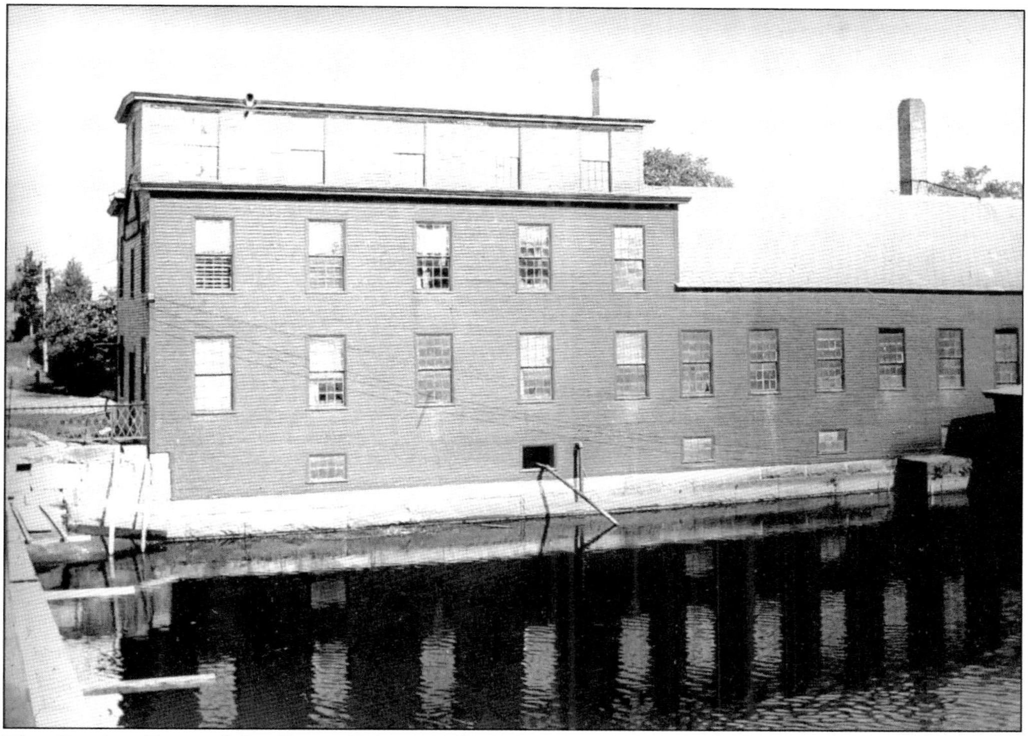

The Scythe Shop of the Dunn Edge Tool Company stood on the west side of Messalonskee Stream between the present town office and the stream.

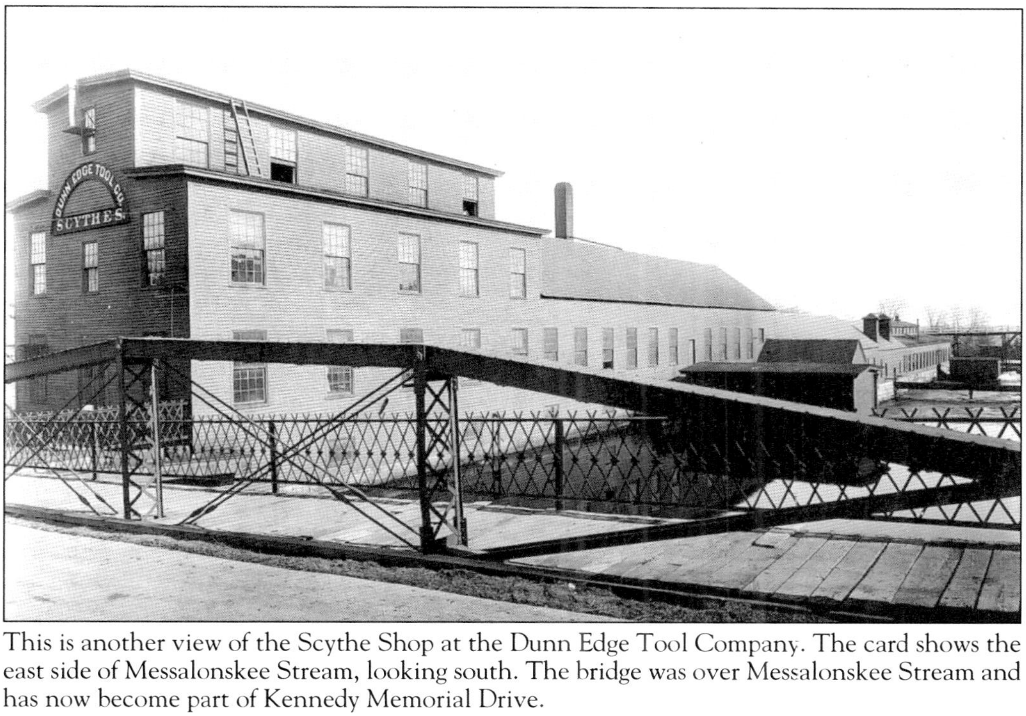

This is another view of the Scythe Shop at the Dunn Edge Tool Company. The card shows the east side of Messalonskee Stream, looking south. The bridge was over Messalonskee Stream and has now become part of Kennedy Memorial Drive.

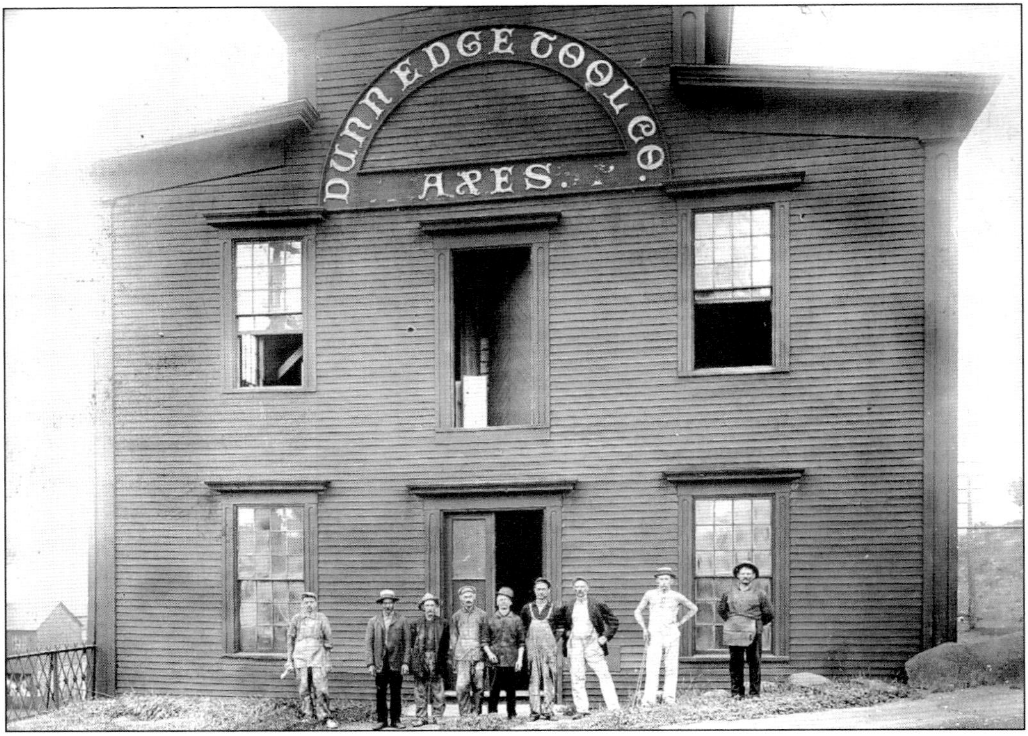

This is the axe building, which stood on the east side of Messalonskee Stream, just north of present-day Kennedy Memorial Drive.

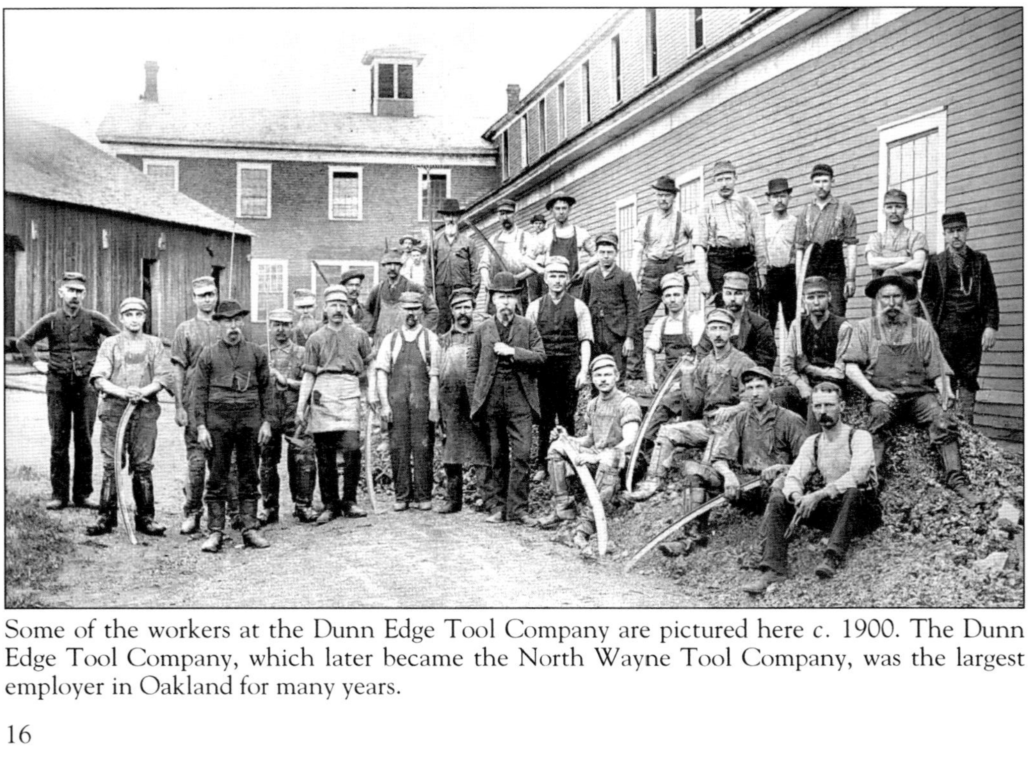

Some of the workers at the Dunn Edge Tool Company are pictured here *c.* 1900. The Dunn Edge Tool Company, which later became the North Wayne Tool Company, was the largest employer in Oakland for many years.

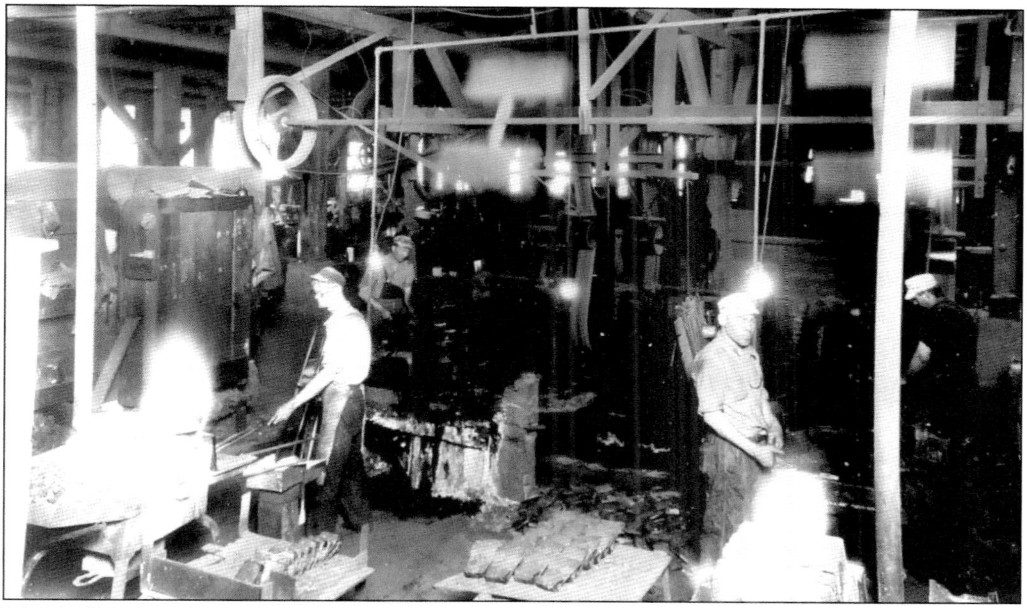

The Spiller Axe Company was another of the many tool producers in Oakland. Steel-forged axe heads can be seen at the bottom center of this photograph. Mark Spiller moved to Oakland in 1880. In 1902, he worked for Emerson & Stevens making axes; he specialized in tempering the tools, which were completely hand-hammered and handmade. His eldest son, Norman, became an axe maker. In 1926, the two purchased land on the Messalonskee River, better known as Emerson's Stream, and formed a company known as M. D. Spiller & Son. In 1937, the name changed to Spiller Axe & Tool Company. At the time, it had 10 full-time employees making 60 dozen axes per week. Norman's son, Harold F., then 19 years old, also joined the company, which continued to operate until 1965.

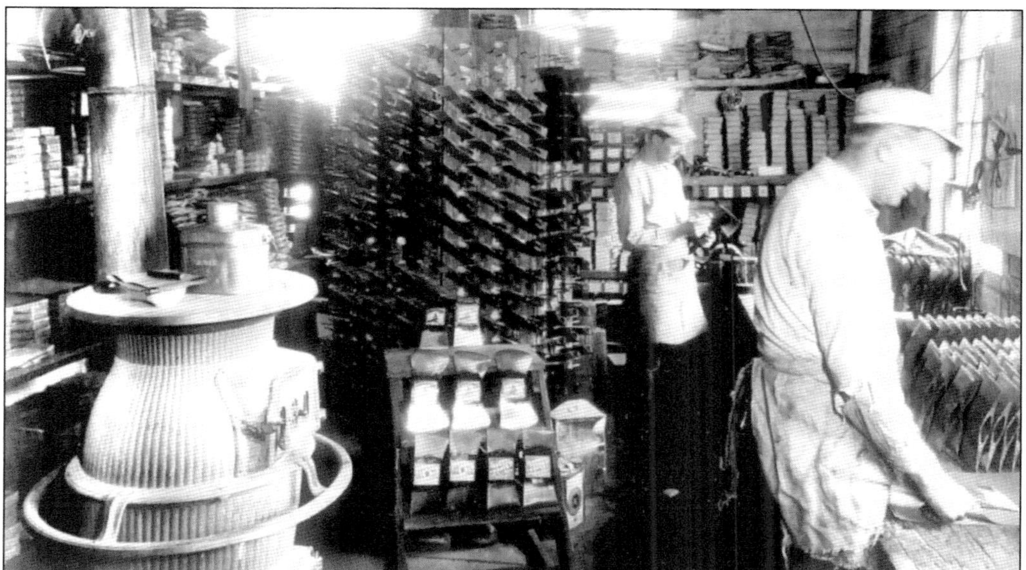

The finished product, seen at the center of the photograph, is marked, packaged, and ready for sale.

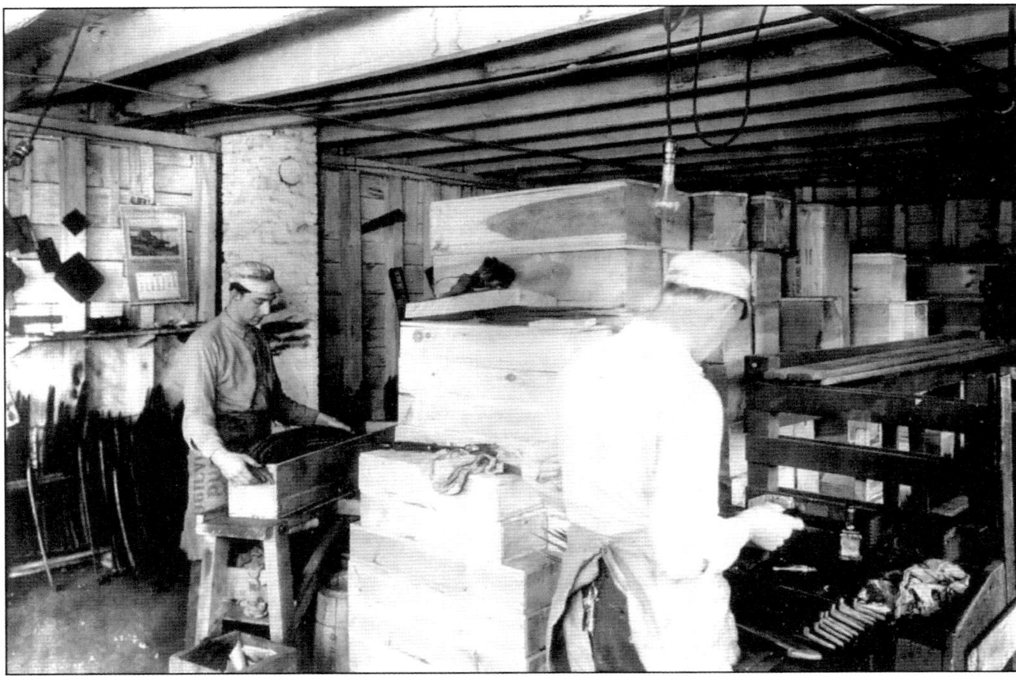

In this photograph, axes are being packed in preparation for shipping.

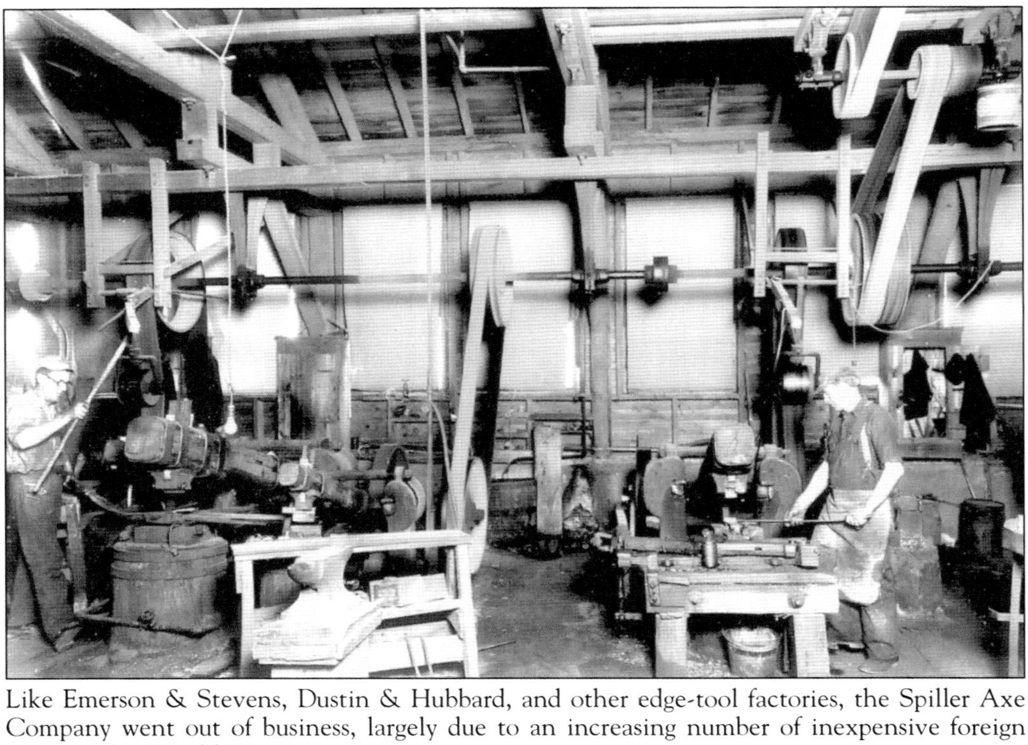

Like Emerson & Stevens, Dustin & Hubbard, and other edge-tool factories, the Spiller Axe Company went out of business, largely due to an increasing number of inexpensive foreign imports after World War II.

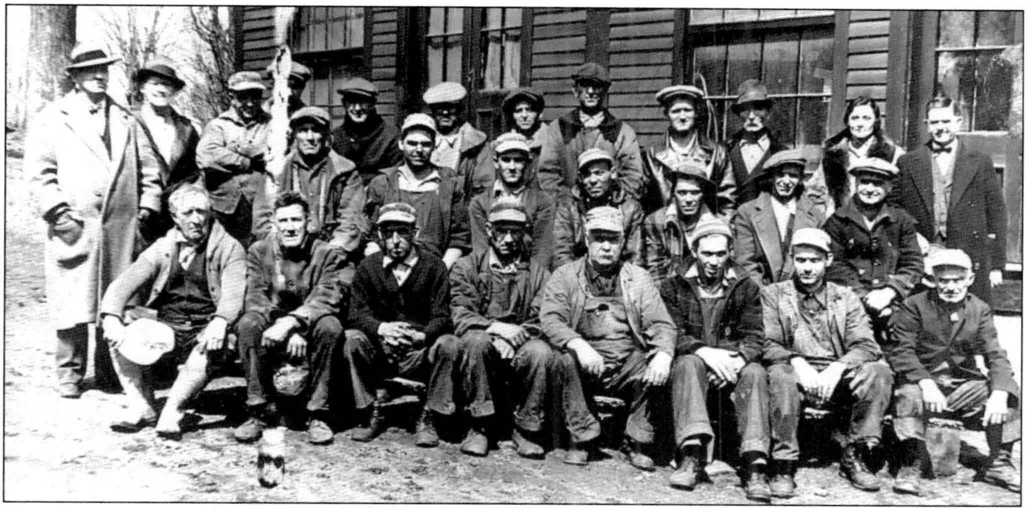

Seen here are employees at Emerson & Stevens Manufacturing Company c. 1930. They are, from left to right, as follows: (first row) Harry Giberson, Edgar ?, Ray Whitaker, Scott Mitchell, Rodney Barrett, Cecil Phair, Roy Barrett, and Bill Penny; (second row) Cecil Pulcifur, "Furpo" Robinson, Everett Watson, Harold Pulcifur, Perlie Pulcifur, unidentified, and Emile Dubois; (third row) Harry Hatfield, Harold York, two unidentified people, Joseph Jordan, Louis Crowel, unidentified, Norman Spiller, Homer Lothrop, Mark Spiller, Helen Oliver, and Ralph Stowell.

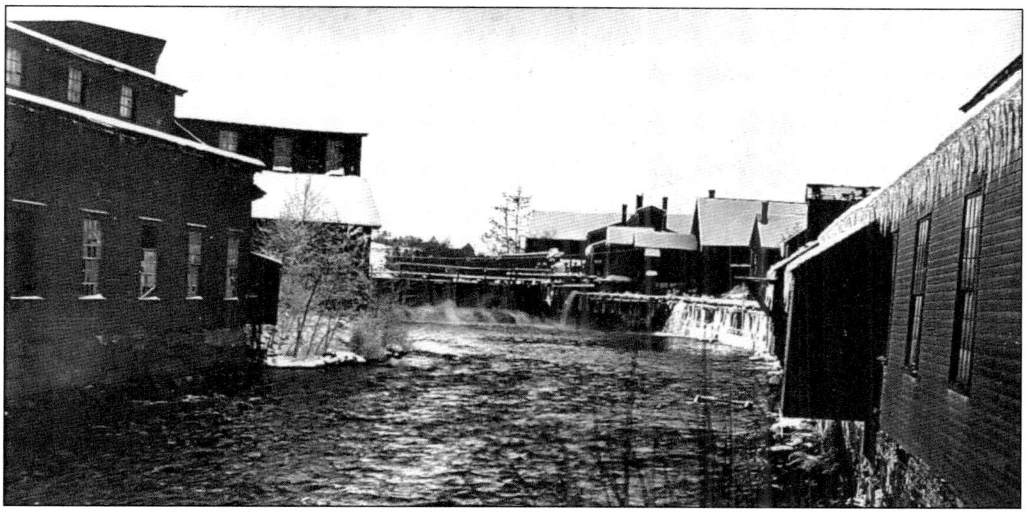

This photograph of the Emerson & Stevens Manufacturing Company was taken from the School Street Bridge c. 1910. Emerson & Stevens, which went into business c. 1870, was located along both sides of Messalonskee Stream and on both sides of the School Street Bridge. The company was founded in 1870 by Luther Dorr Emerson, Joseph E. Stevens, W. R. Pinkham, and George W. Stevens. It was located on Lord's Dam, which was named for Daniel B. Lord, who had an axe factory near this location in 1850. Axe brands produced by Emerson & Stevens included the Pioneer, the Diamond, the Lumberman's Pride, the Pine Tree, and the Cock of the Woods. The brands of scythes included the best grades, such as the Diamond, the Hurricane, the Smuggler, and the All Hammered, and the cheaper grades, such as the Black Clipper, the Green Clipper, and the Red Clipper.

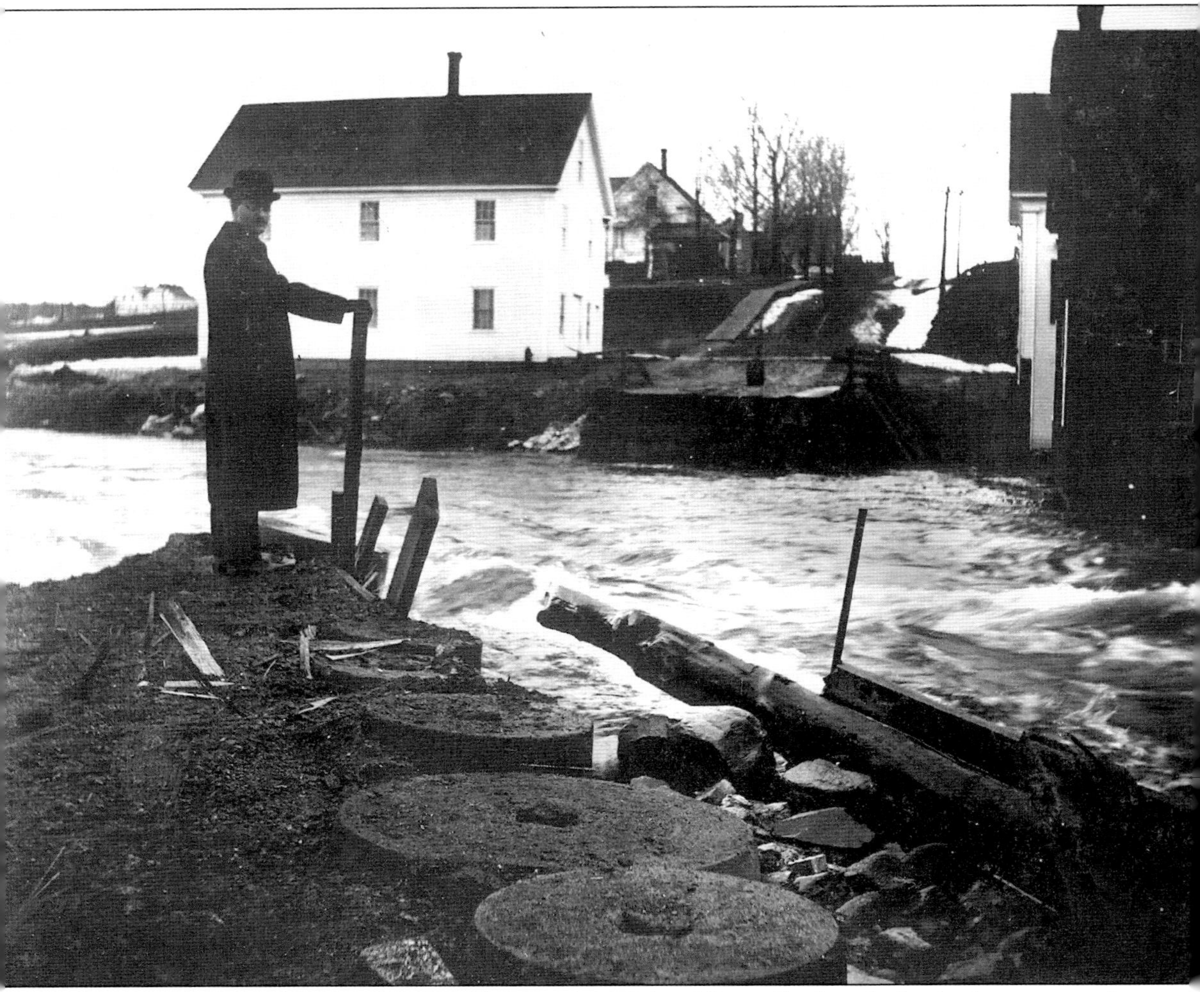

In this *c.* 1900 photograph believed to be of the School Street Bridge, the bridge has apparently washed away—a frequent occurrence in the 1800s—or is being replaced. According to town reports, the School Street Bridge was replaced in 1900. This view, looking east toward Water Street, may show the area near that bridge. The grindstones in the foreground were probably used in an edge-tool factory, as the Emerson & Stevens Manufacturing Company was located very near where the well-dressed gentleman stands.

Two

TRANSPORTATION

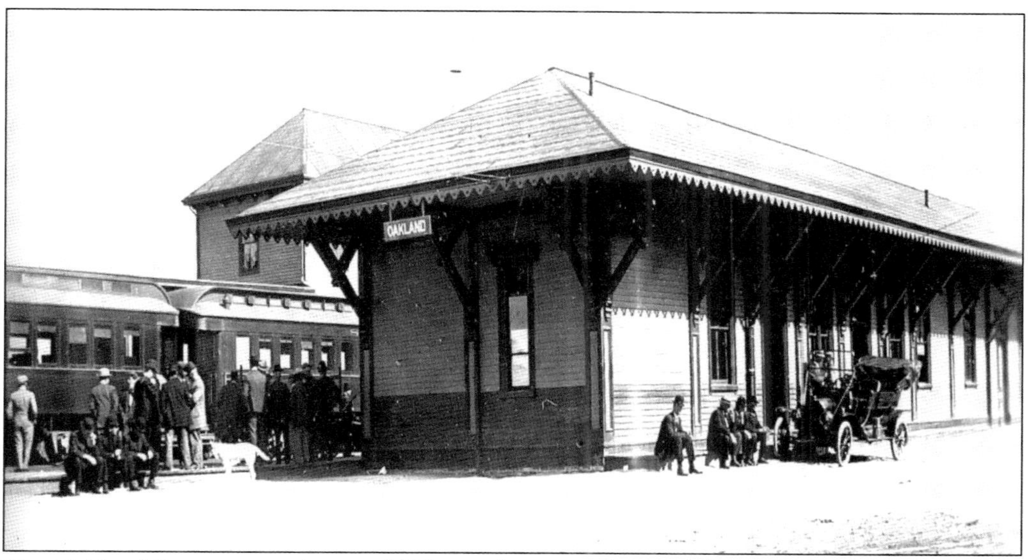

The Oakland Station, seen here *c.* 1905, stood just northeast of the junction of Main and Oak Streets. In the rear was the freight office (which appears in another photograph on page 23). The Androscoggin & Kennebec Railroad came through West Waterville, now Oakland, in December 1849; it was bought out by the Maine Central Railroad in 1881. Downtown had been located near the lake, but when the railroad came through, the area around the depot developed and became the new downtown. Passenger trains ran through Oakland until 1957. In 1850, the cost for a ticket to Waterville was 15¢.

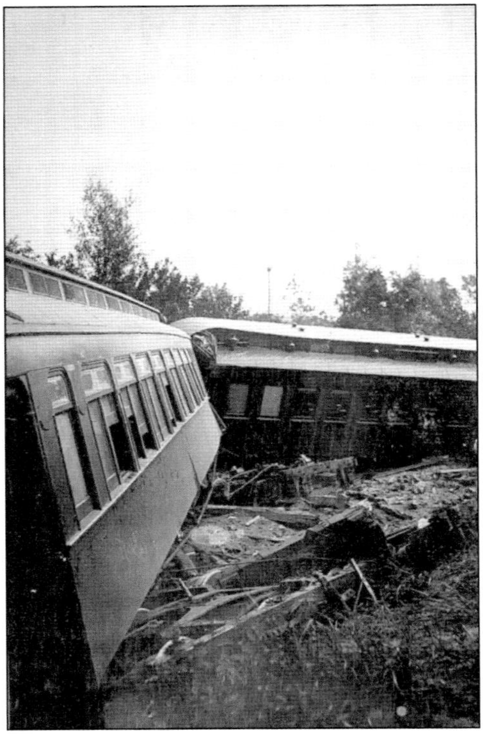

Things did not always go easily on the railroad, as evidenced by this train wreck, which occurred on June 29, 1907. The historical society has numerous photographs of other train wrecks that, like this one, look very serious but, in fact, resulted in very few injuries.

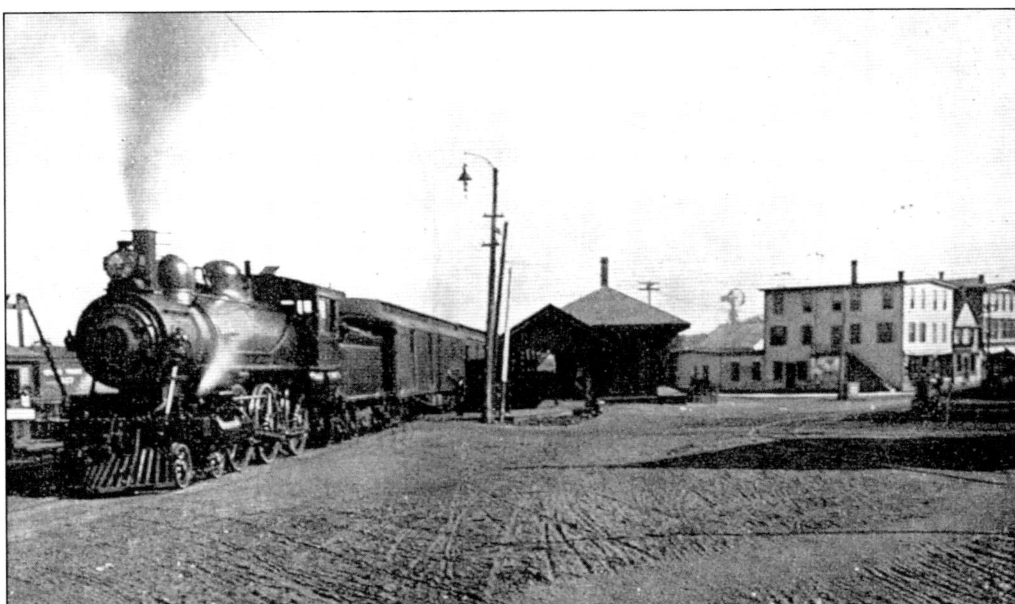

Railroad Station, Oakland, Me.

This train, pictured at the depot on Main Street *c.* 1910, is on the Maine Central Railroad track; another track to the left (west) was the Somerset Railroad track. The Somerset was headquartered in Oakland and ran tracks through Skowhegan and Bingham to Moosehead Lake. Thus, the railway became the main gateway to the Moosehead resort region.

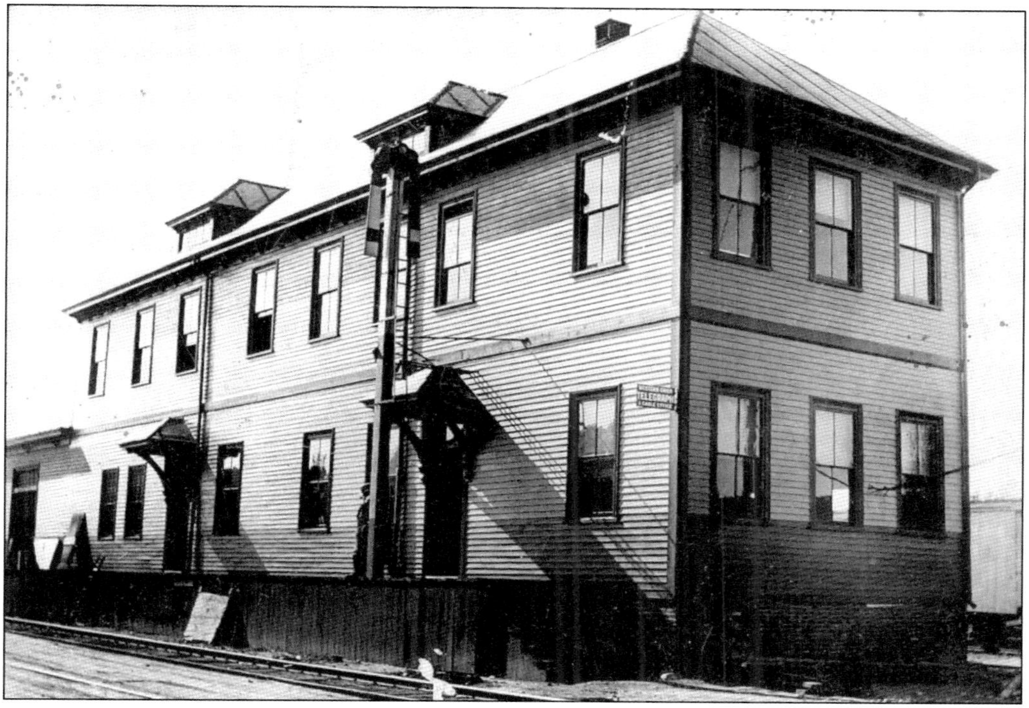

This building, seen here *c.* 1910, was located on the north side of the tracks near Main and Oak Streets. It served as the offices and freight depot for both the Maine Central Railroad and the Somerset Railway. The far left portion of the building was torn down in 2003.

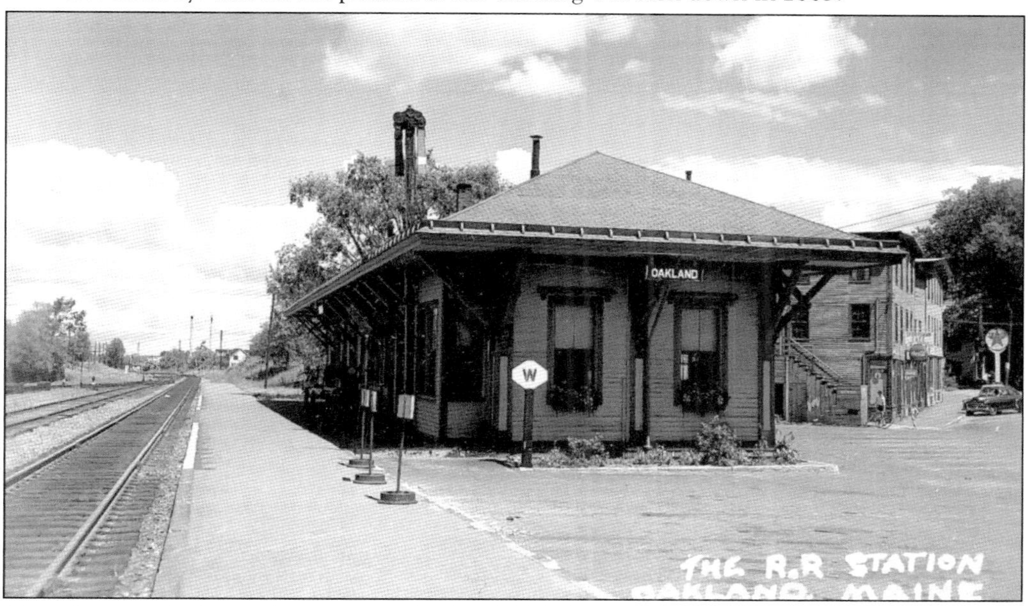

This photograph shows the depot in the late 1940s. The track closest to the depot points east and heads for Waterville; the other track points north and heads to Bingham. By this time, the Somerset line had been cut back to Bingham from a terminus at Moosehead Lake. The Somerset Railroad merged with the Maine Central Railroad *c.* 1910.

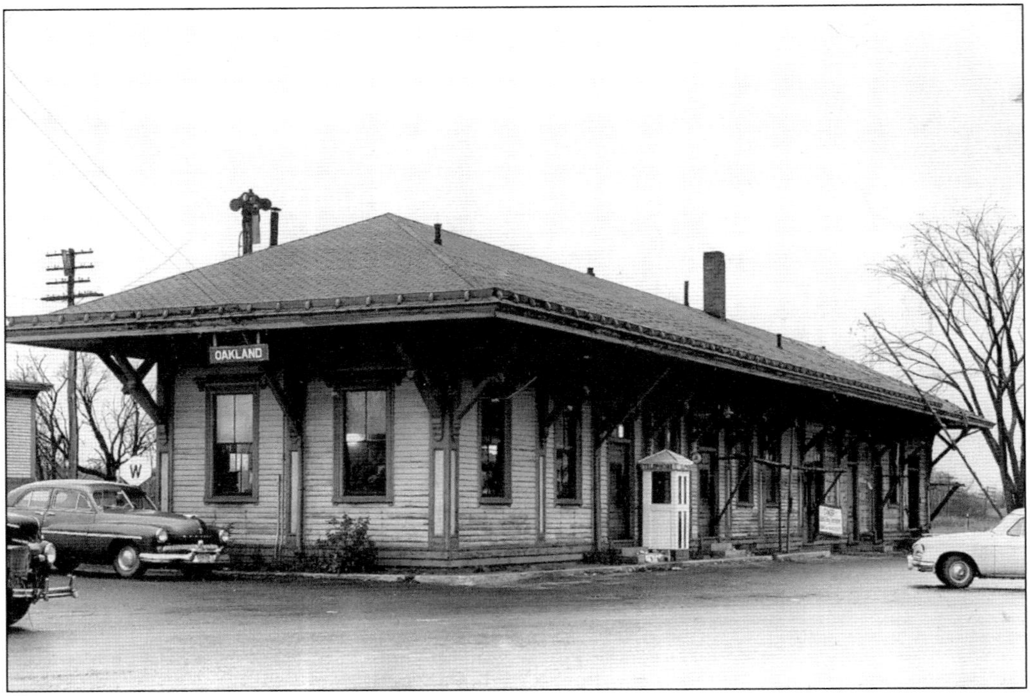

Seen here in the early 1950s, the depot is somewhat in disrepair. Taxis waited for passengers alighting from the trains. Passenger train service ended in Oakland *c.* 1962.

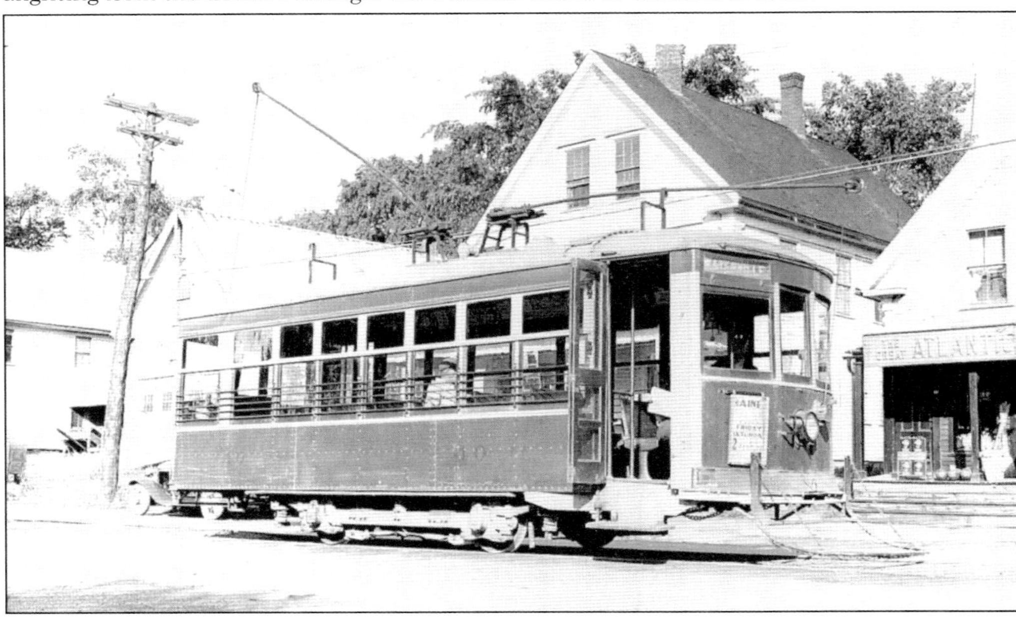

This photograph shows Car No. 40 in Haymarket Square on July 1, 1935, about two years before the Waterville, Fairfield & Oakland Street Railway went out of business. At the time, travelers could go from Fairfield, Maine, to Norfolk, Virginia, on electric street railways, and many people commuted to work in Waterville on the Waterville, Fairfield & Oakland Street Railway. (Photograph courtesy of Ray Applegate, Great Barrington, Massachusetts.)

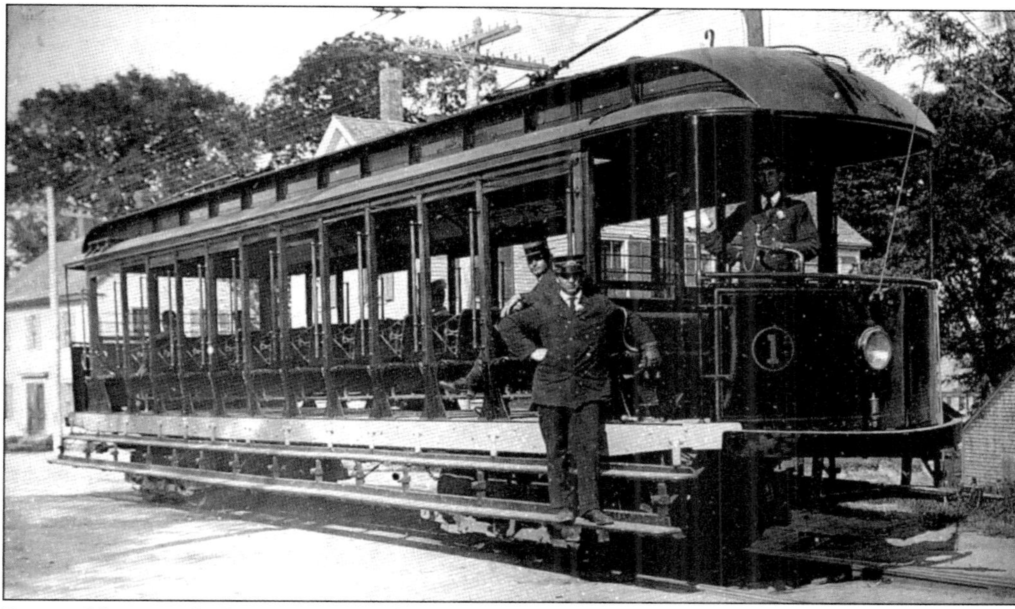

Pictured here with Car No. 1 are, from left to right, George Kennedy of Waterville, Joseph Jordan, and Erland Brann. In the summertime, open cars were used. The conductor would move the backs of the seats so passengers always faced forward; the car itself never turned around. To reverse direction, instead of turning, the conductor simply connected one trolley wire and disconnected another from the overhead electric wire. At the end of the line, the connected wire was disconnected, the unconnected one was connected, and the car ran in the opposite direction.

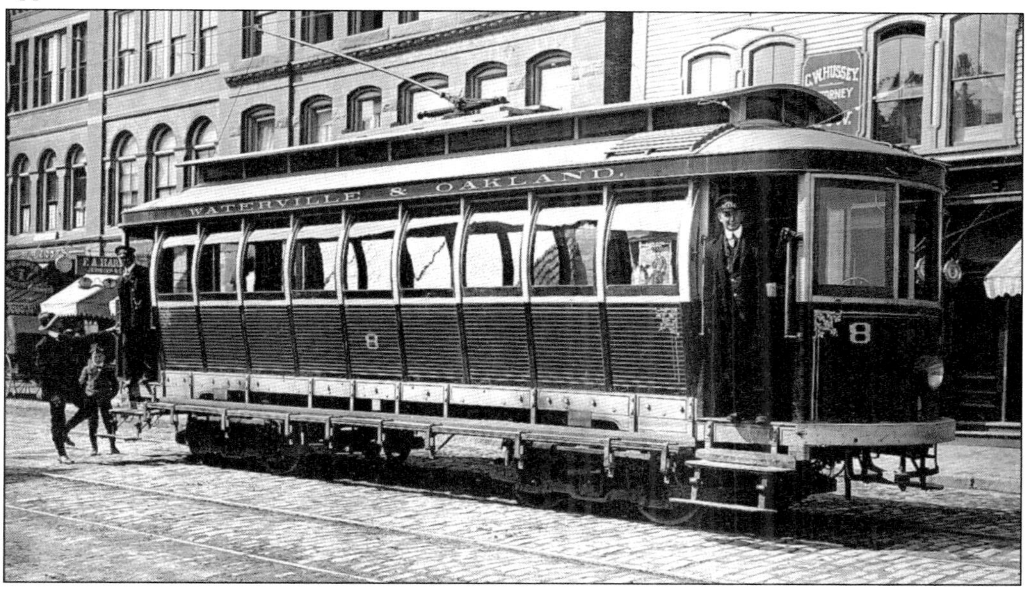

Pictured with Car No. 8 are Mel Beane and Joseph Jordan. The Waterville and Oakland line operated from 1902 to 1911; it merged with the Waterville and Fairfield line in 1911, becoming the Waterville, Fairfield & Oakland Street Railway Company. In 1937, the company went out of business, and transportation services to Waterville were replaced by Duplessis Bus Lines.

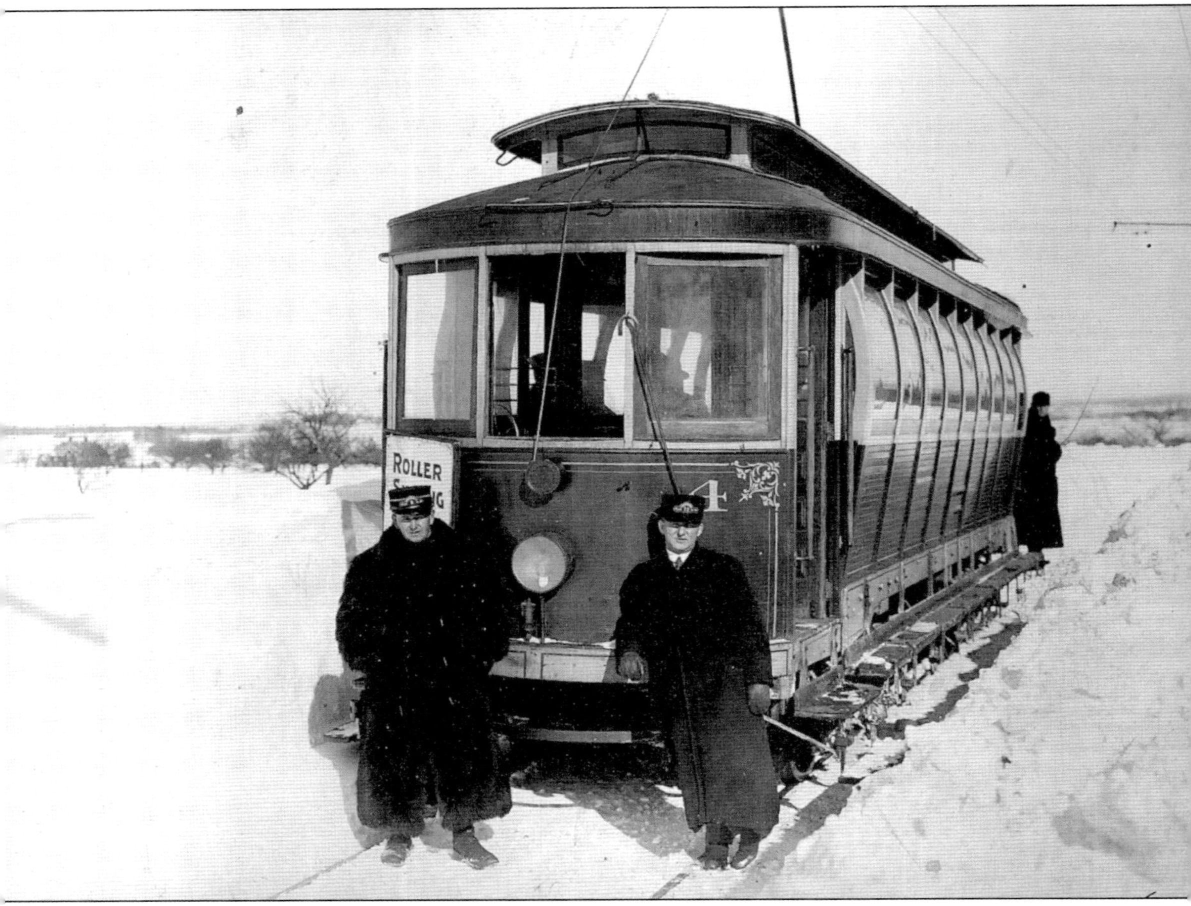

This photograph shows Joseph Jordan and Mel Beane *c.* 1910. The Waterville, Fairfield & Oakland line ran cars to and from Oakland all year round. In 1903, five and a half miles of track were laid from Oakland to Waterville. The line ran from the car barn (Messalonskee Hall) in Oakland down Church Street to Main Street, crossed Fairfield Street near the present fire station, and then ran on into Waterville. The trip to Waterville took 30 minutes, and cars left for Waterville every 15 minutes. Stops included Cascade Park and the Central Maine Fairground in Waterville (where the Seton Unit of MaineGeneral Medical Center is now located). The last run was on October 10, 1937, at 10:35 pm.

Three

Business and Industry

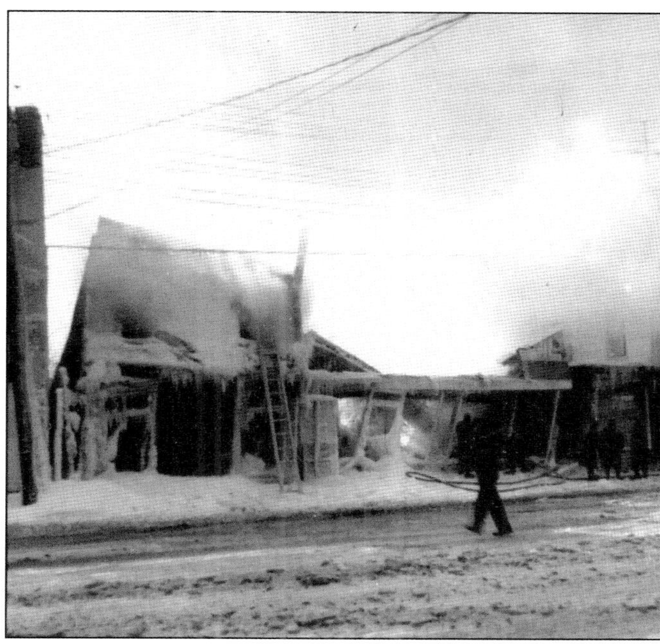

Located on Main Street at Depot Square, this building, which housed Morse's Clothing Store and True's Pharmacy, burned on February 22, 1963. On this site, the Trues built a single-story building, which now houses Higgins and Bolduc, an insurance company.

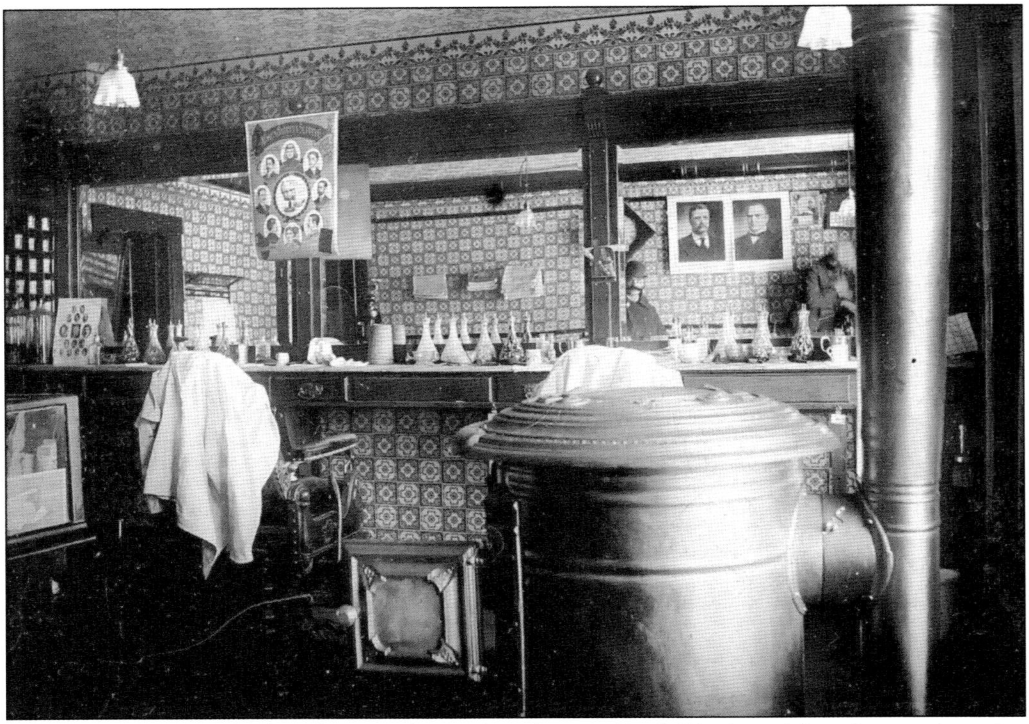

George W. Wilson's barber shop was located in the new Bank Block on Main Street when this photograph was taken *c.* 1897. The shop apparently was in operation from *c.* 1885 until 1934.

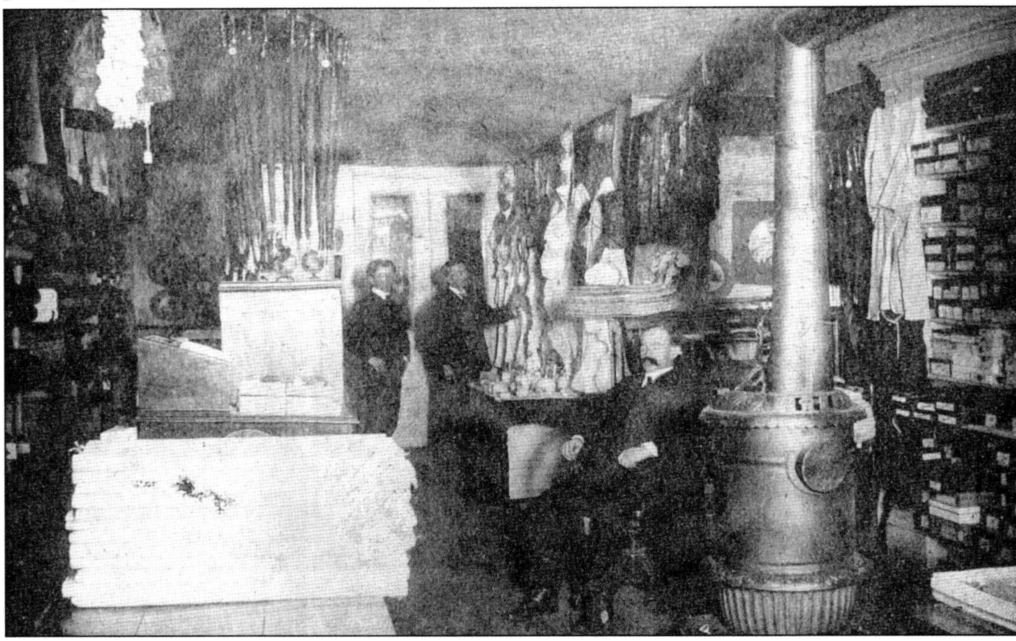

Ridley & Flanders was a dry-goods and fancy-goods store on Main Street at Depot Square. It was in operation by 1903 and remained into the 1920s. Seen in the front of this photograph is Charles Ridley; in the back are Walter E. Sullivan (left) and Wallace Flanders (right).

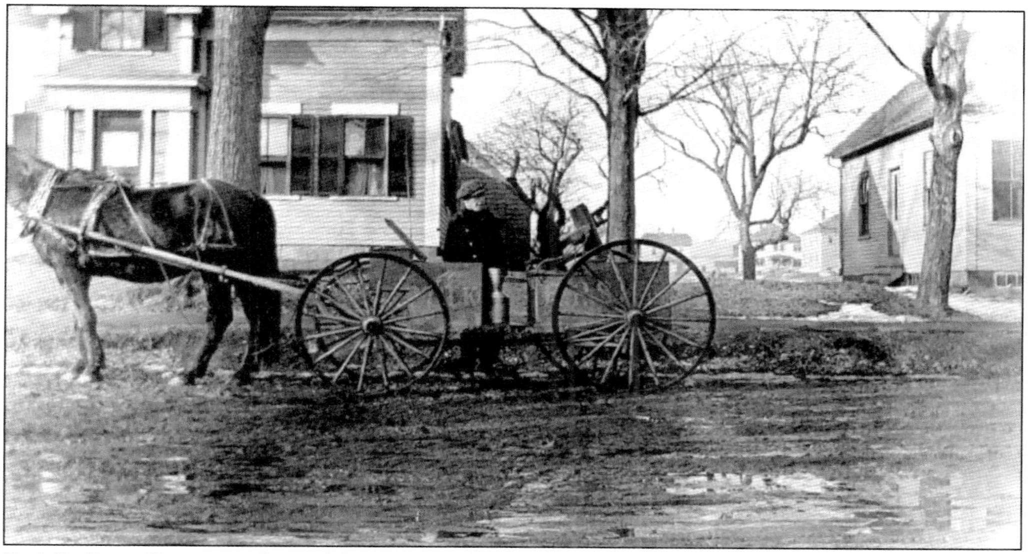

Earl P. Sawtelle is seen here delivering milk, probably on Church Street, c. 1900. This was in the era before home delivery by major dairies, and long before the end of home deliveries!

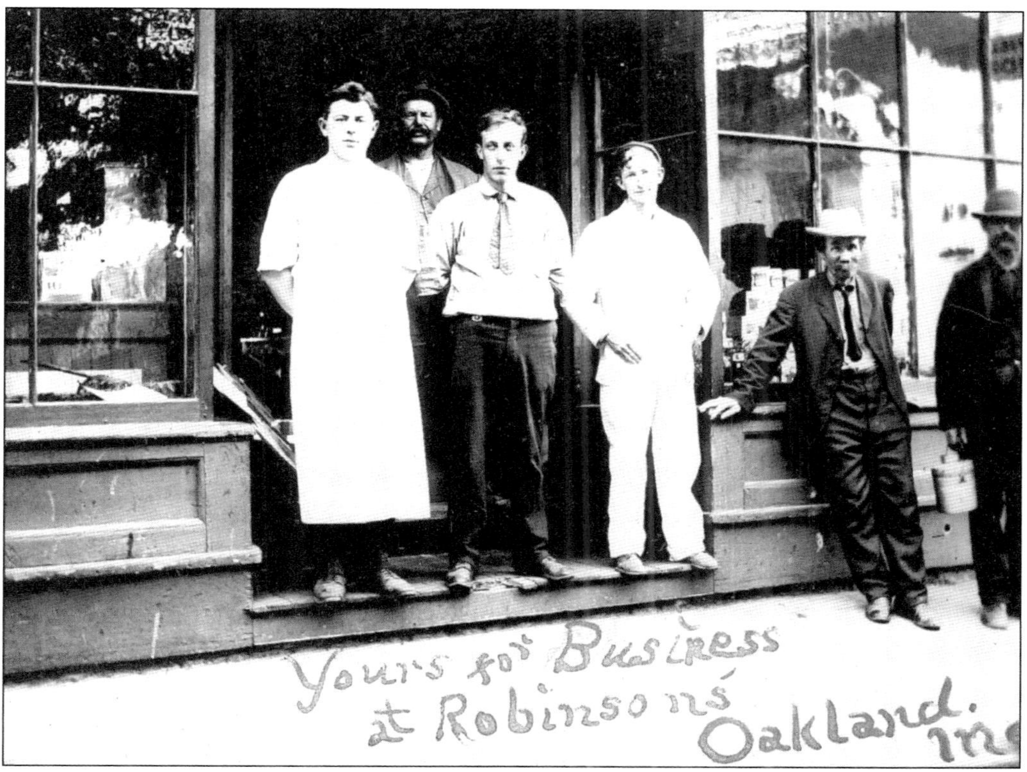

Robinson's grocery store was located on Church Street near the depot and the present-day barber shop from c. 1887 on. Robinson's slogan was "Yours for business at Robinson's."

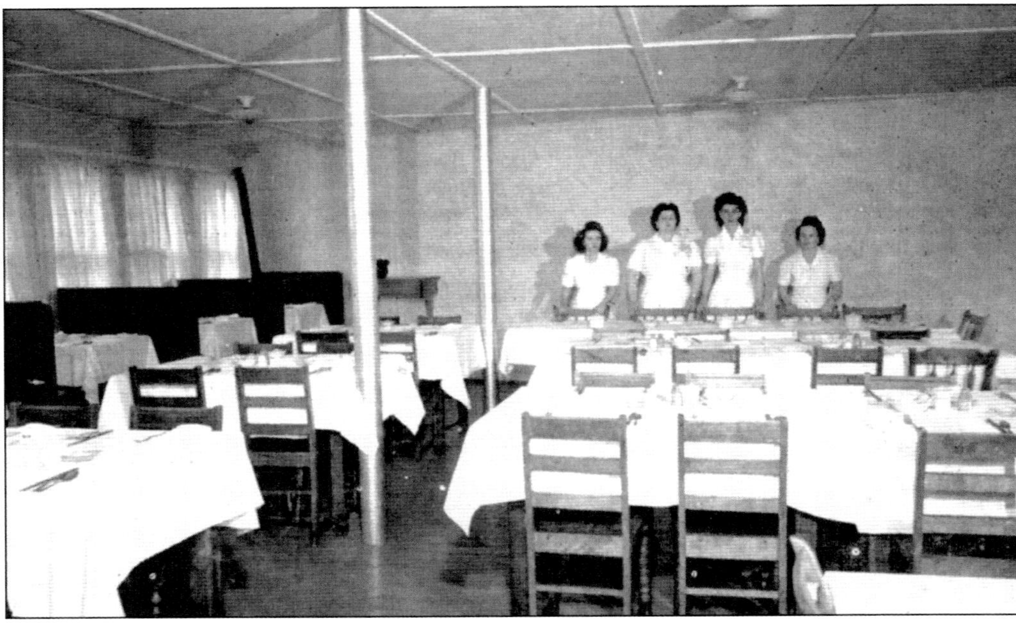

Hal's Restaurant was located in the building that has housed Blake's Family Hardware since the mid-1960s. The restaurant's slogan was "[t]he house of Hal's—where good food reigns king." The notation on the back of this photograph reads, "Hal's Restaurant, Main Street, Oakland, Maine. In the heart of the Belgrade Lake region. Mecca of Summer Campers."

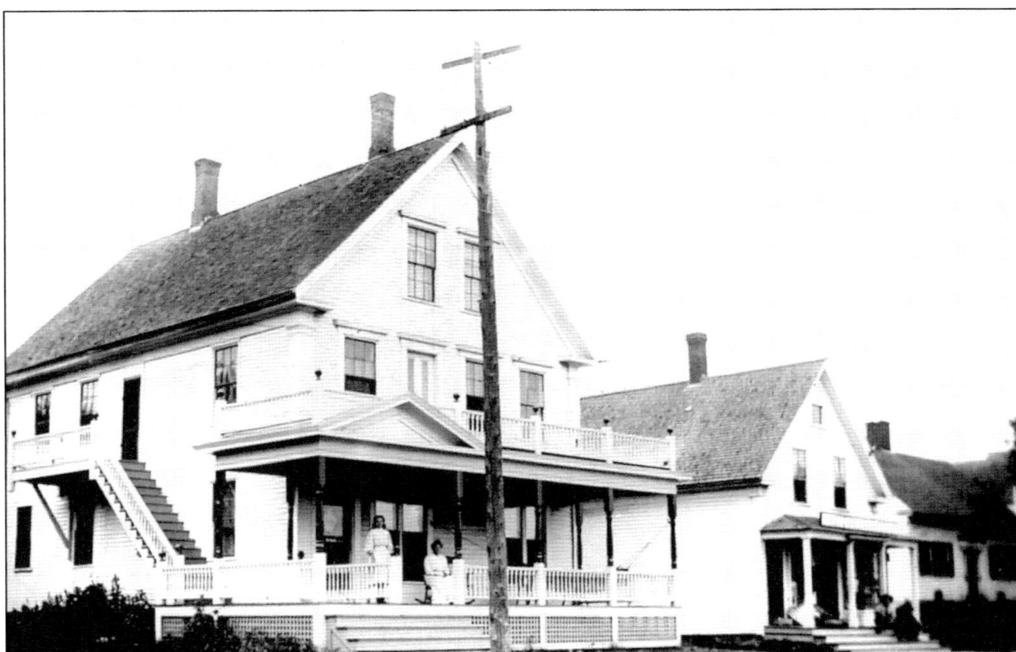

George P. Boynton's house and store were located in the Upper Mills, near the junction of Church and Water Streets. The store later became an A&P store. The building just visible on the right still stands.

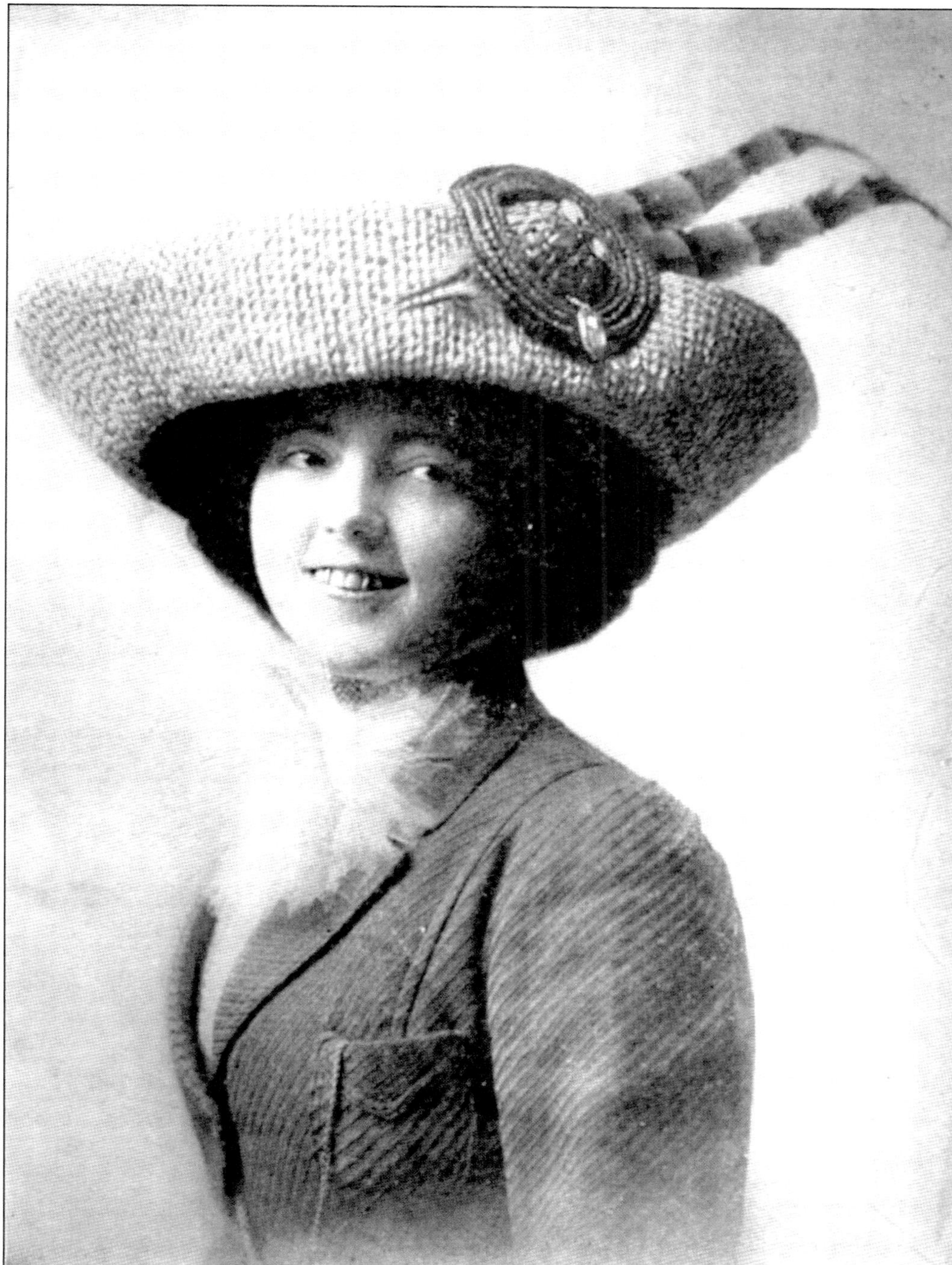

This is Bertha Strickland's *c.* 1910 business card. It reads, "Announcement—Spring and Summer Millinery, Ready for Your Inspection On and After Apil [*sic*] 1. Bertha Strickland, 35 Main Street, Oakland."

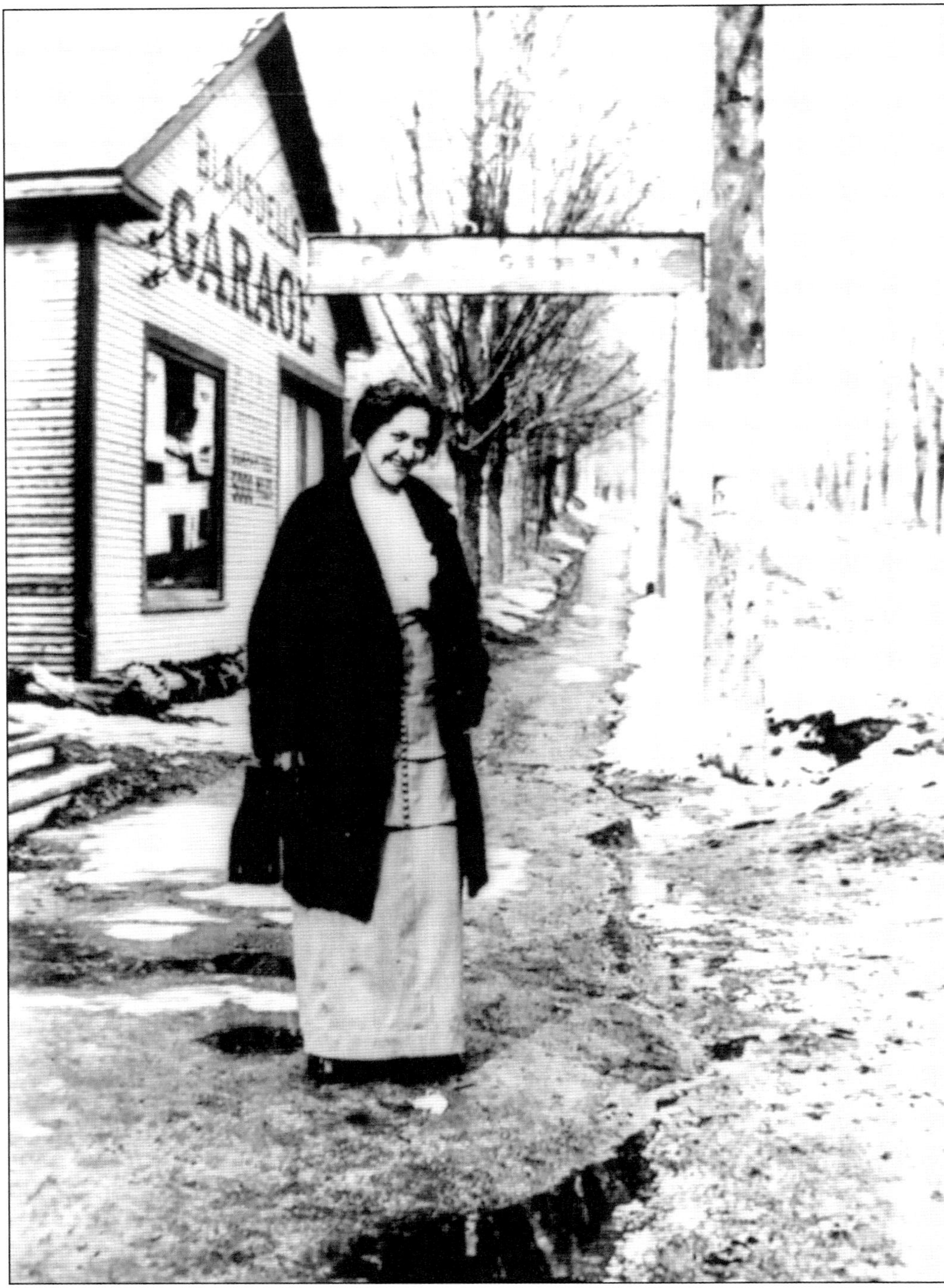

Mildred Boynton stands in front of Blaisdell's Garage in Haymarket Square, the first Ford garage in Oakland, in the early 1920s. Blaisdell's Garage was in operation from 1917 until 1928. Blaisdell was a dealer and also did automobile repairs in his shop just north of Boynton's grocery on Church Street.

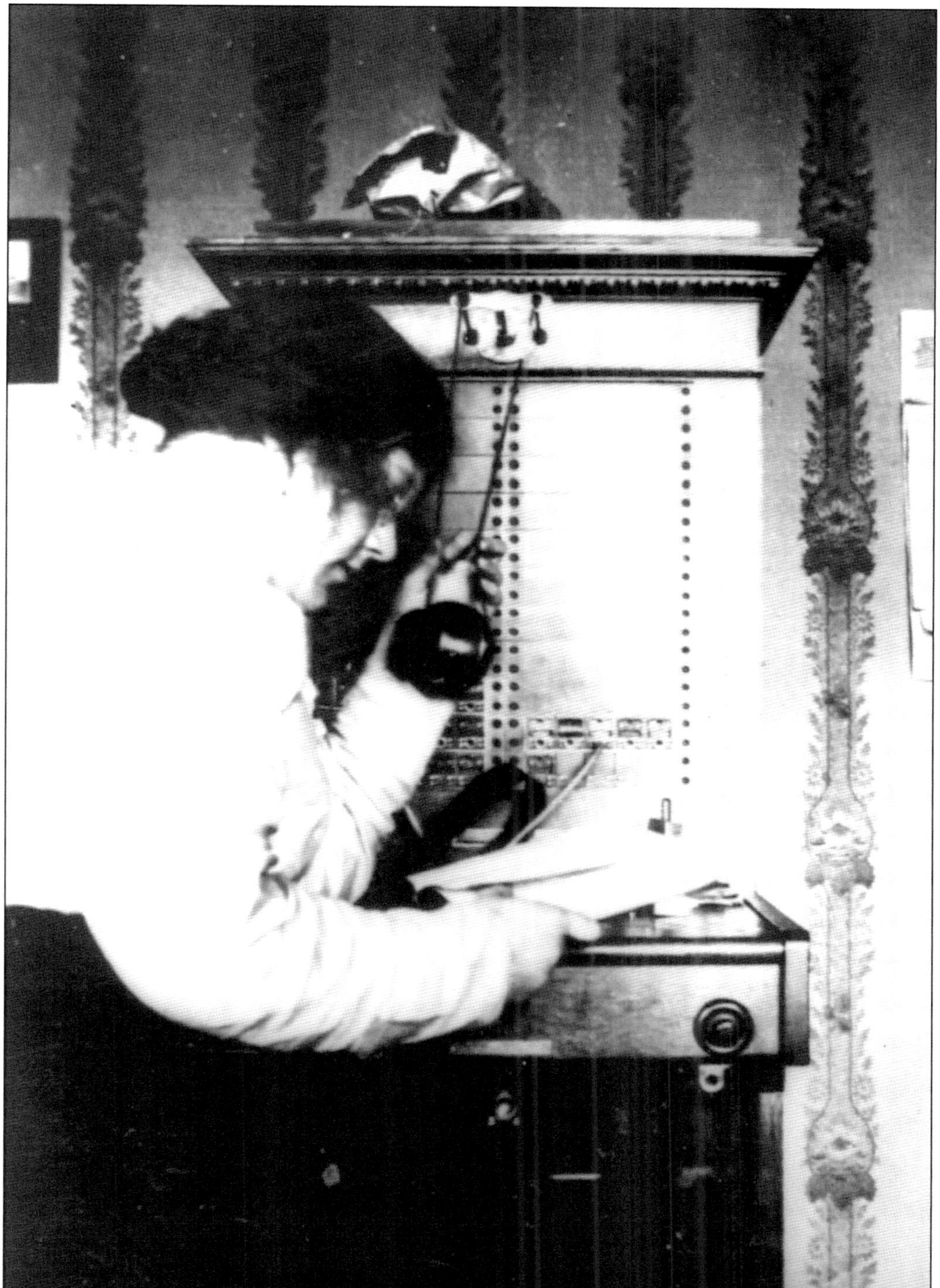

The first telephone exchange and switchboard in Oakland had operator Ruth Tozier connecting calls. The exchange was located upstairs in the Blake Block as late as the 1920s.

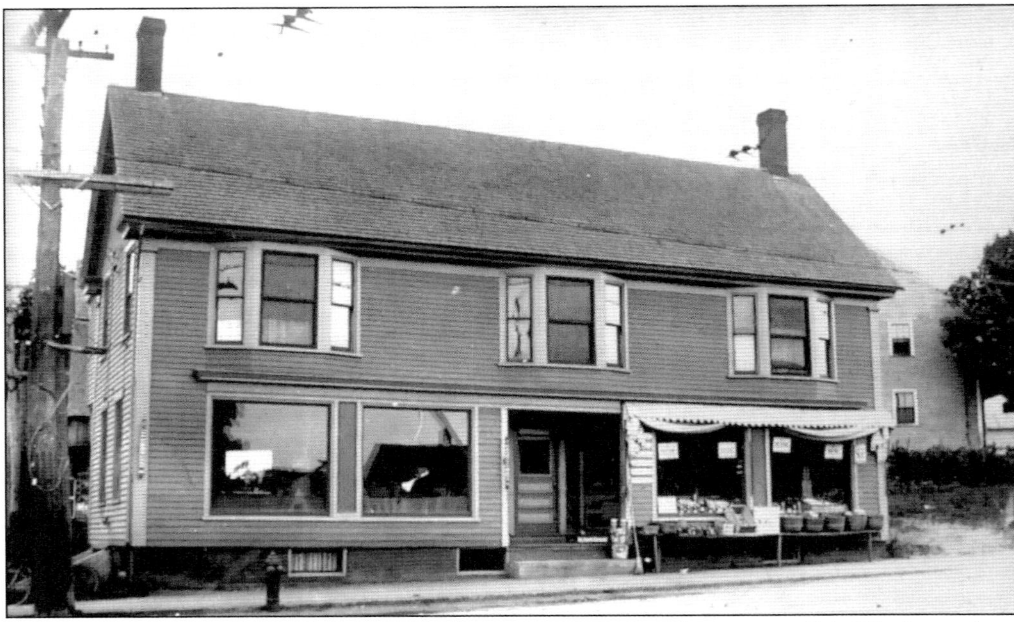

This building is located on the Dusty Block on Main Street at the corner of Middle Street (now Center Street). It has housed dozens of small businesses over the years, including Michaud's Red and White (pictured on the next page).

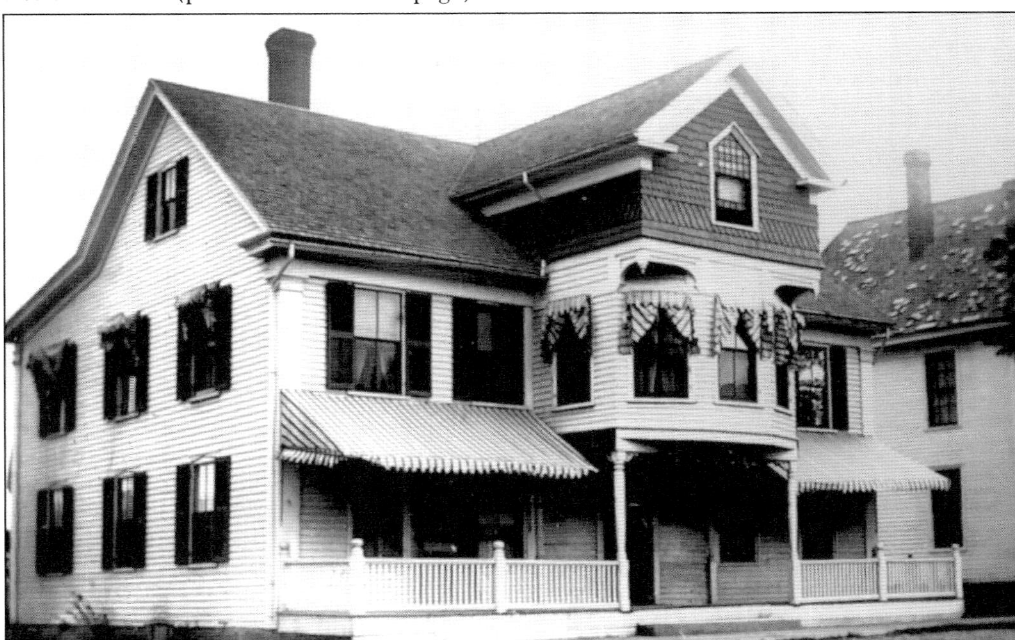

The Oakland Hotel was located on Main Street and was owned by Ora Sibley. An advertisement in the Maine Register in 1899 said, "Twenty-five rooms. Electric lights and bells. Telephone. Good Livery Stable connected with the house. Gentlemen's Horses constantly on hand for sale." The hotel stood across the street from the current Blake's Family Hardware, probably where Buddies' grocery is located today.

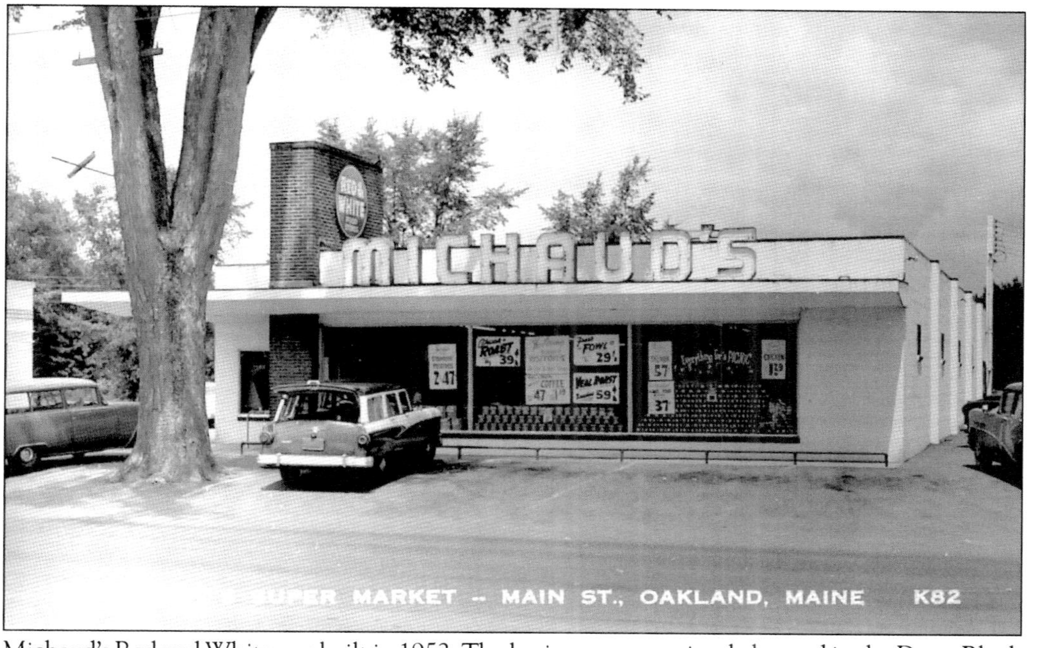

Michaud's Red and White was built in 1952. The business was previously located in the Dusty Block across and up the street. The building is now Buddies' and has been remodeled and enlarged.

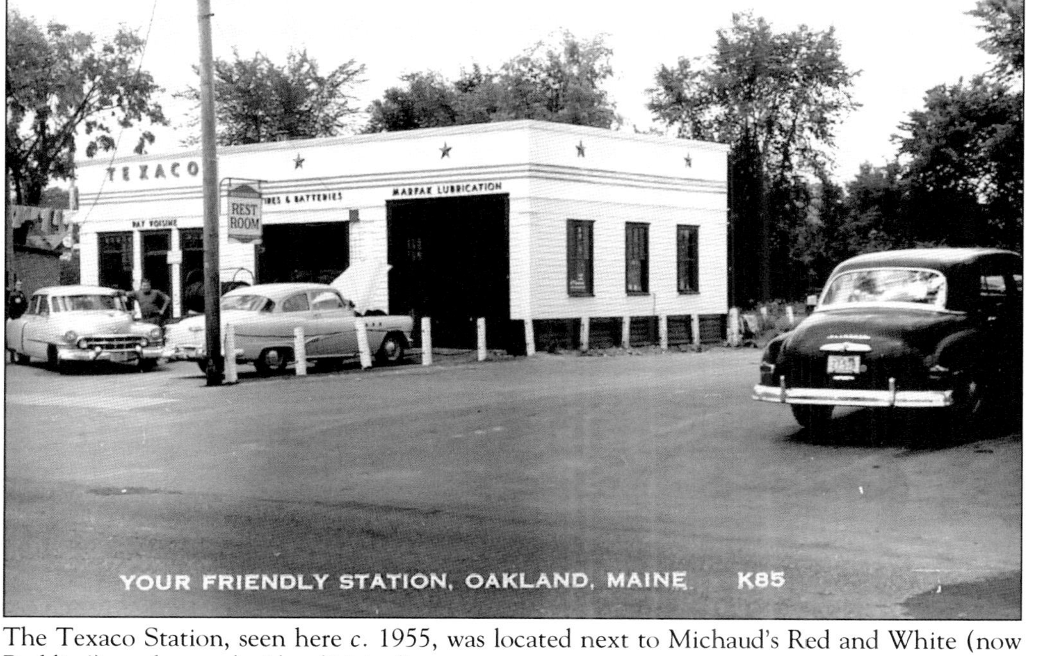

The Texaco Station, seen here *c.* 1955, was located next to Michaud's Red and White (now Buddies') on the north side of Main Street.

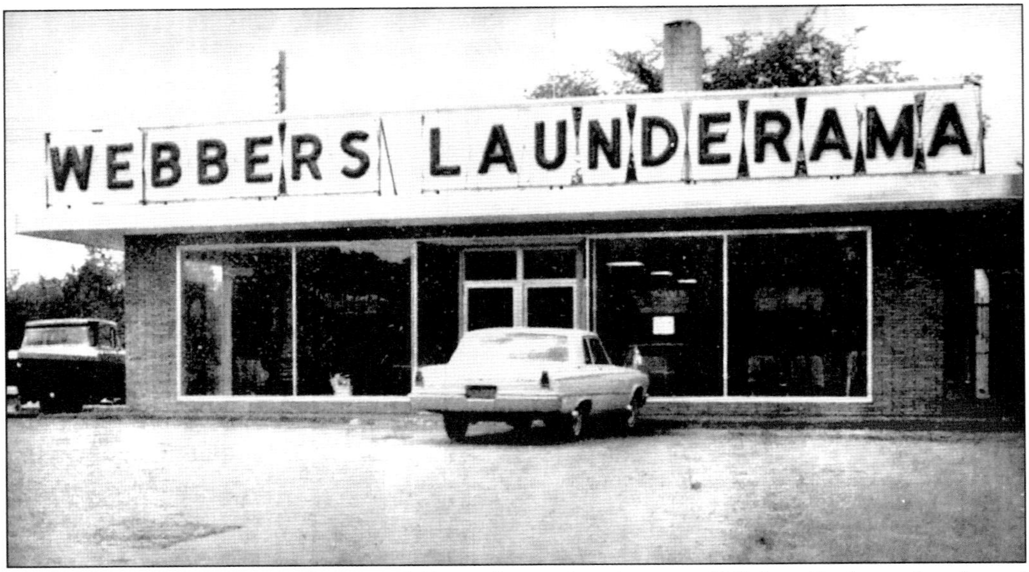

Webber's Launderama, seen here *c.* 1962, was located to the east of Michaud's. A much enlarged and remodeled version of the Launderama burned in 2003. The Oakland (Sibley's) Hotel may have been on this site earlier in the 20th century.

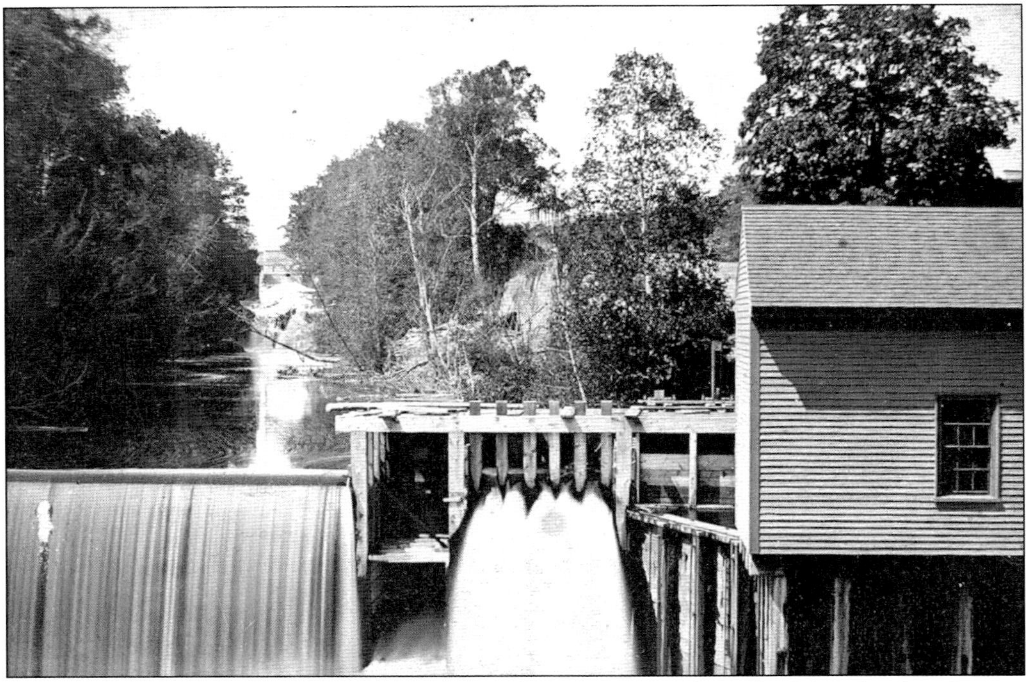

This photograph shows the thriving industry that sprung up along the Messalonskee Stream near the Cascade. There are actually several waterfalls along the Messalonskee: the 100-foot Cascade seen in the distance at the center and numerous milldam falls, including the one shown here near the Cascade Woolen Mill *c.* 1905.

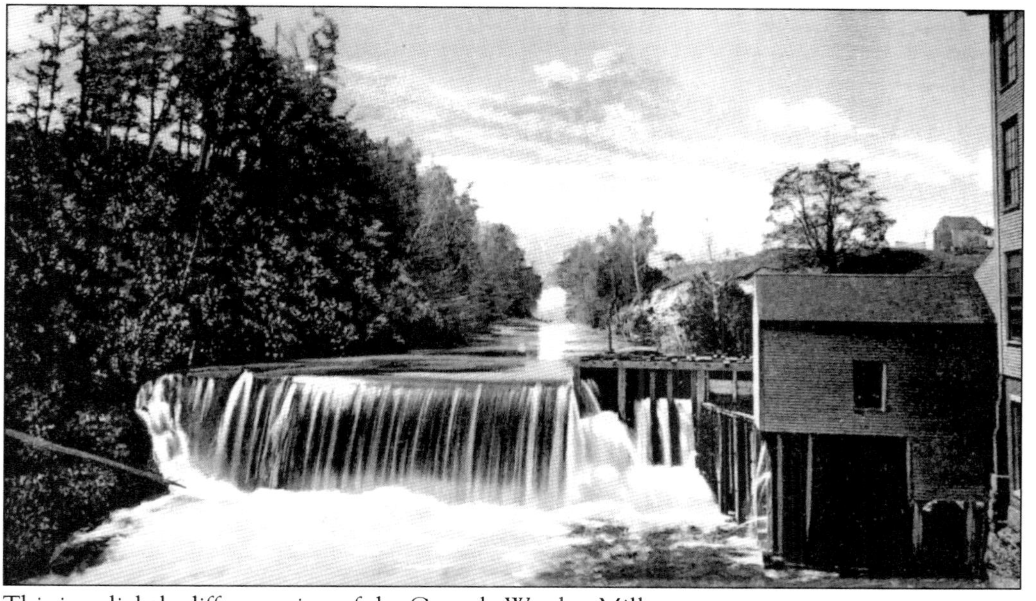

This is a slightly different view of the Cascade Woolen Mill.

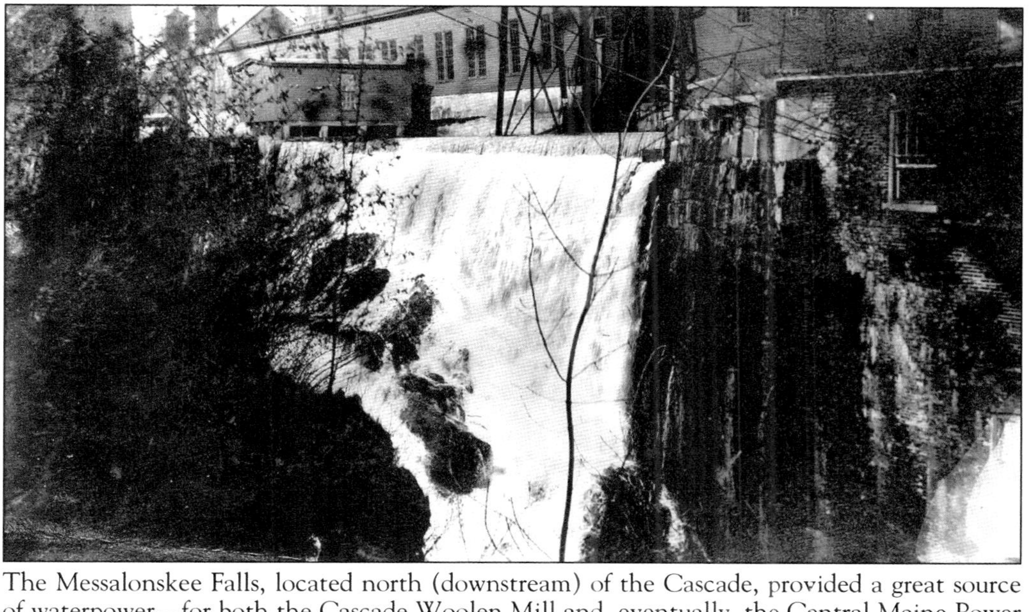

The Messalonskee Falls, located north (downstream) of the Cascade, provided a great source of waterpower—for both the Cascade Woolen Mill and, eventually, the Central Maine Power Company—from the late 1800s through the mid-20th century.

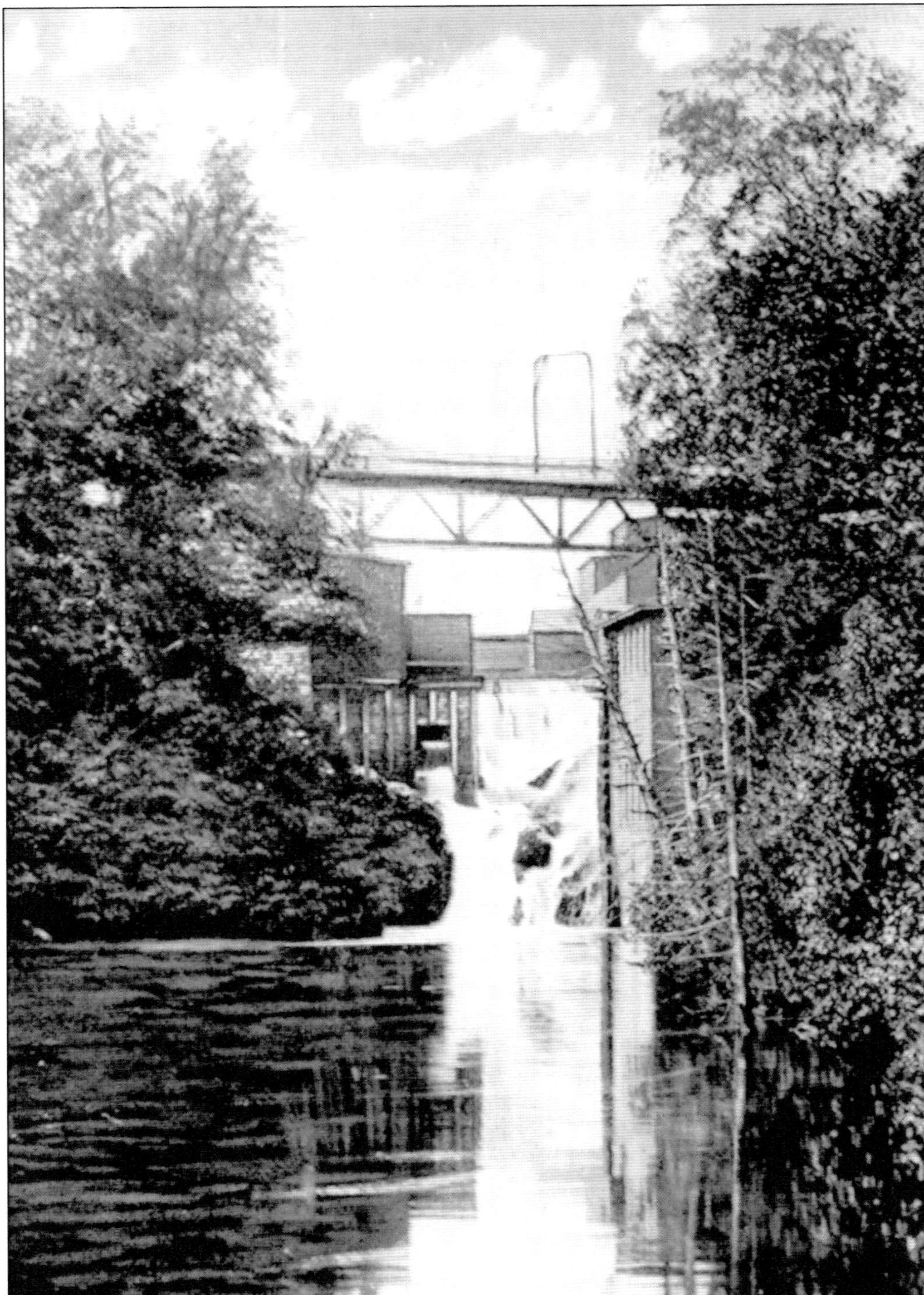

This dramatic view shows the 100-foot Cascade and the street railway trestle over Messalonskee Stream.

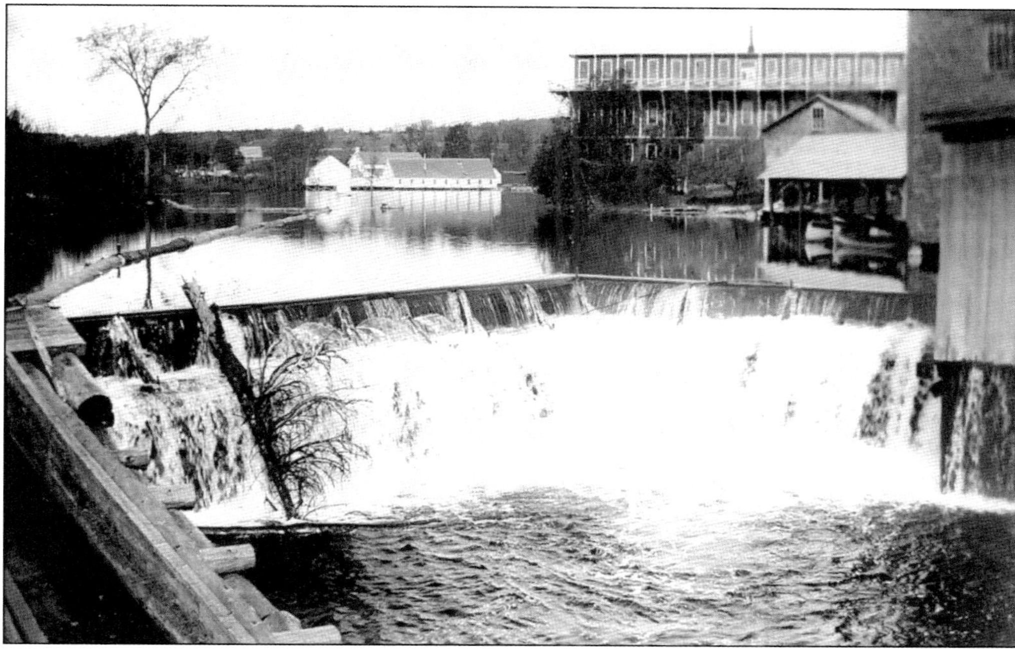

Many factories, ranging from sawmills and gristmills to chair and axe factories, have operated at the outlet of Messalonskee Lake over the years. When this dam was built in the late 1700s, the water level in Messalonskee Lake rose several feet, prompting residents of Belgrade, at the south end of the lake, to file a complaint with the Massachusetts General Court about the flooding of their farmlands. (Maine was a part of Massachusetts at the time.)

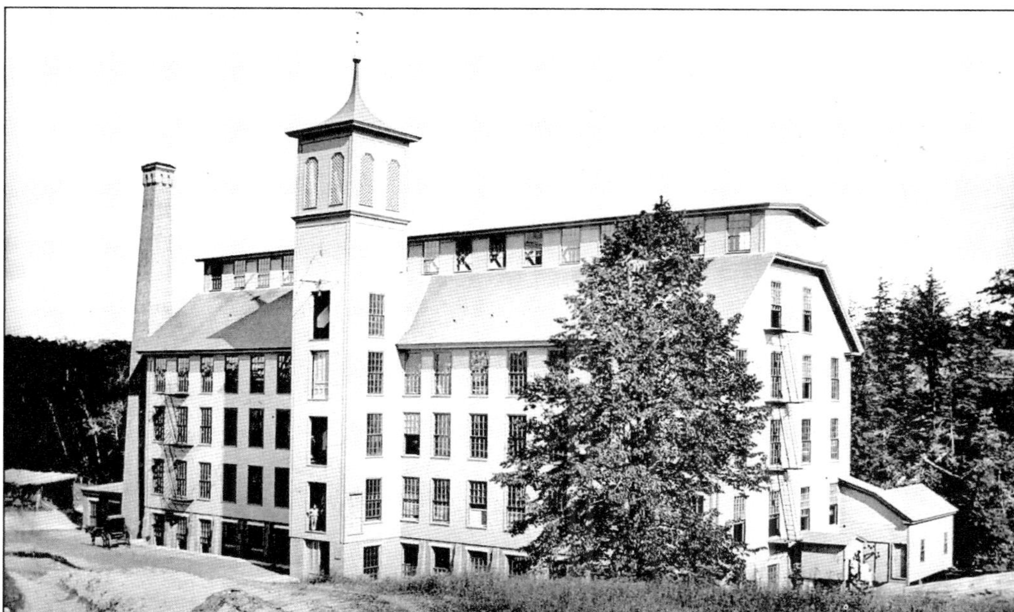

The Cascade Woolen Mill, seen here c. 1900, manufactured fine woolen cloth. It closed in the 1980s, again due to inexpensive foreign imports. Though the building is still there, little business or manufacturing is going on inside now.

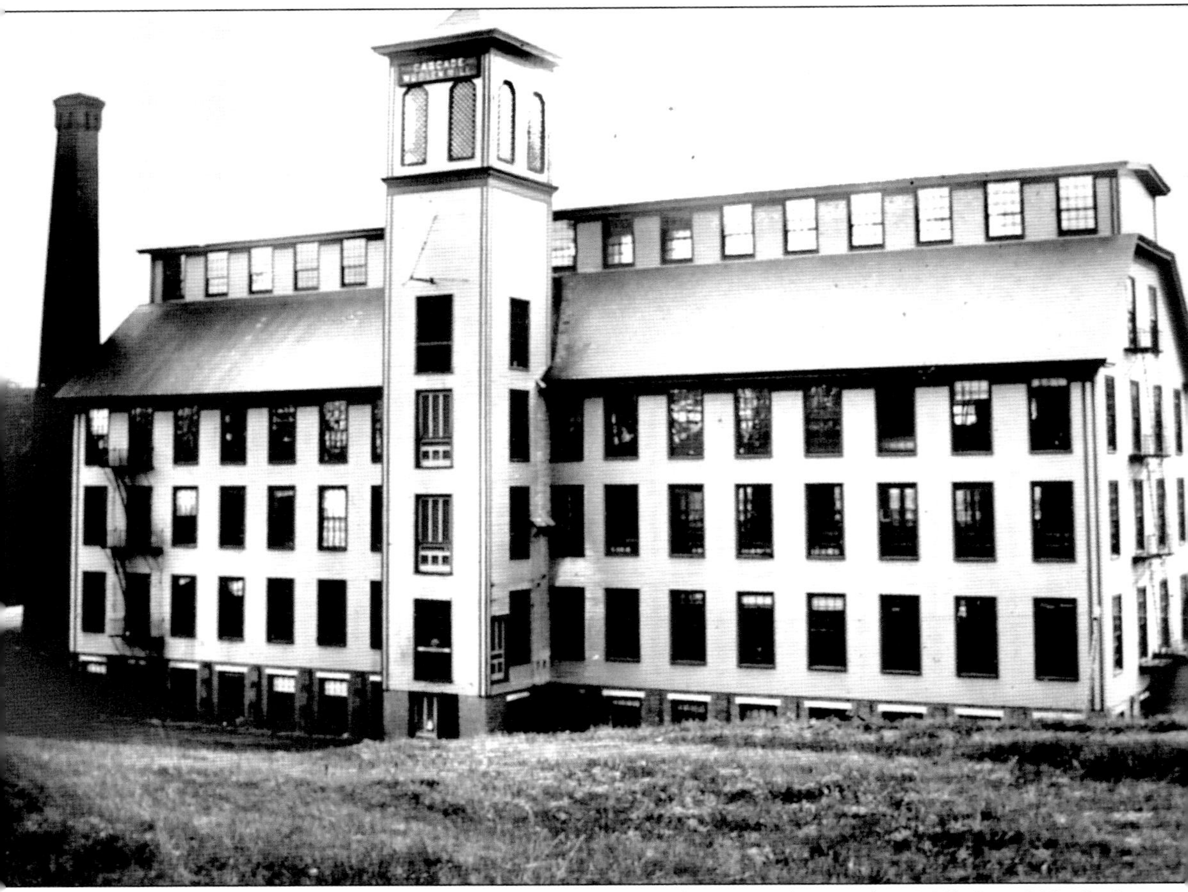

This c. 1905 photograph offers a different view of the Cascade Woolen Mill. In 1882, Seth Milliken, Reuben B. Dunn, John Ayer, David Campbell, and Josiah Mayo formed the mill corporation, naming the mill after the cascading falls just south of the site. The original five-story building still stands. The mill employed more than 200 people in the 1950s.

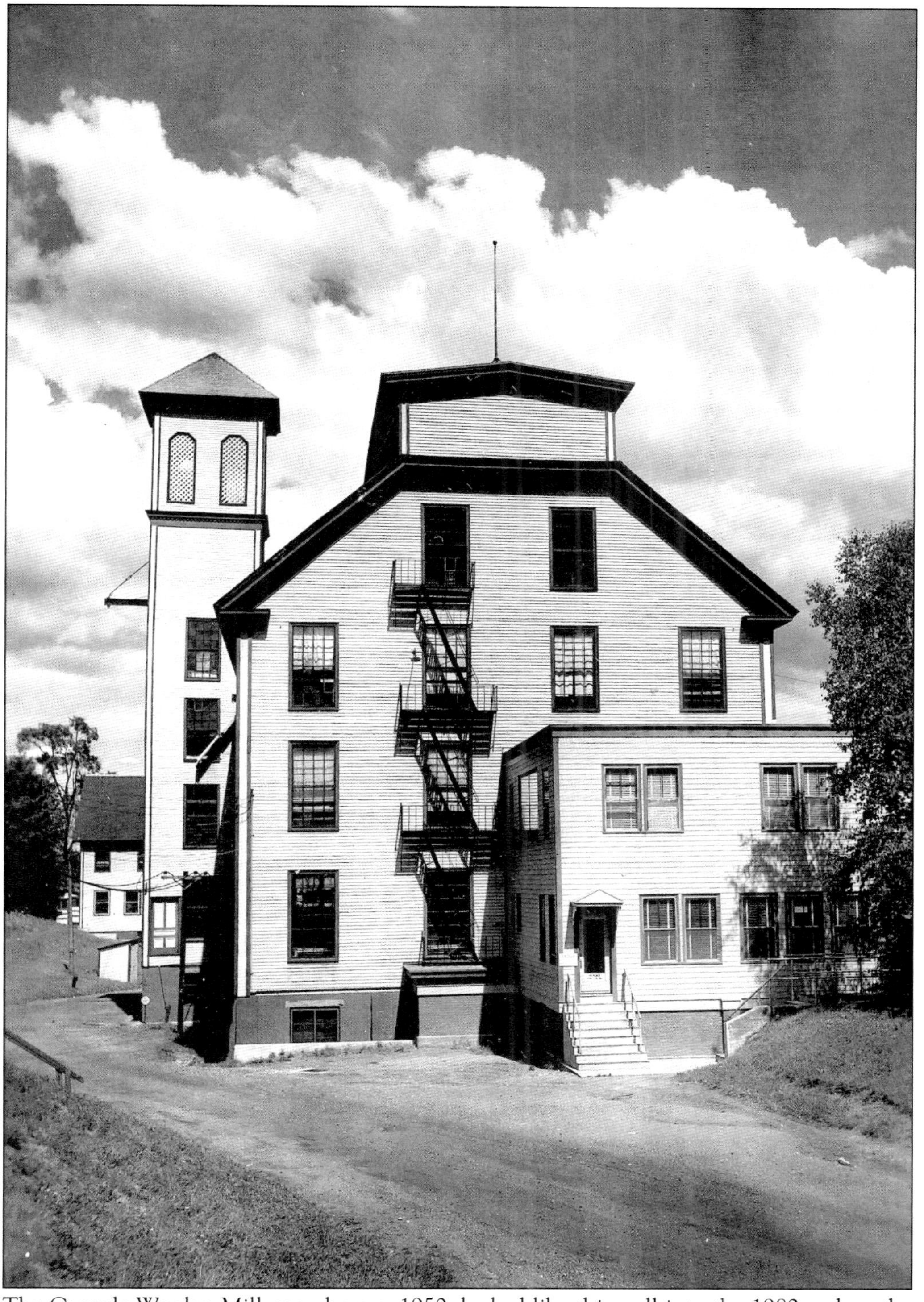

The Cascade Woolen Mill, seen here *c.* 1950, looked like this well into the 1980s, when the mill closed for good. About 250 jobs were lost when this last major factory closed.

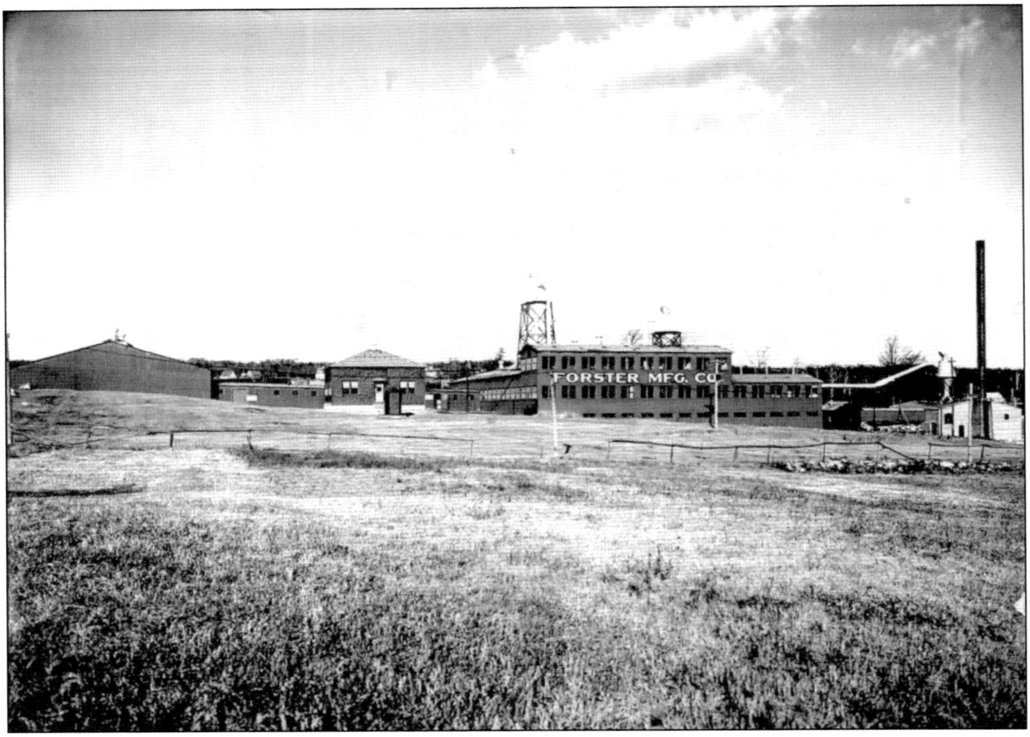

The Forster Manufacturing Company manufactured toothpicks and other woodenware.

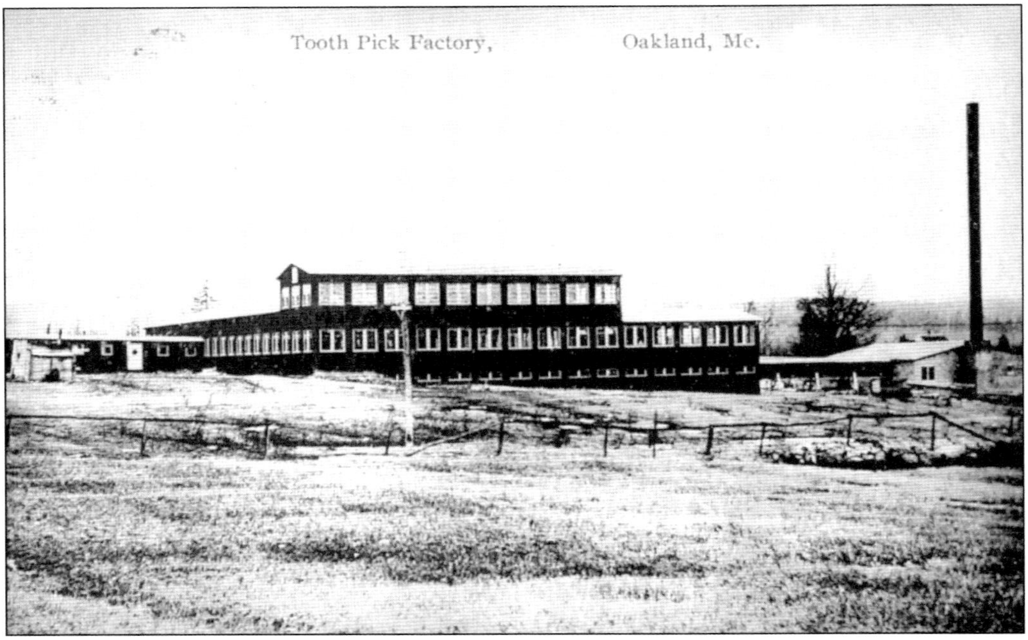

For generations, the Forster Manufacturing Company was known simply as "the Toothpick" by older residents. It became, in turn, Berst-Forster-Dixfield, Diamond Match, Diamond National, and, finally, Diamond International, before going out of business in the 1970s.

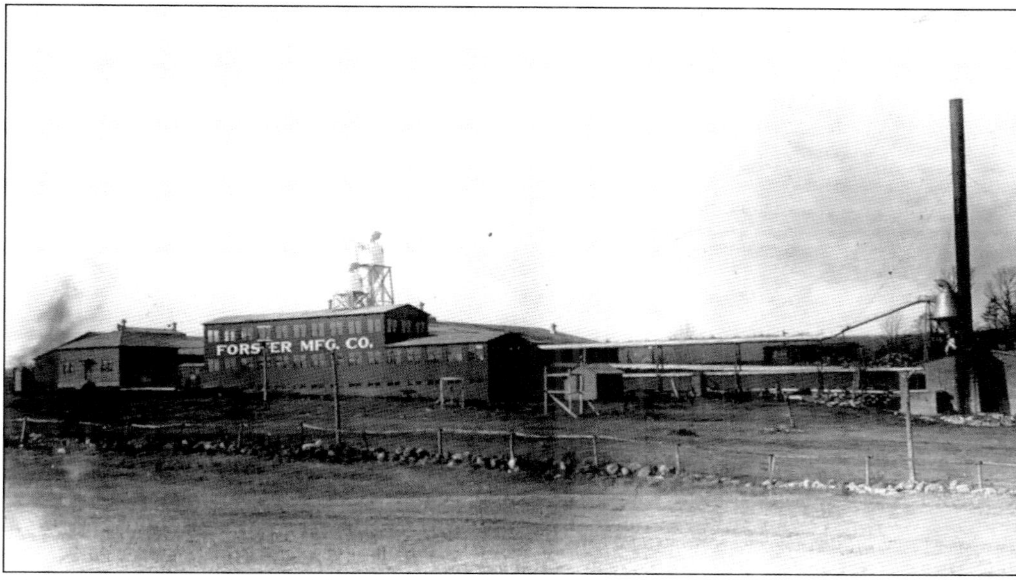

This view shows the Forster Manufacturing Company as it looked *c.* 1920.

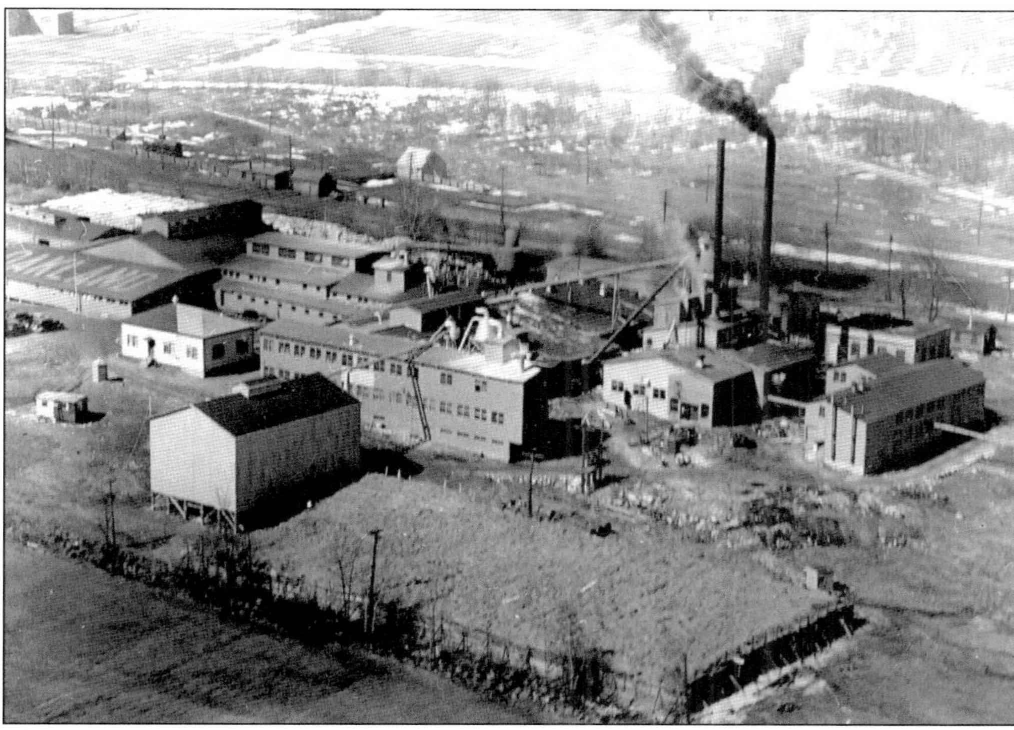

The Diamond Match Company is seen here *c.* 1950. Notice the present-day Williams Elementary School in the upper left. Today the new Messalonskee Middle School stands in the open ground at the top center.

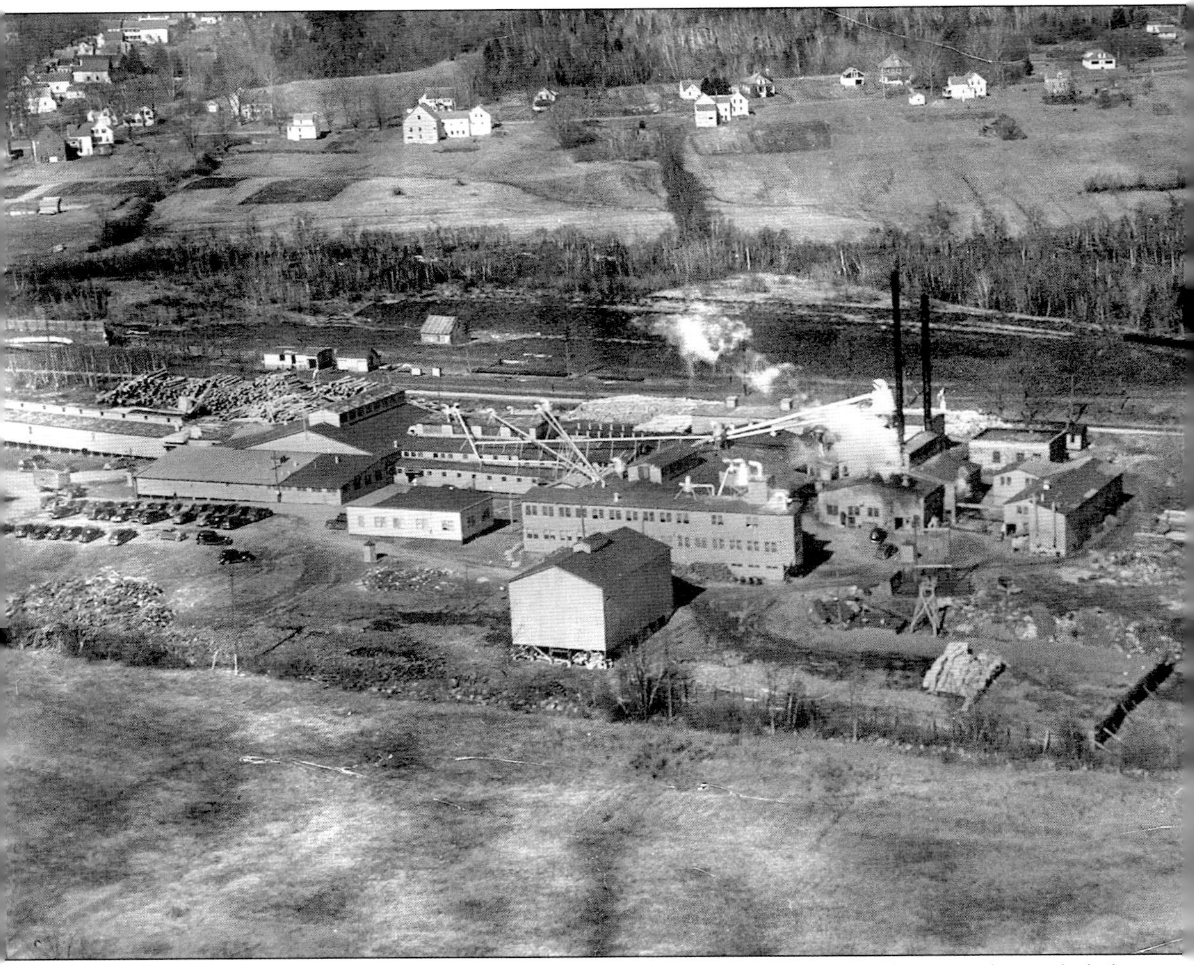

This photograph of the Diamond Match Company, also taken c. 1950, provides a slightly different view, looking west. Today the site is occupied by Industrial Metal Recycling. Homes on Oak and High Streets are clearly visible in this aerial photograph.

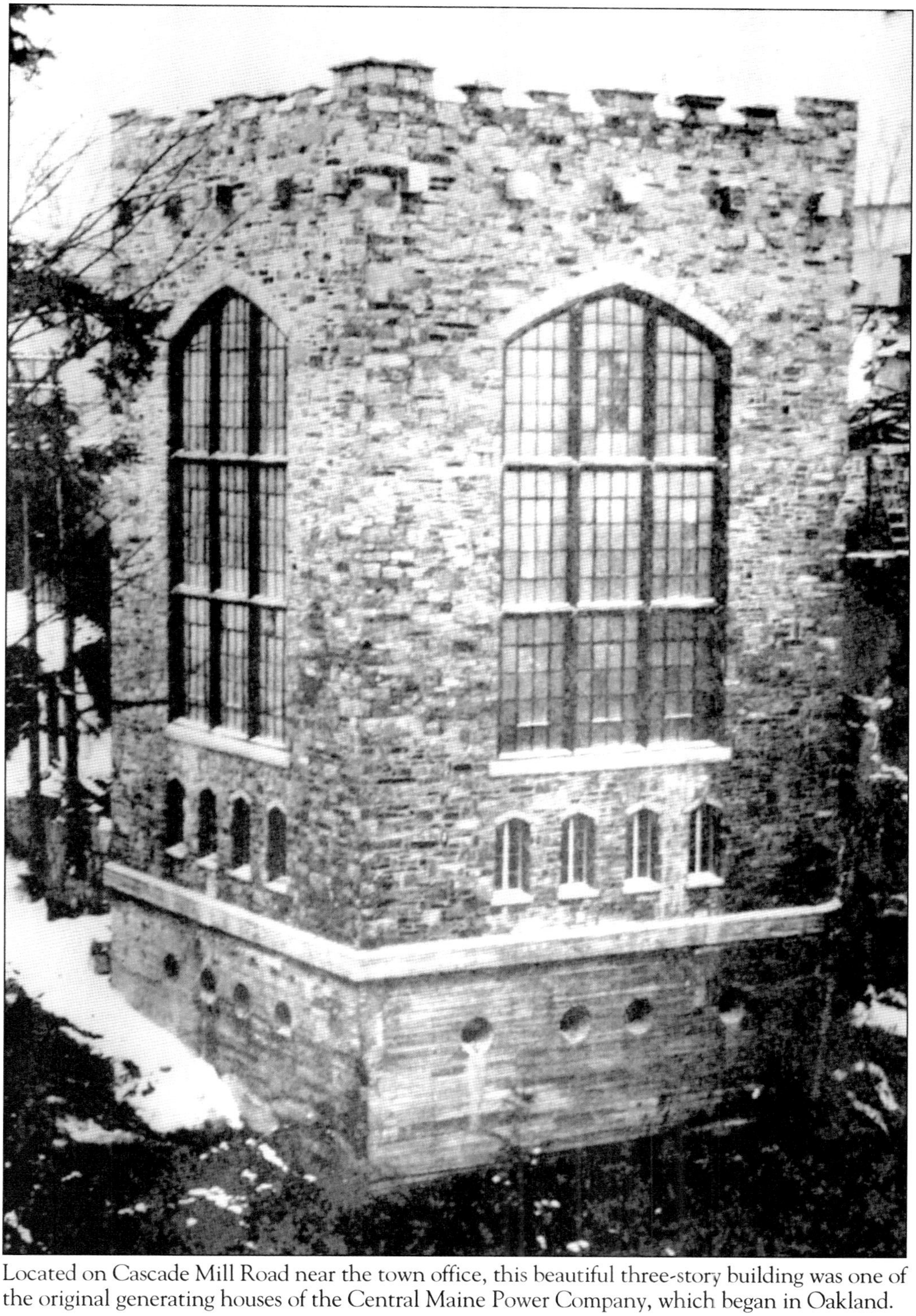

Located on Cascade Mill Road near the town office, this beautiful three-story building was one of the original generating houses of the Central Maine Power Company, which began in Oakland.

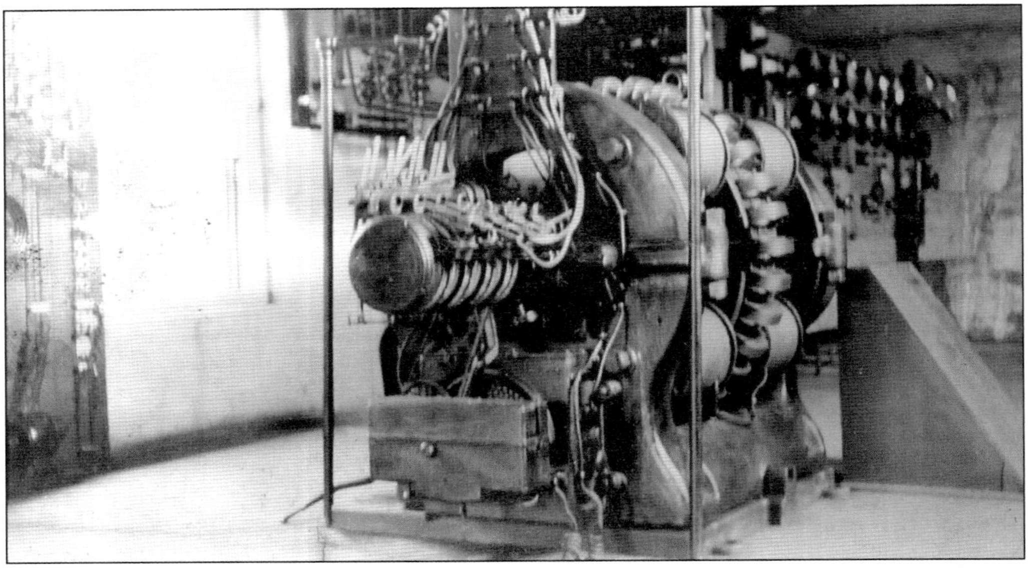

According to the Central Maine Power Company, these photographs (and the one on the top of page 47) are of the Oakland Water Company; however, the Oakland Area Historical Society believes they are of the generator house on Messalonskee Stream.

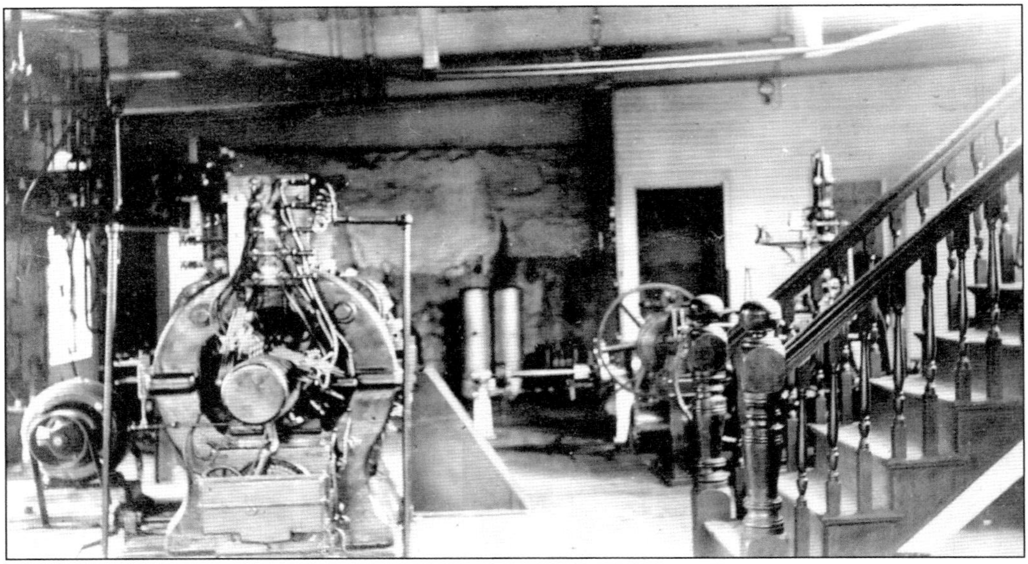

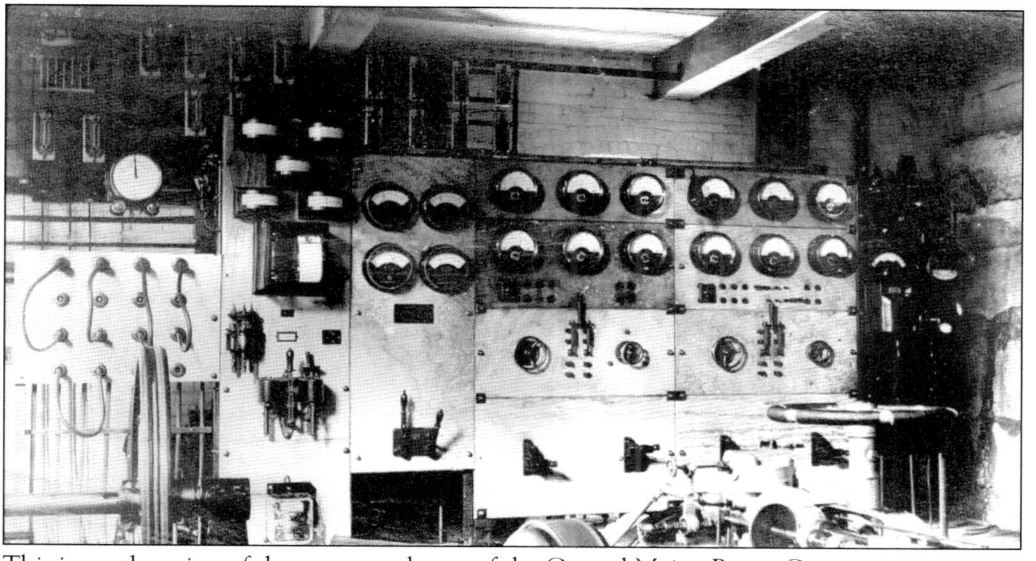

This is another view of the generator house of the Central Maine Power Company.

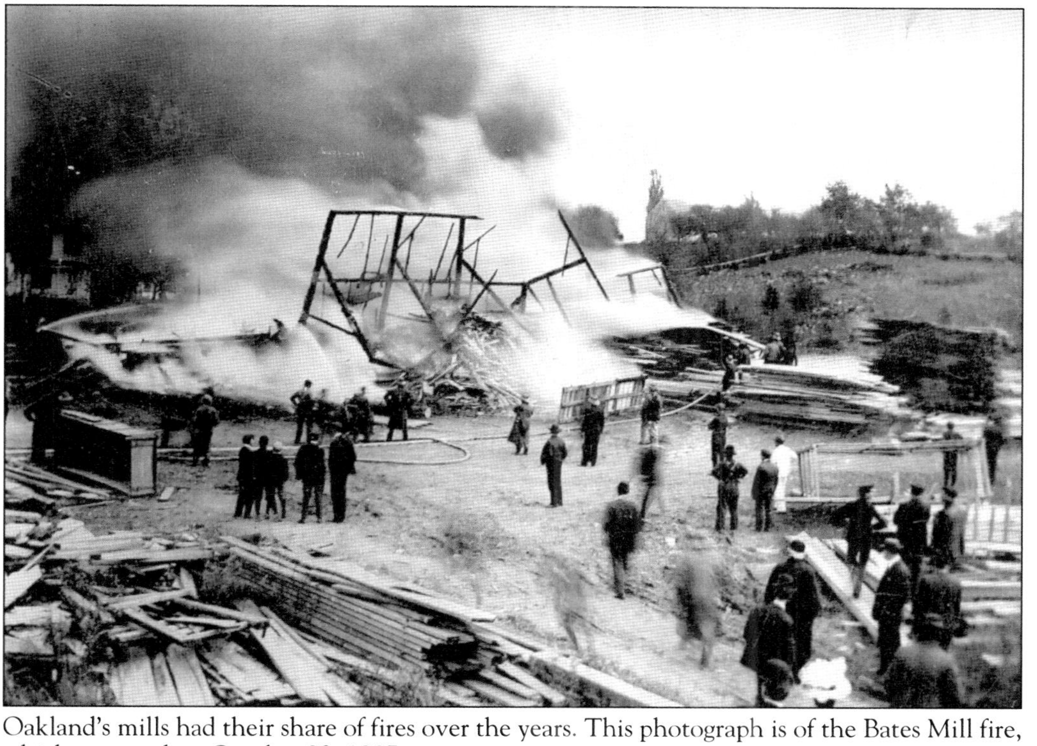

Oakland's mills had their share of fires over the years. This photograph is of the Bates Mill fire, which occurred on October 23, 1907.

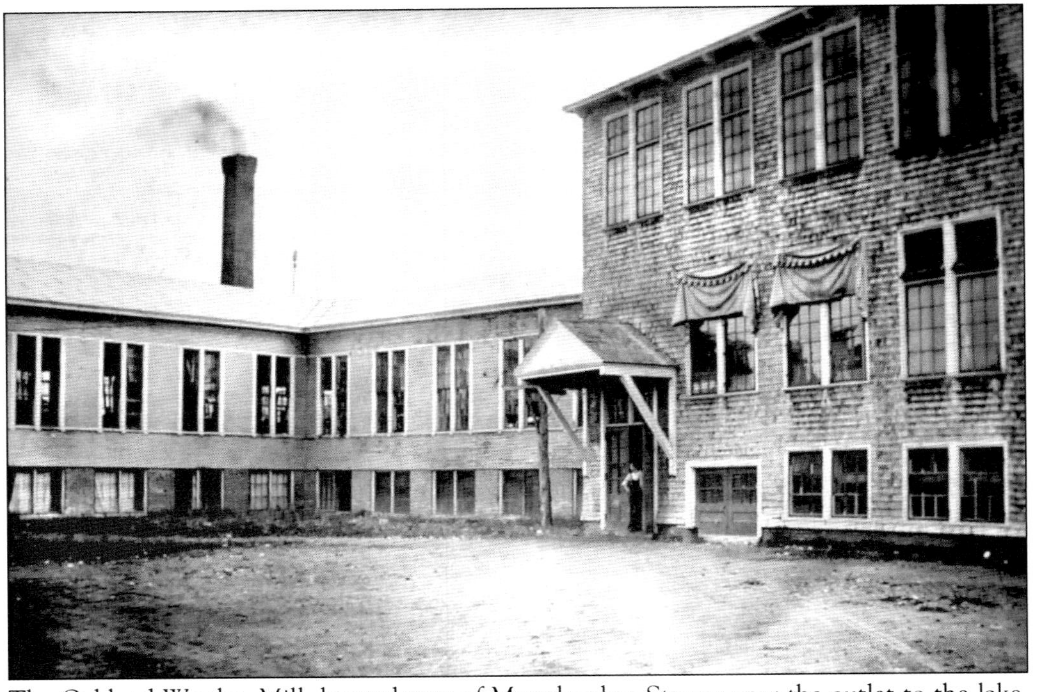

The Oakland Woolen Mill, located west of Messalonskee Stream near the outlet to the lake, apparently burned *c.* 1935 and was not rebuilt. Thus, it became one of the early Oakland factories to go out of business.

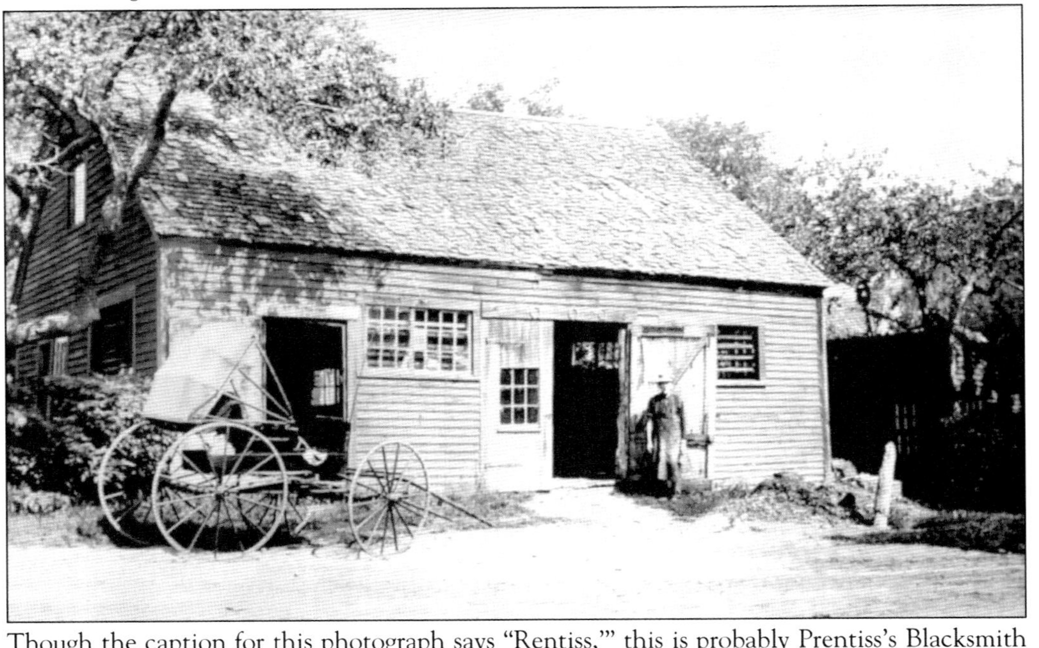

Though the caption for this photograph says "Rentiss,'" this is probably Prentiss's Blacksmith Shop. William H. Prentiss was a blacksmith in West Waterville as early as 1867 and as late as 1918. His shop was located near the Dunn Edge Tool Company. This photograph shows his shop *c.* 1905.

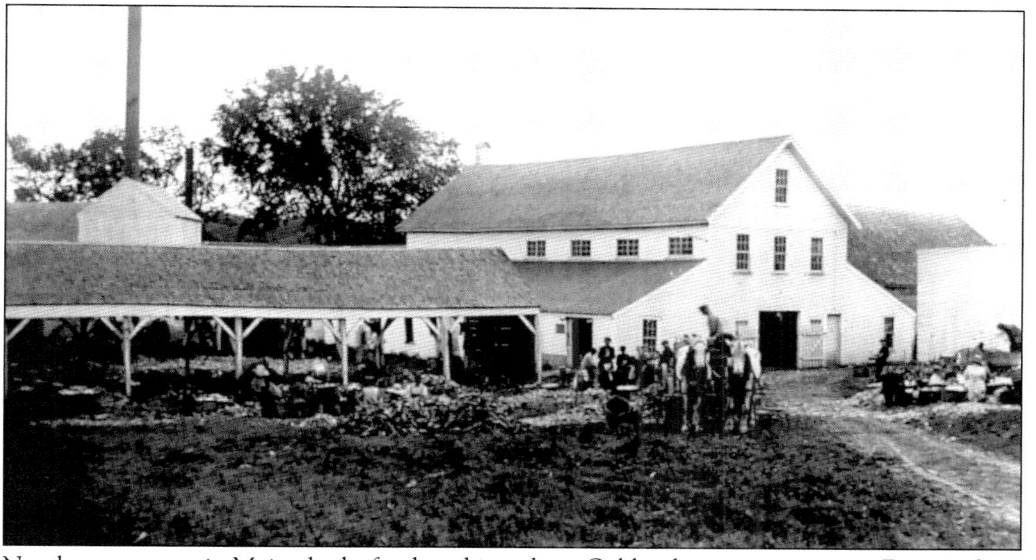

Nearly every town in Maine had a food-packing plant. Oakland was no exception. Farmers from all around would bring their corn, peas, or beans to the Portland Packing Company on Belgrade Avenue, where the vegetables were cooked and packed into tin-coated steel cans.

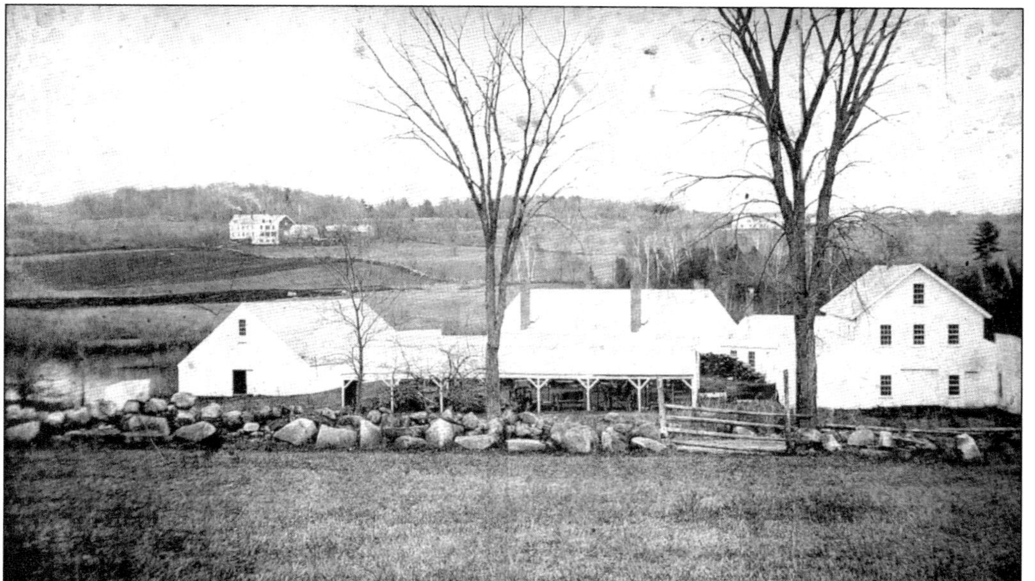

The Portland Packing Company on Belgrade Avenue was located near Lake View Cemetery on Messalonskee Lake, roughly where the boat landing is today.

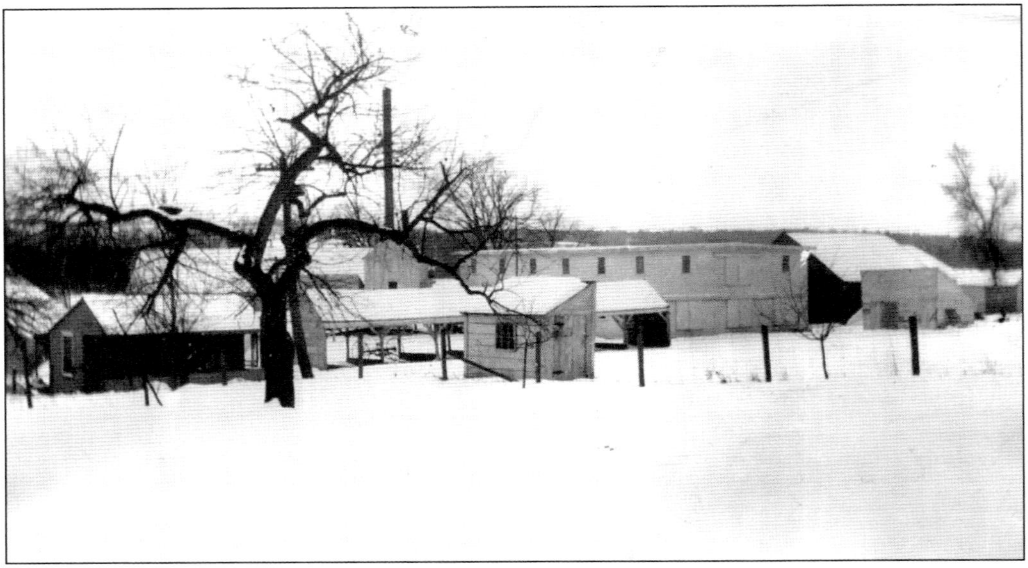

This is another view of the Portland Packing Company.

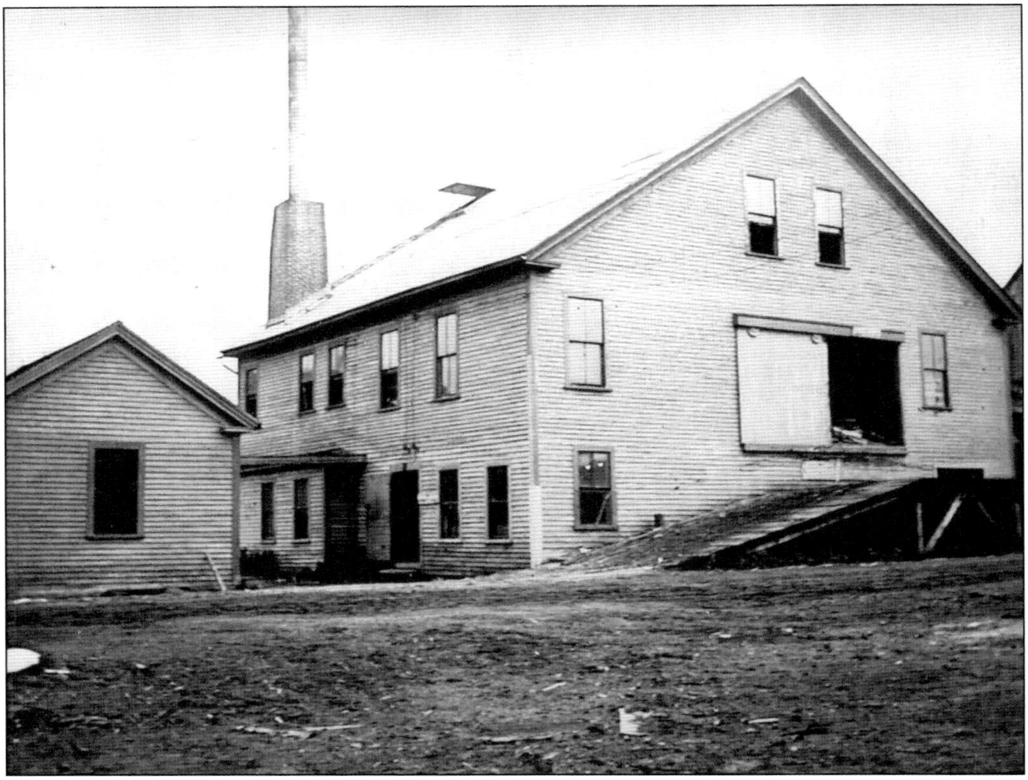

The Shovel Handle Shop on Heath Street was one of many small industries in Oakland, past and present. In fact, today there are no major industries left in town, but there are numerous small factories that employ a new generation of workers from Oakland and surrounding towns.

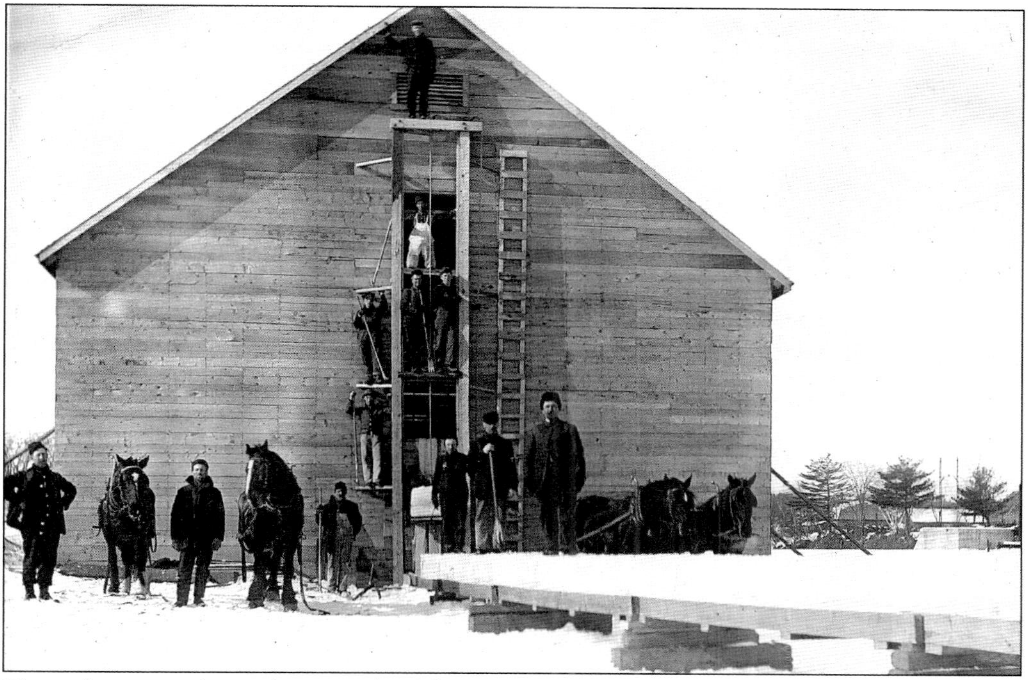

The icehouse was located just south of the cemeteries on Messalonskee Lake. In the era before refrigeration and air conditioning, ice was cut from rivers and lakes, stored in icehouses under piles of sawdust (which prevented melting), and sold during the spring, summer, and fall months. Many icehouses were located on the lower Kennebec River, south of Augusta, but nearly every stream and lake in Maine had its own.

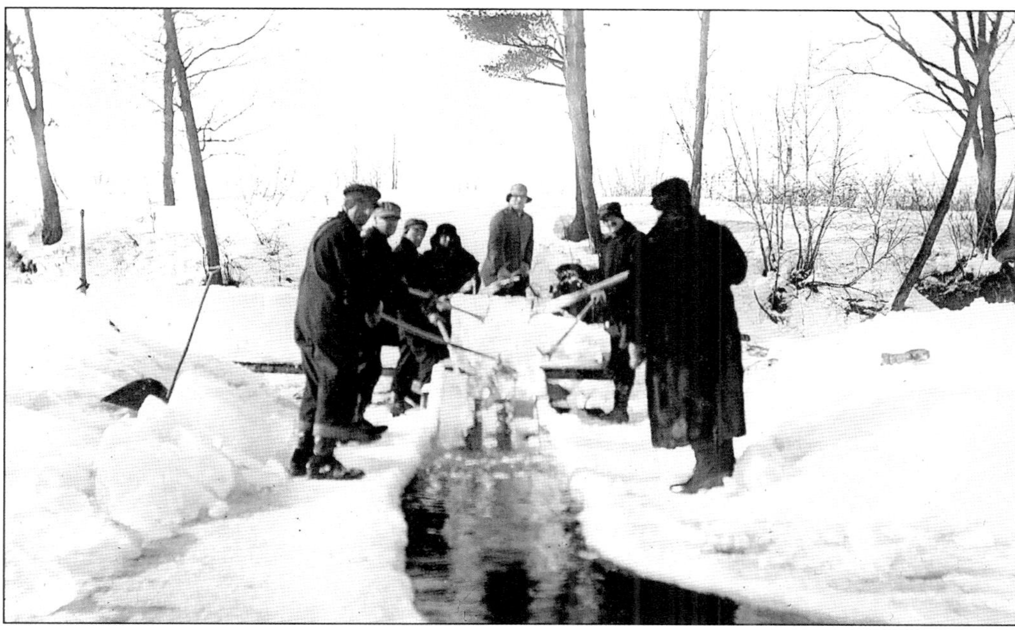

This photograph shows ice being cut on the lake. The ice was cut with large horse-drawn blades and then floated to the icehouses along the channels produced by the cutting of the ice.

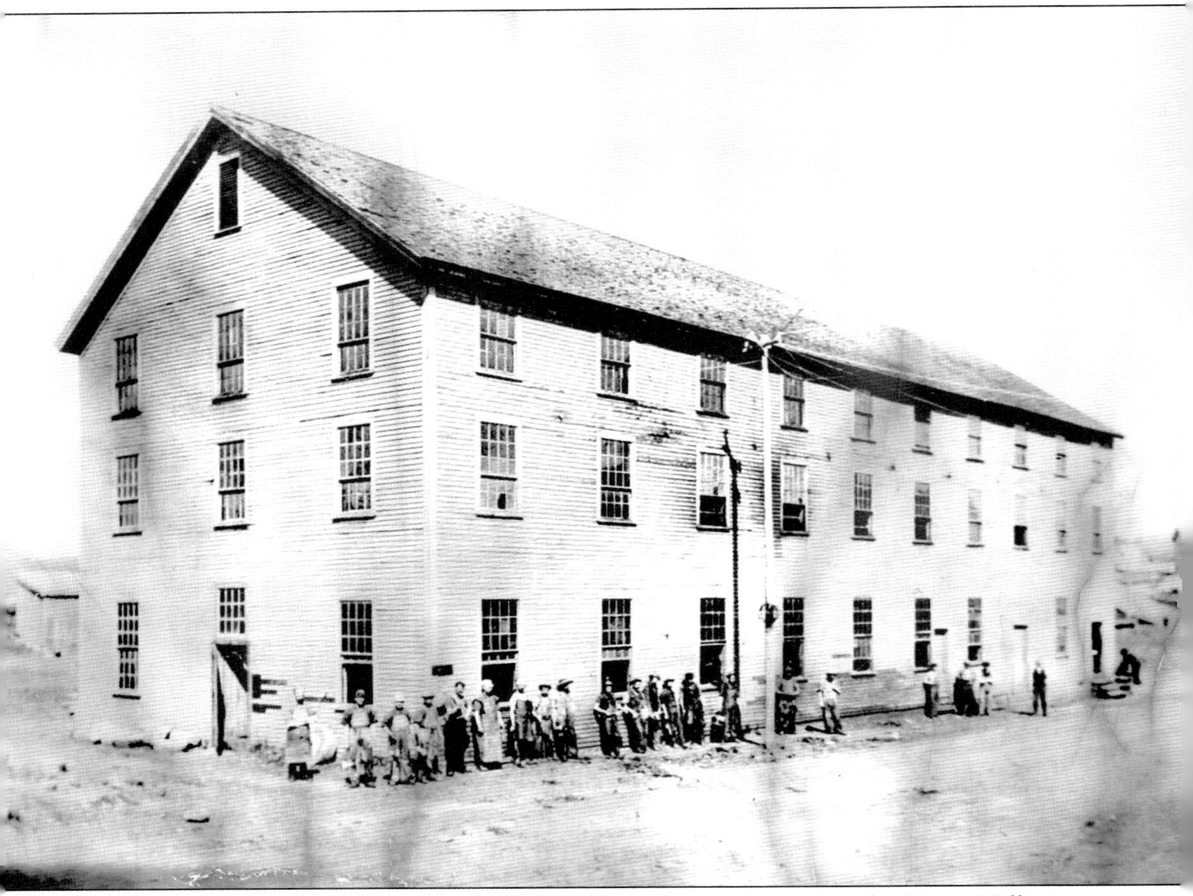

This building may have been the Bachelder Chair Factory, located in the Upper Mills.

Four

People, Organizations, and Recreation

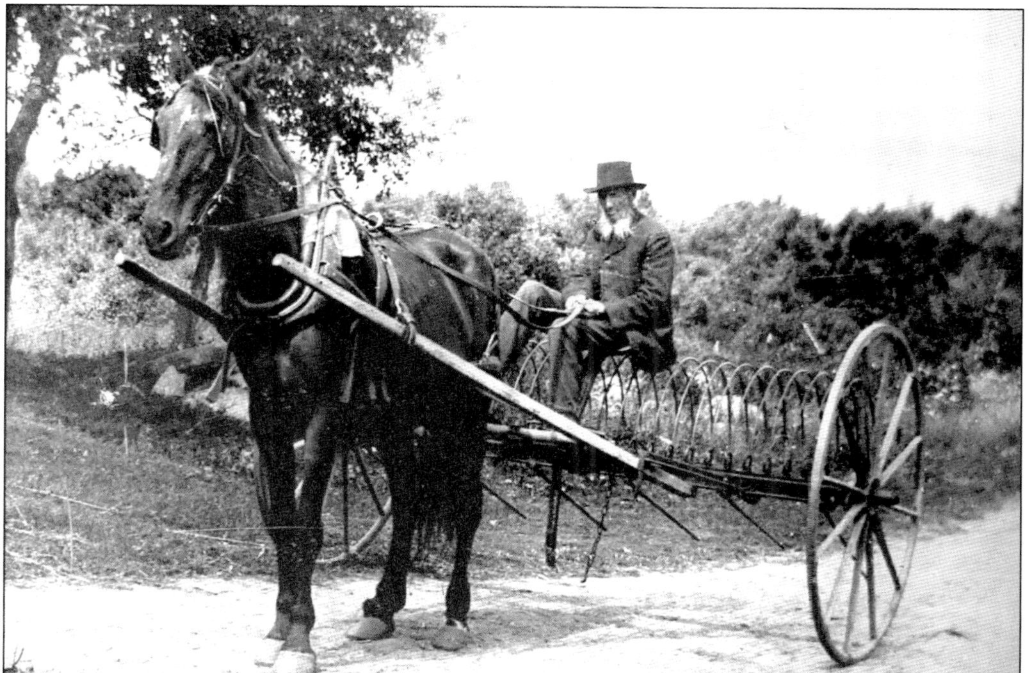

Benjamin F. Gleason bought land in 1854 and married Caroline V. McIntire in 1855. He was the great-grandfather of Lucile Small of Oakland. His land was located on Belgrade Road at the corner of Town Farm Road. His son, Arthur Gleason, lived in the house for many years. Local residents used to buy eggs from him.

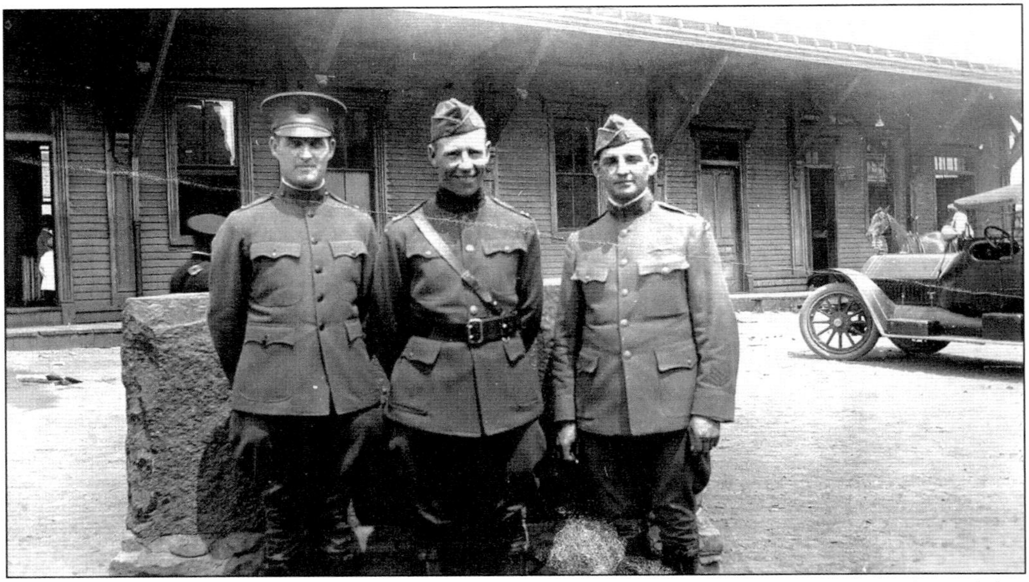

Pictured here are World War I veterans Albion Blake, Earl Goodwin, and Walter Blake, probably in their World War I uniforms. Oakland held a giant parade honoring its war heroes in 1919, many photographs of which are included later in this book.

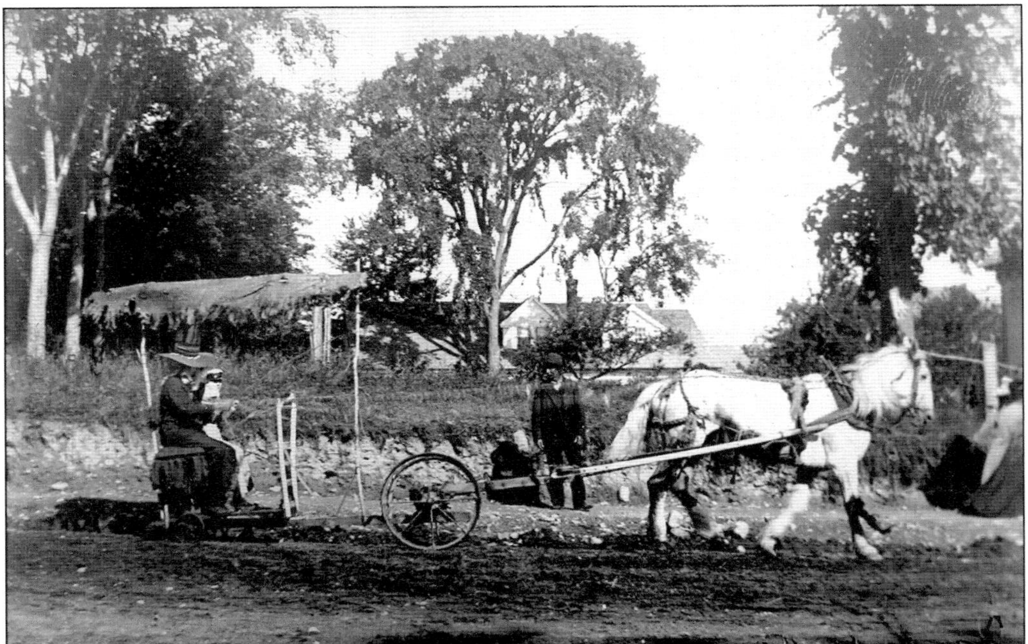

Charles Bailey's team is seen here on July 4, 1900. Bailey was born in March 1851 and died on May 10, 1922. He married Anna L. Moor on September 24, 1877. The 1885 town directory said he was a carpenter. He had a home on Elm Court (which may have been in Waterville) in 1903. The Maine Register lists him as a farmer and building mover with two children, Silas E. and John E.

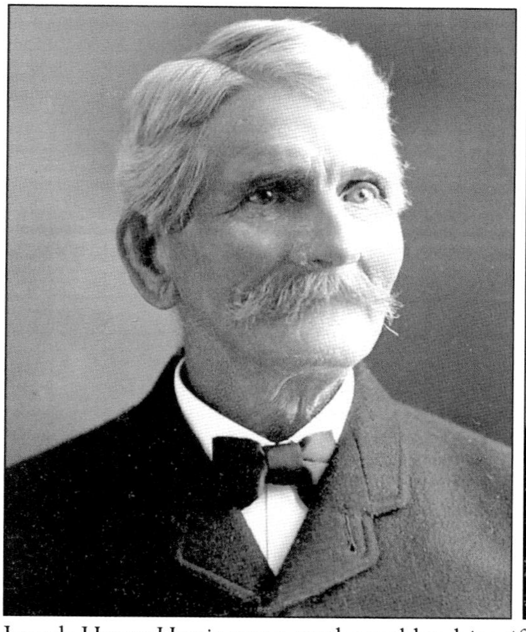

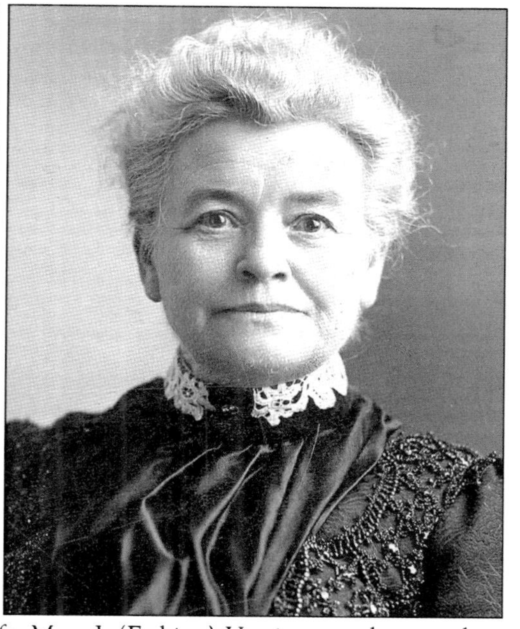

Joseph Henry Harris was a scythe welder; his wife, Mary J. (Erskine) Harris, was a homemaker. They lived on School Street near Church Street. Their children were Charles C. Harris and Joseph E. Harris. Joseph E. married Mabel A. Caswell in 1885 and was a cashier at Messalonskee National Bank also in 1885.

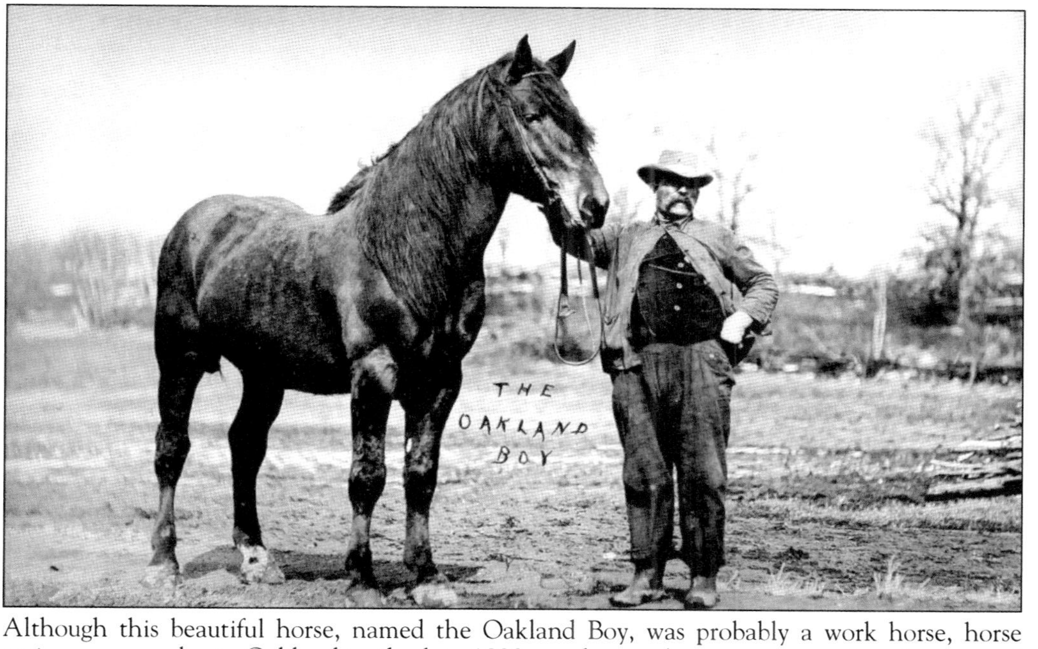

Although this beautiful horse, named the Oakland Boy, was probably a work horse, horse racing was popular in Oakland in the late 1800s, and many horses were raced at the Central Maine Fairgrounds in Waterville (near the present-day Seton Unit of the MaineGeneral Medical Center).

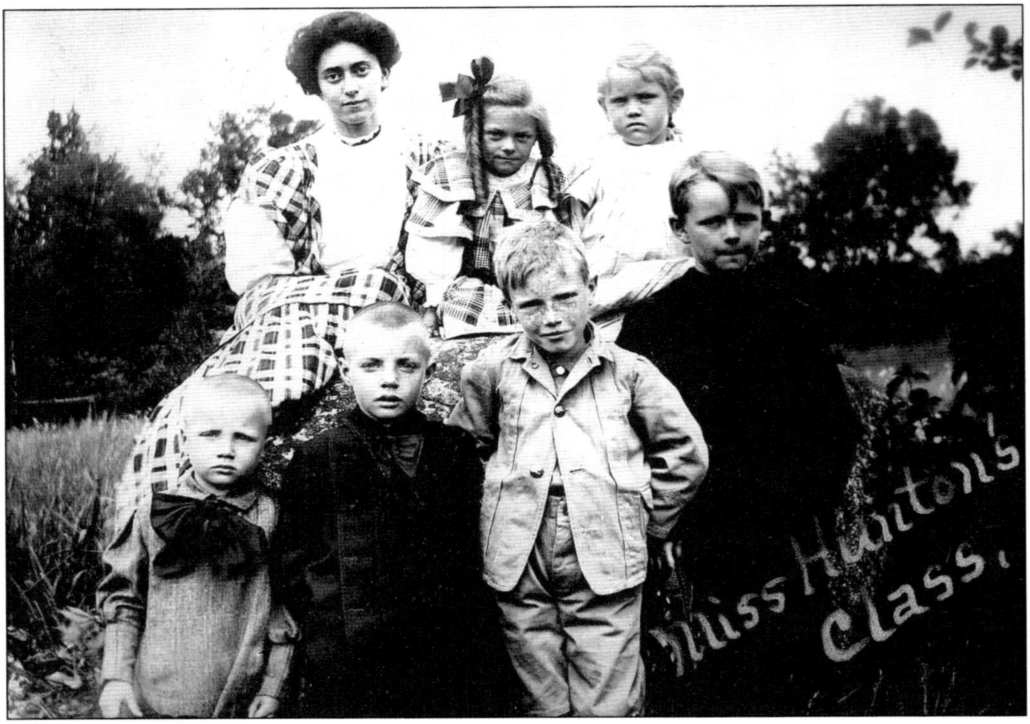

Seen here is Miss Hunton's class at the Free Will Baptist Church's Sunday school picnic at McGrath Pond on July 29, 1909.

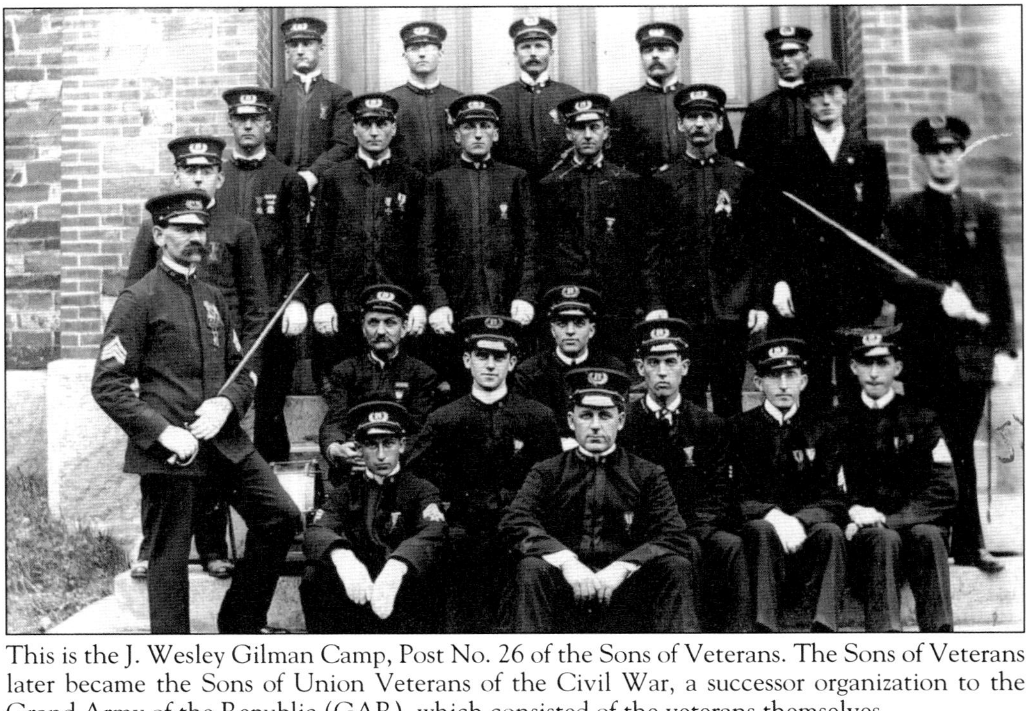

This is the J. Wesley Gilman Camp, Post No. 26 of the Sons of Veterans. The Sons of Veterans later became the Sons of Union Veterans of the Civil War, a successor organization to the Grand Army of the Republic (GAR), which consisted of the veterans themselves.

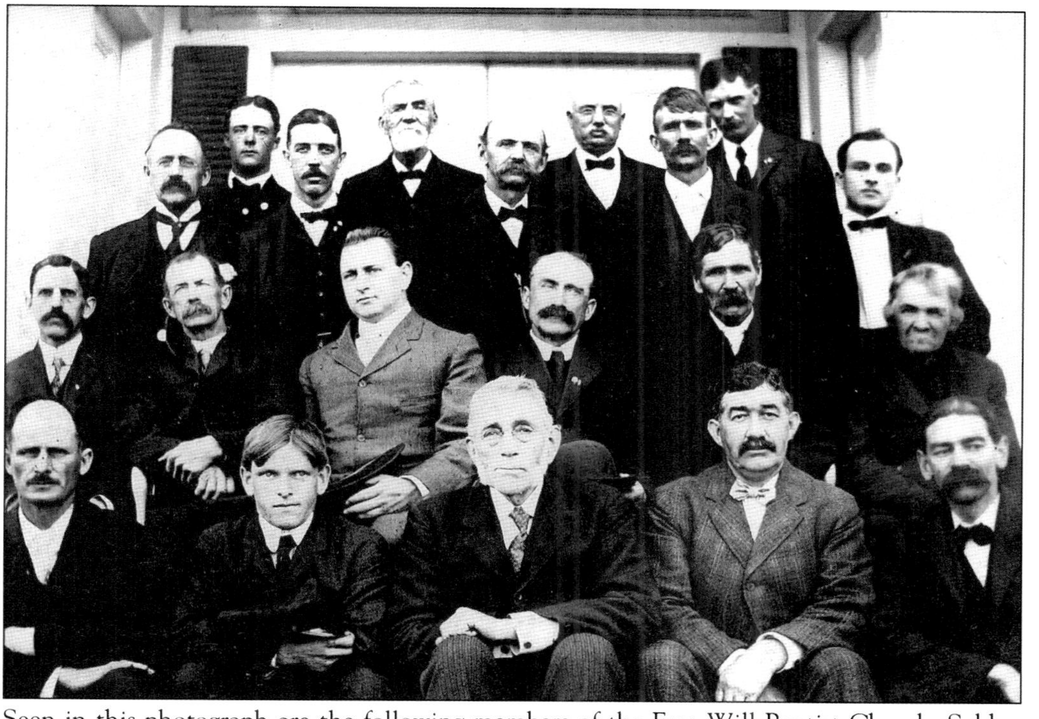

Seen in this photograph are the following members of the Free Will Baptist Church: Selden Manter of Sidney, son of George Manter (first row, second from the left); Rev. Aura C. Gerrish (first row, center); T. W. Longley of Sidney (second row, fourth from the left); and George Manter of Sidney (rear, in the center). Charles Lewis, George Manter's grandson, provided the identifications for this photograph.

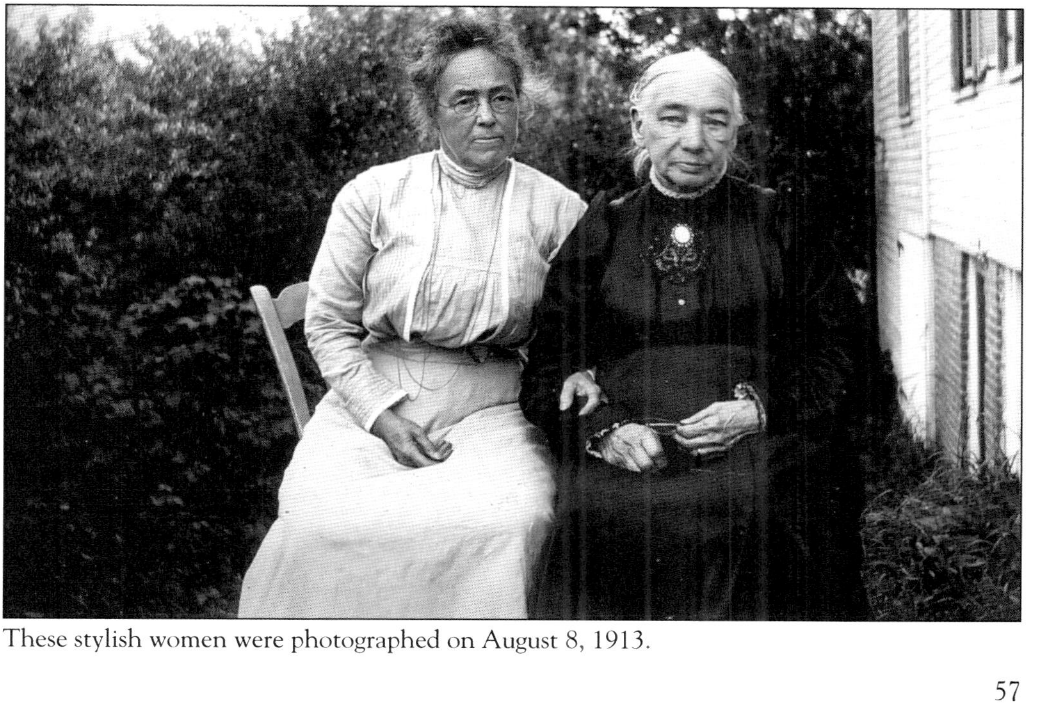

These stylish women were photographed on August 8, 1913.

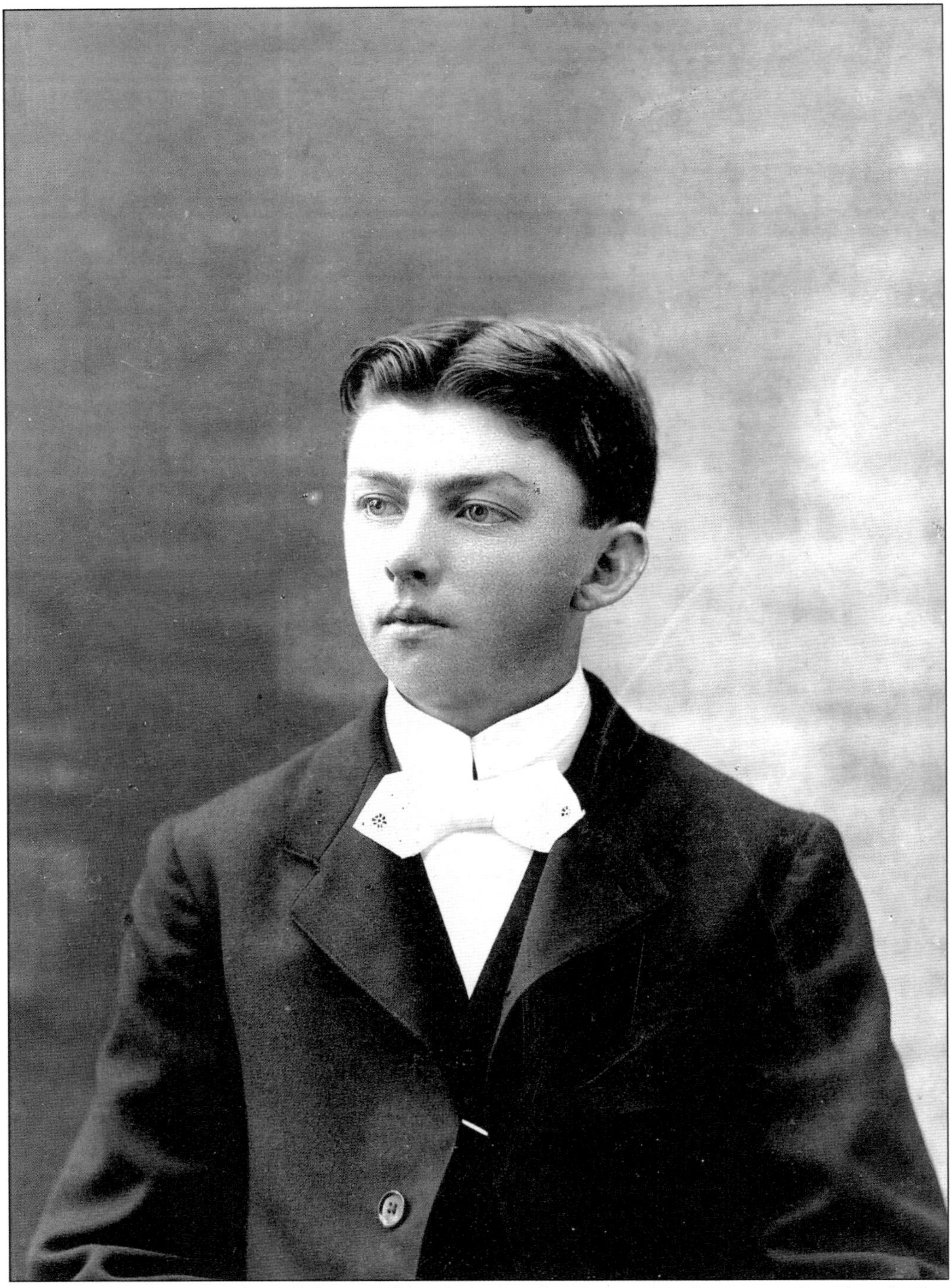

Walter E. Sullivan graduated from Oakland High School in 1897. A note enclosed with this photograph reads, "Picture of Walter Sullivan, Oakland; uncle to Eileen Dudley, Marguerite Nason, Thena Gilbert—given by June Otten, Camden."

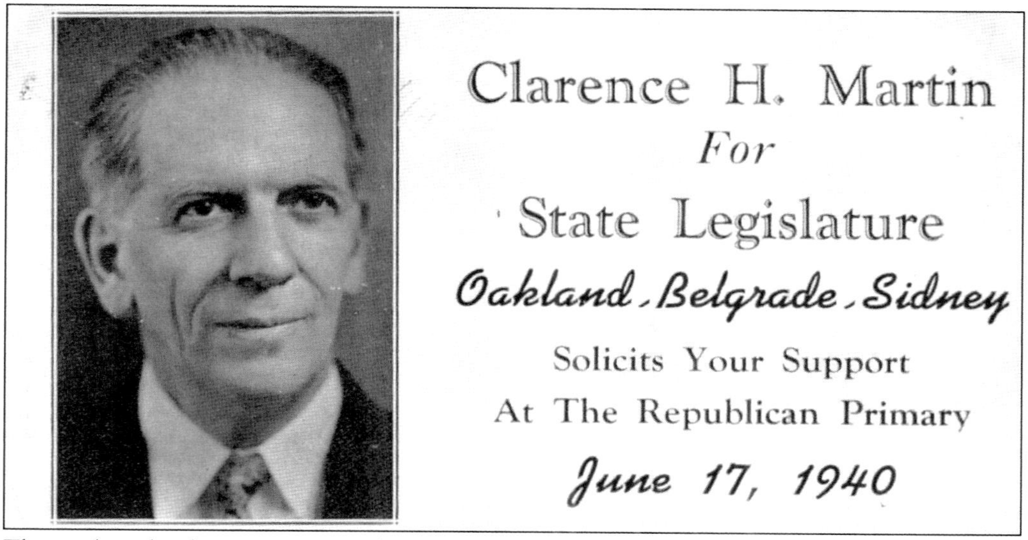

This political advertisement reads, "Clarence H. Martin for State Legislature, Oakland, Belgrade, Sidney, Solicits Your Support At The Republican Primary, June 17, 1940." Martin ran a newsstand and soda fountain on Church Street near the railroad crossing. He had taught school in Oakland before that.

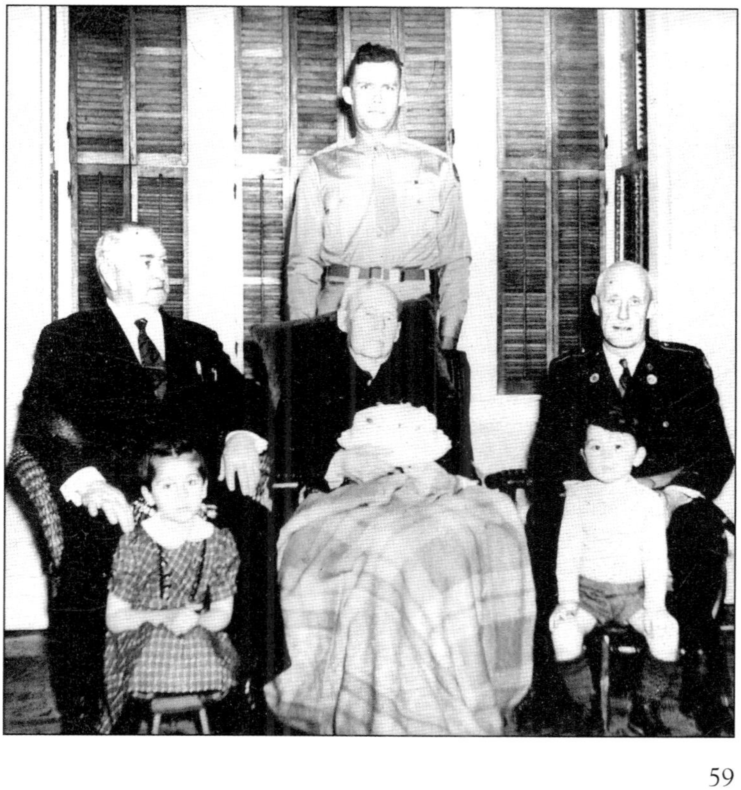

Pictured here are some of Oakland's veterans. From left to right are the following: (first row) Jeannette McGowan and Larry Williams; (second row) Sargie Warren (Spanish-American War), George Benson (Civil War), and Roy Tracy (World War I); (third row) Robert Lothrop (World War II). George Benson died in 1944.

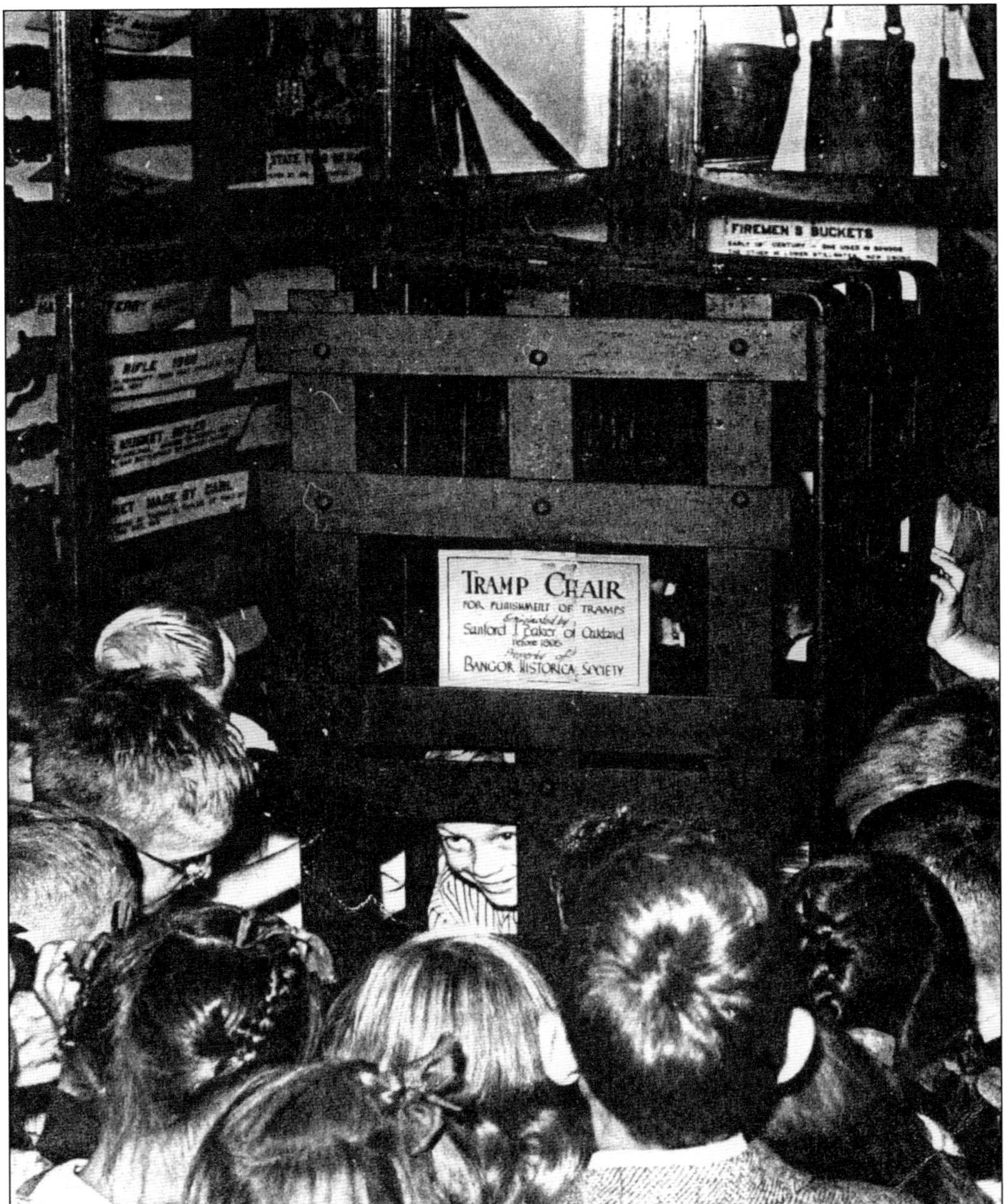

The Tramp Chair was invented by Sanford Baker. This strange contraption, once located at the Bangor Historical Society, was supposed to *house* the homeless temporarily until they could be physically removed from the town. In the late 1800s, towns were responsible for the support of the indigent, and if a town could *transport* its indigent to another town, the receiving town had to pay their support.

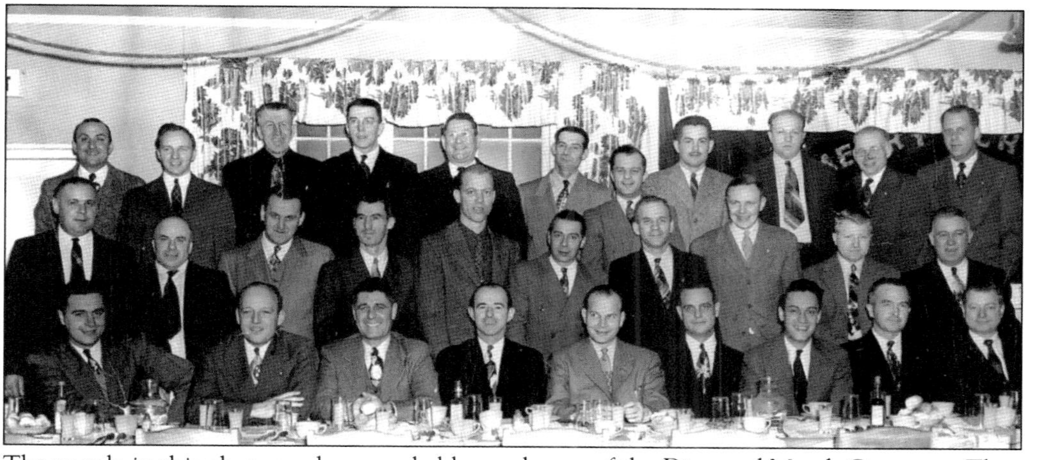

The people in this photograph are probably employees of the Diamond Match Company. They include Charles Pooler, Cyrus Davis, Harold Buzzell, ? Isbister, Ernest Goodspeed, Roy Bowen, and Arthur Noyes.

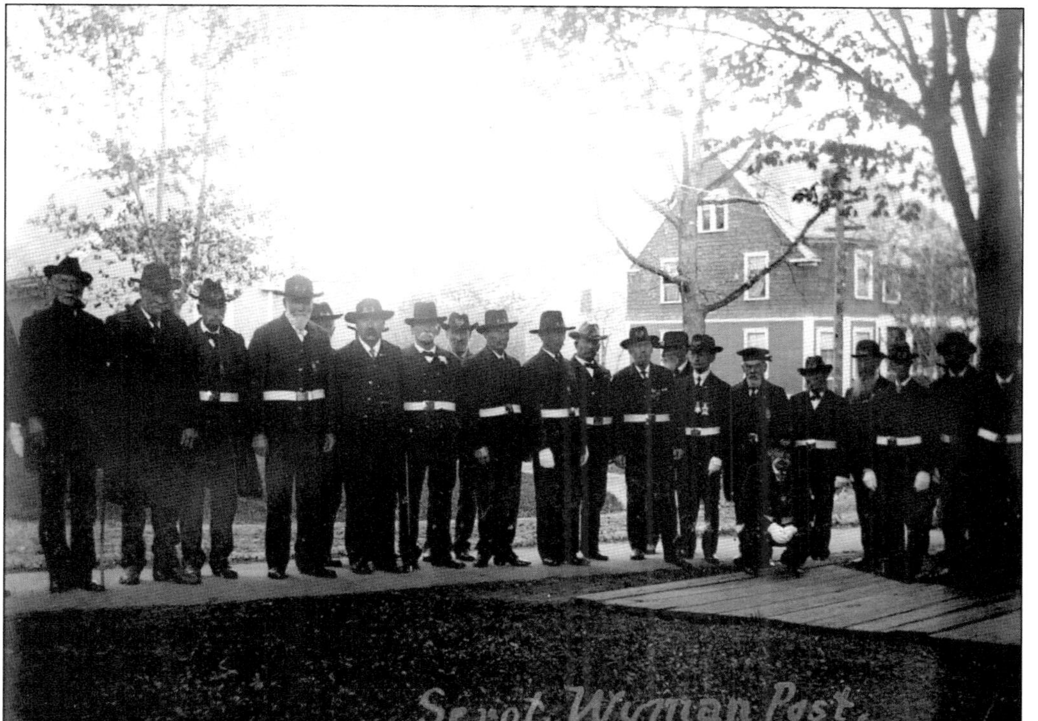

The Grand Army of the Republic was made up of Civil War veterans. Oakland's GAR Sergeant Wyman Post No. 97 was responsible for building Soldier's Memorial Hall in 1870. Oakland's last Civil War veteran, George Benson, died in 1944.

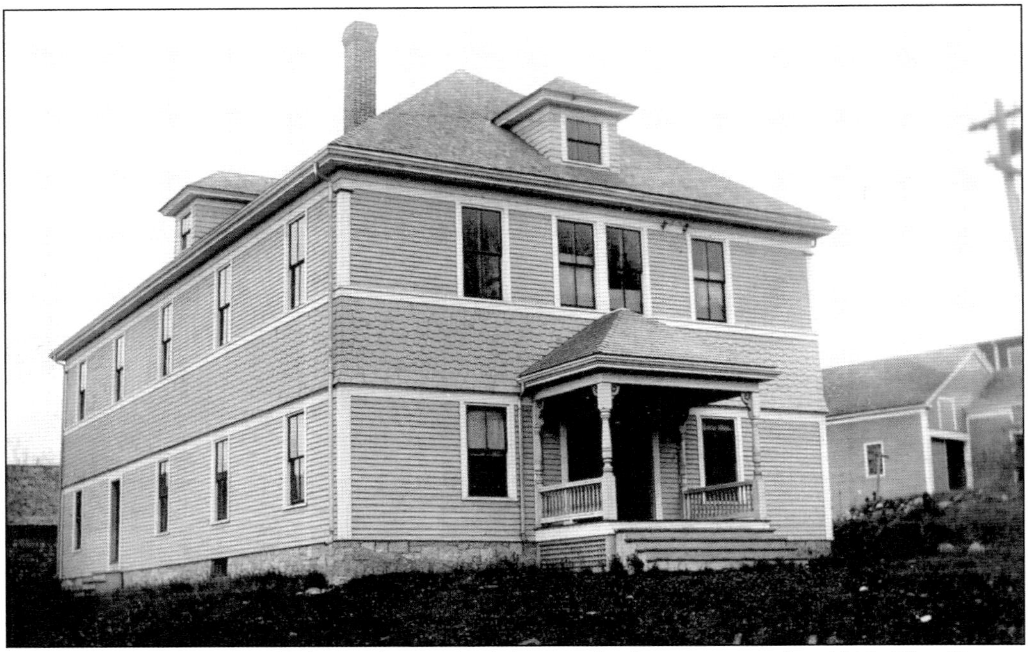

The Cascade Grange Hall, located near the lake, was built sometime after 1913. The Grange itself was organized in Oakland in 1875 and held meetings in Liberty Hall, a building near the junction of Alpine Street and Middle Road.

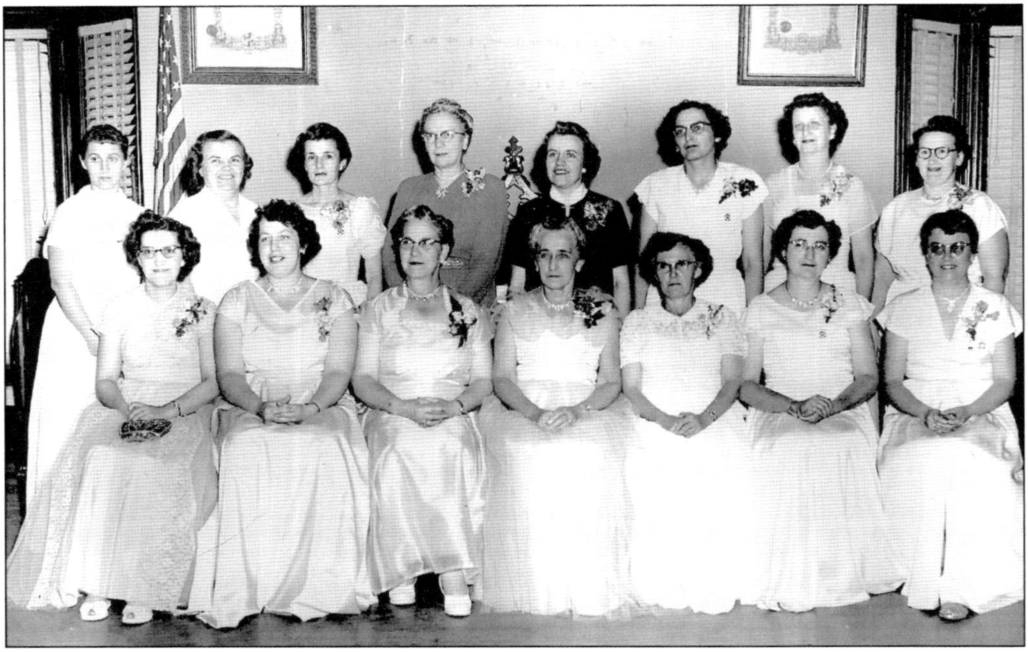

Pictured at the Acme Rebekah Lodge *c.* 1950 are, from left to right, the following: (first row) Edith Cunningham, ? Boyles, Evelyn Boyles, Eleanor Day, Evelyn Soper, Alys Watson, and Margaret Bowen; (second row) Dorothy Miner, Rosella Isbister, Ethel Hutchinson, Elizabeth Hills, Bernley Hambleton, Dorothy Jordan, Emeline Bard, and ? Soule.

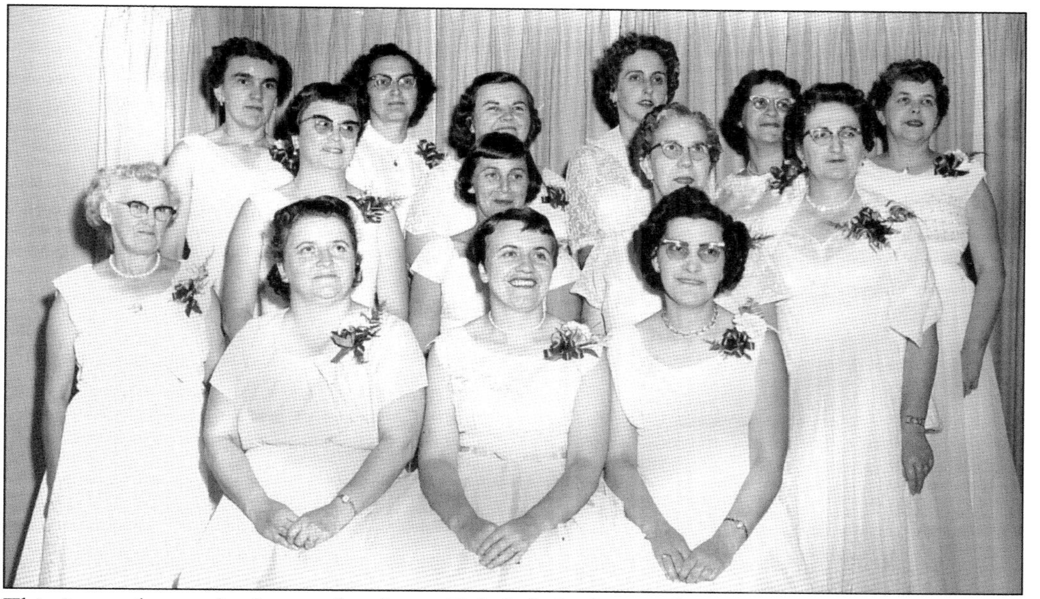

This is another gathering at the Acme Rebekah Lodge in the 1950s. The women pictured are, from left to right, as follows: (first row) Ruth Buzzell, Bernley Hambleton, and Edith Cunningham; (second row) Evelyn Soper, Margaret Bowen, Dorothy Miner, Evelyn Boyles, and Alys Watson; (third row) Myrtle Bickford, Dorothy Jordan, Rosetta Isbister, two unidentified people, and Audrey Livingston.

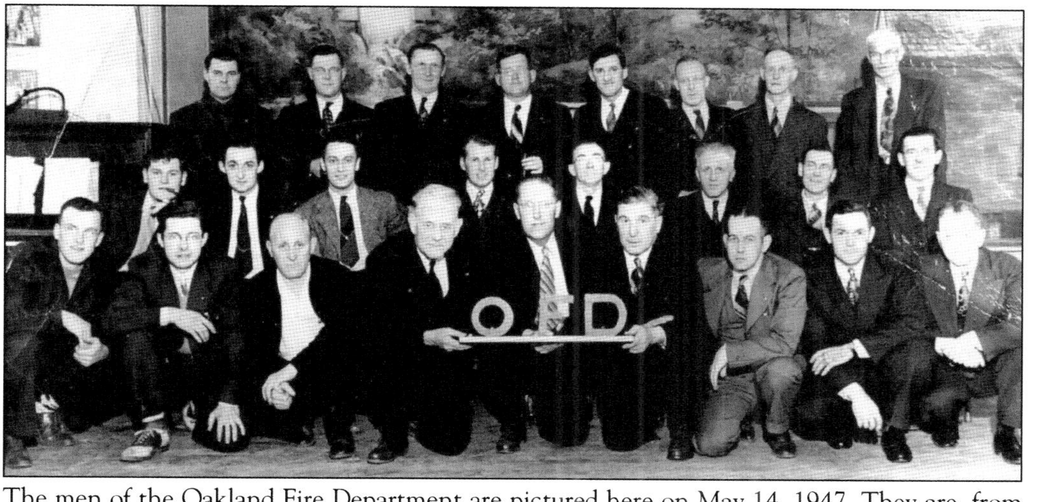

The men of the Oakland Fire Department are pictured here on May 14, 1947. They are, from left to right, as follows: (first row) Clifton Collar, hook and ladder; Theodore Kerr, driver 1; Simon Stevens, hook and ladder; Merton Leech, second assistant chief; Alva D. Kerr, chief; Ben Brown, second assistant chief; Chester Blake, driver 1; Robert Clark, driver, secretary, and treasurer; and Lyman Nason Dunn, hose; (second row) John D. Mahue, hose; Winslow Toby, hook and ladder; Bernard Carey, hose; Charles Hutchinson, driver 1; Walter Brooks, hook and ladder; Ben Luce, hose; Dennis Hamlin, hose; and Everett Watson, hose; (third row) Ed Livingstone, hook and ladder; Ed Pullen, hook and ladder, president; Henry Brown, hook and ladder; Harry Brawn, hose; Emery Soule, hose; Del Tucker, hose; Norris Bush, hose; and W. Danis Foreman, hook and ladder.

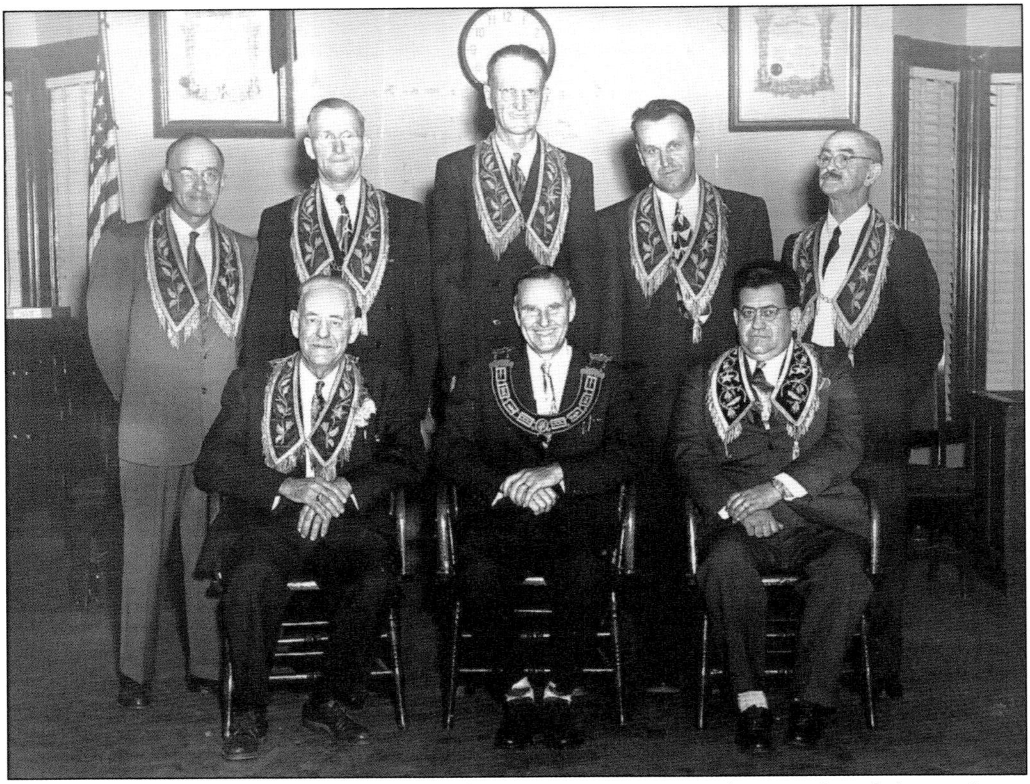

Seen here are members of the Odd Fellows Organization *c.* 1964. They are, from left to right, as follows: (first row) Merton Leech, ? Carrol, and Perry Morse; (second row) Earl Sawtelle, Roy Dudley, Ralph Stevens, Roy Bowen, and unknown.

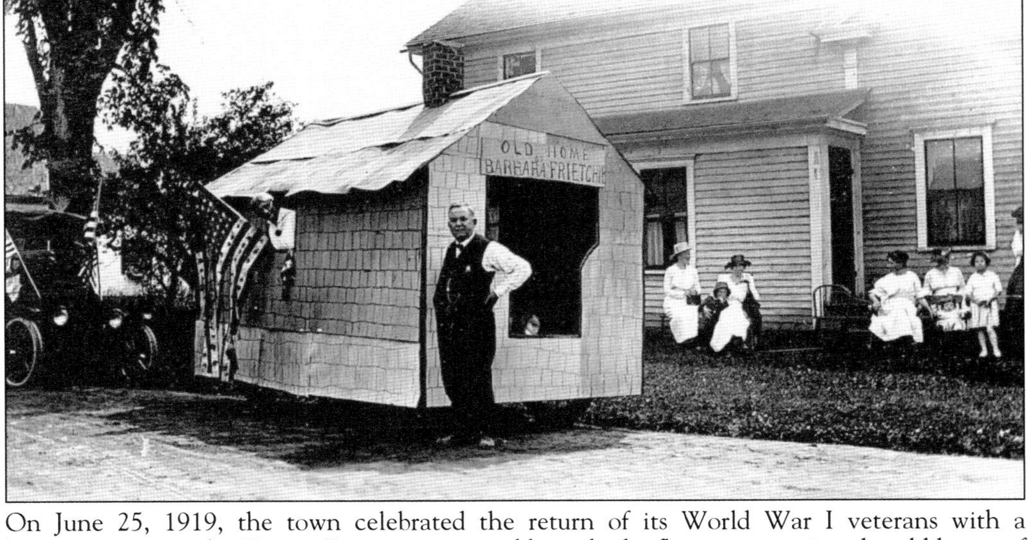

On June 25, 1919, the town celebrated the return of its World War I veterans with a homecoming parade. George Boynton, pictured here, had a float representing the old home of Barbara Fritchie of American Revolution fame. The parade was extensively described by the Waterville *Morning Sentinel* on June 26, 1919.

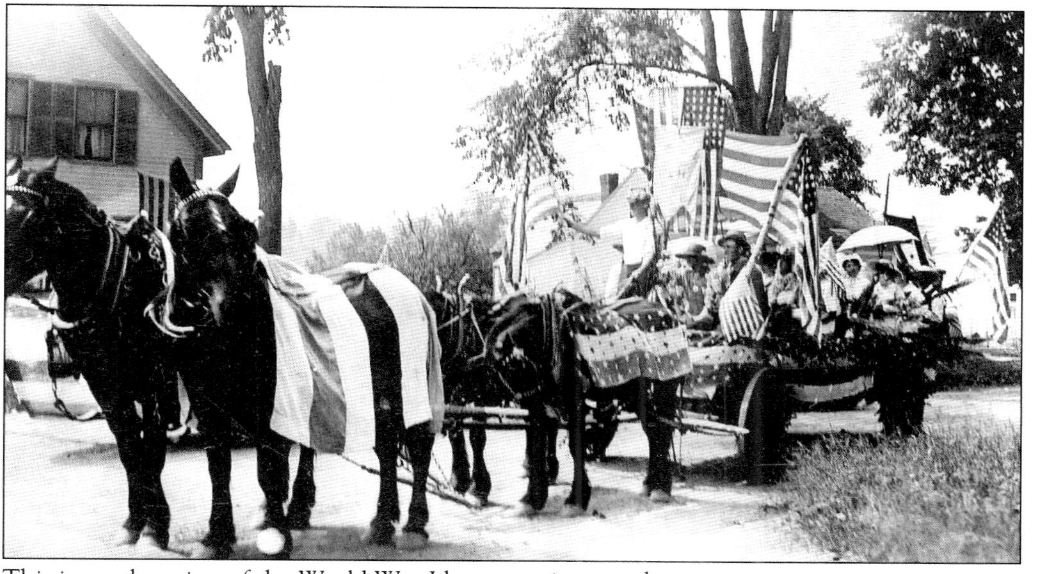

This is another view of the World War I homecoming parade.

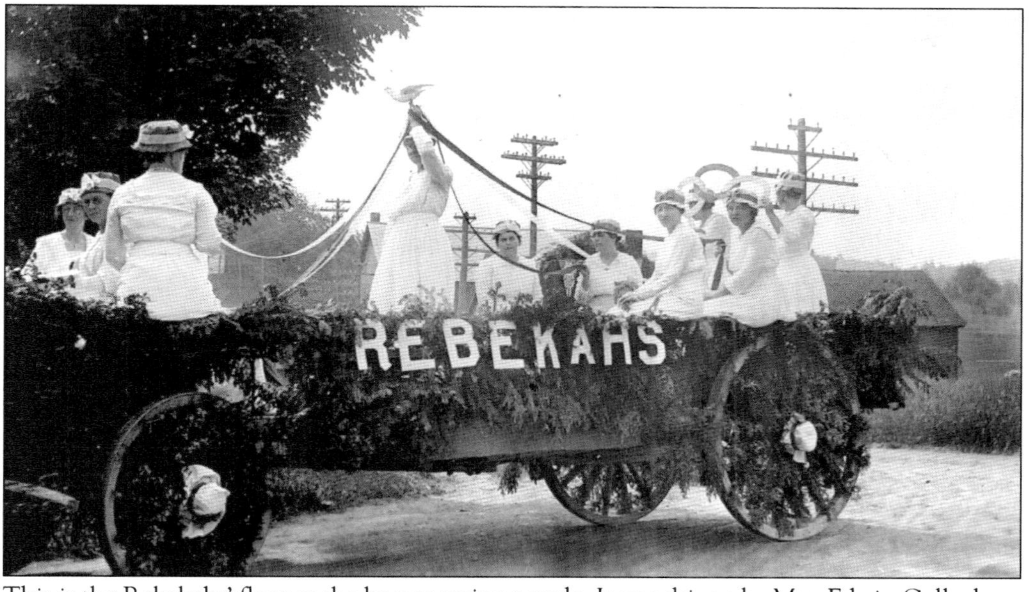

This is the Rebekahs' float at the homecoming parade. It was driven by Mrs. Edwin Gallagher.

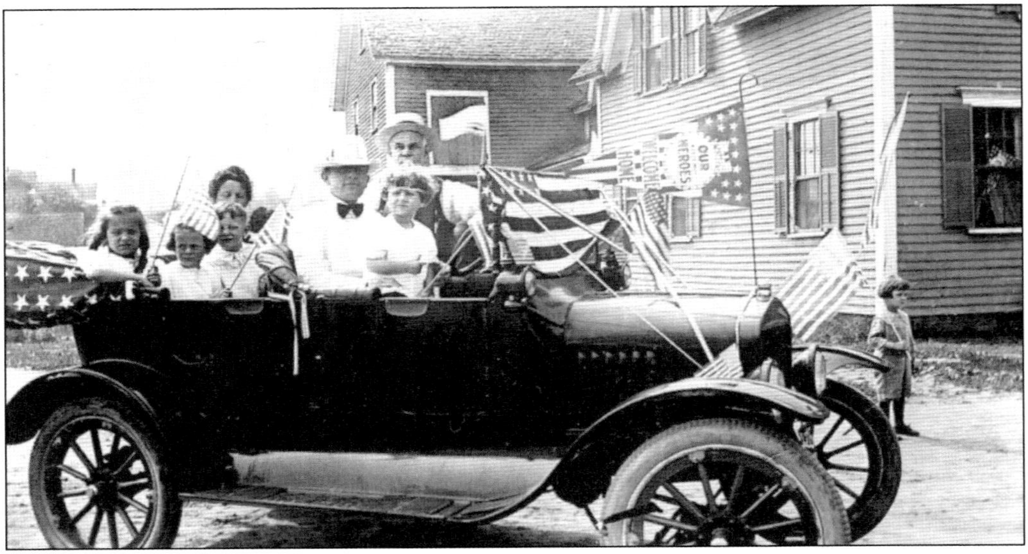

George Wilson drives one of the latest models of cars in the homecoming parade.

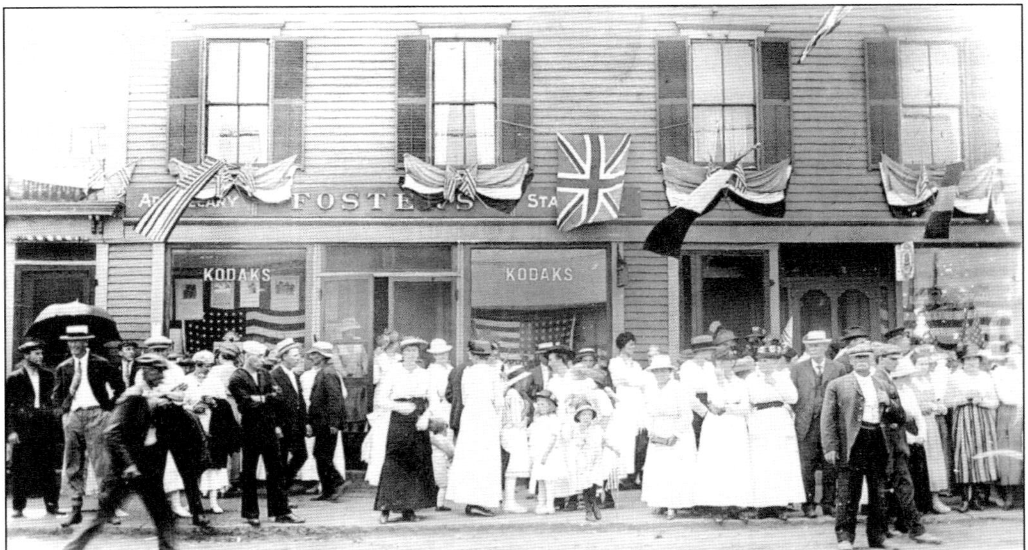

This was the scene in front of Foster's Drug Store on Main Street during the homecoming parade.

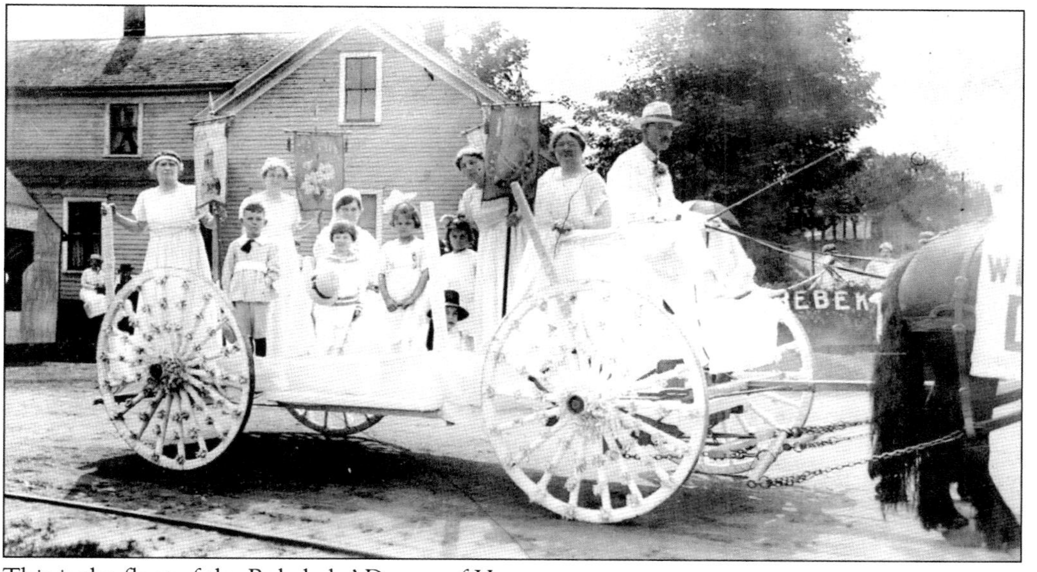

This is the float of the Rebekahs' Degree of Honor.

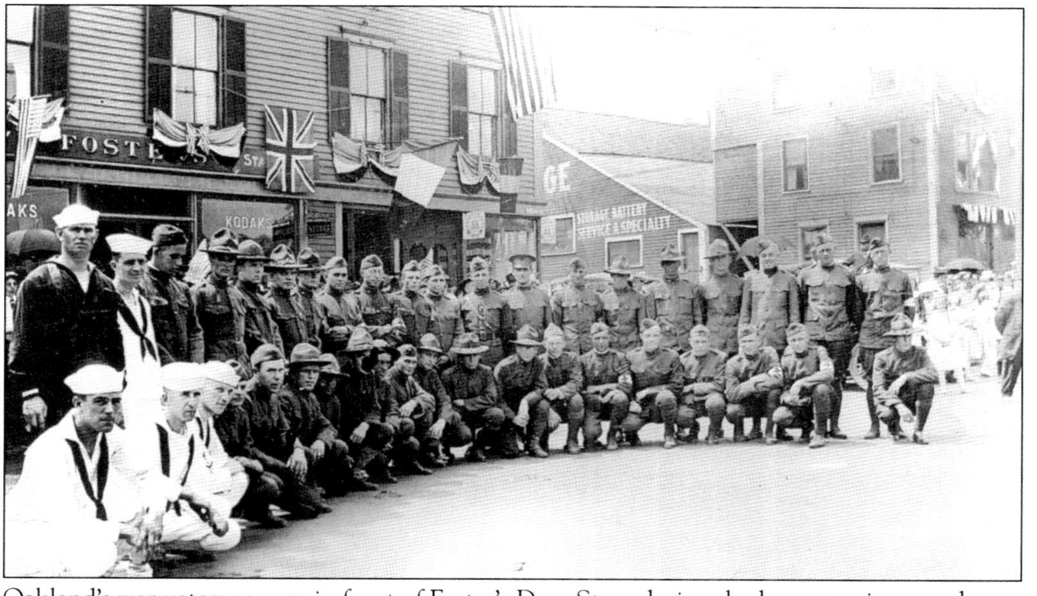

Oakland's war veterans pose in front of Foster's Drug Store during the homecoming parade.

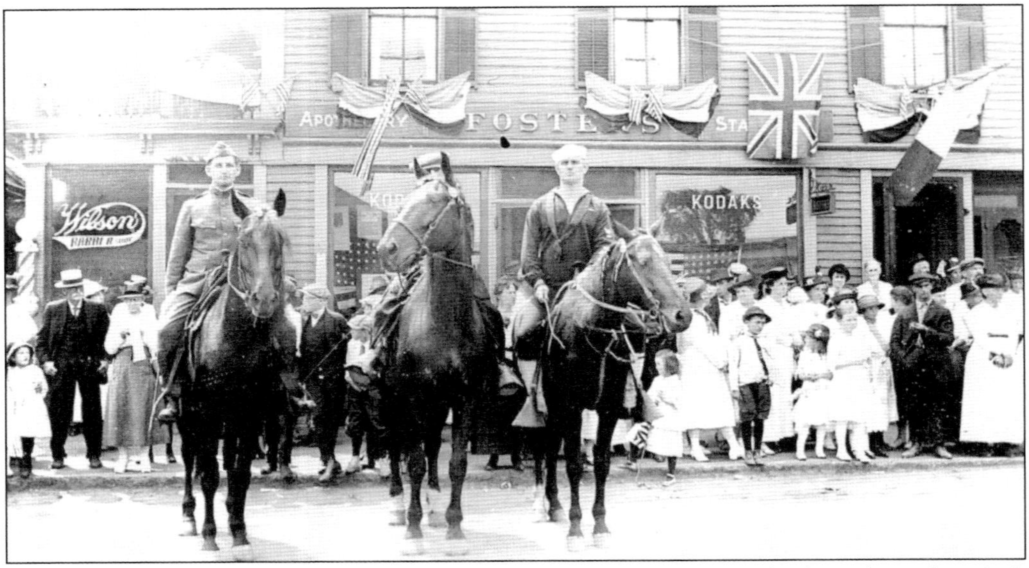

Seen here at the homecoming parade are, from left to right, Walter Blake (army), unidentified, and Henry Hutchinson (navy).

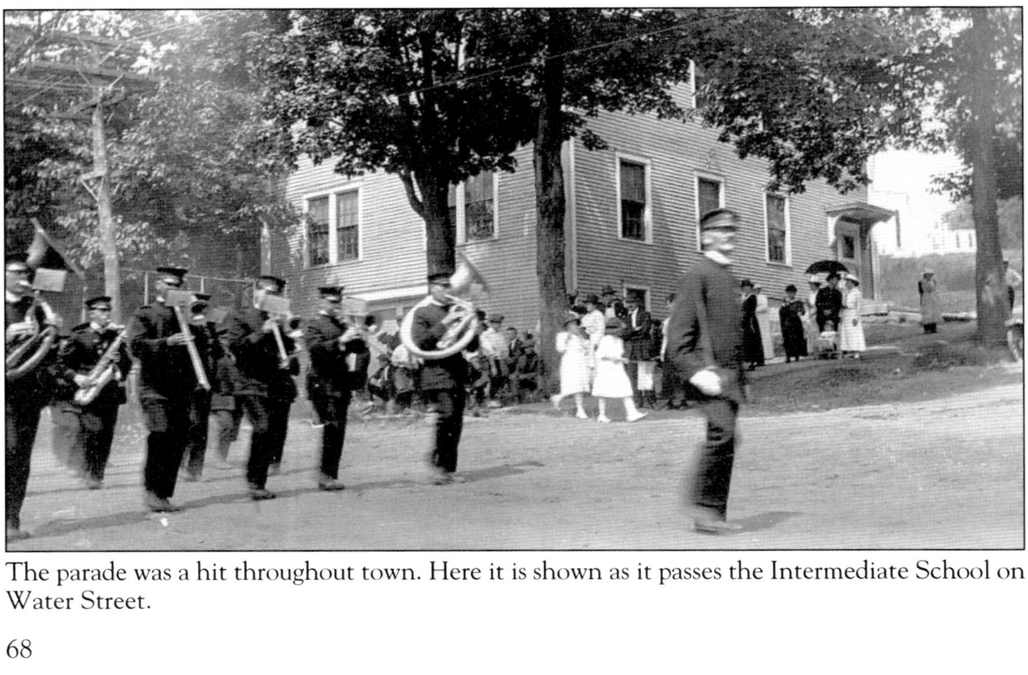

The parade was a hit throughout town. Here it is shown as it passes the Intermediate School on Water Street.

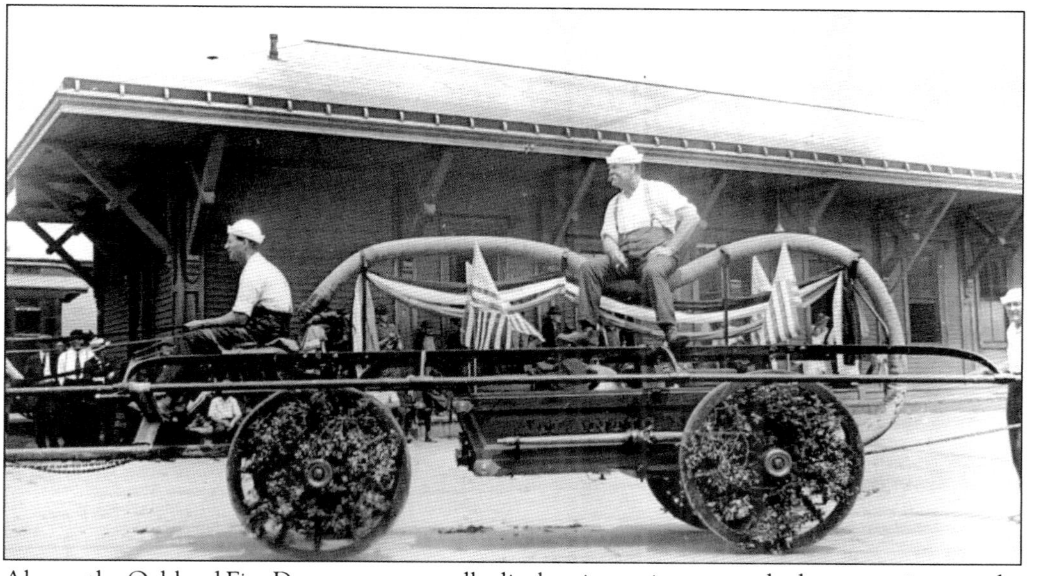

Above, the Oakland Fire Department proudly displays its equipment at the homecoming parade. Below is another photograph of the fire department on parade day.

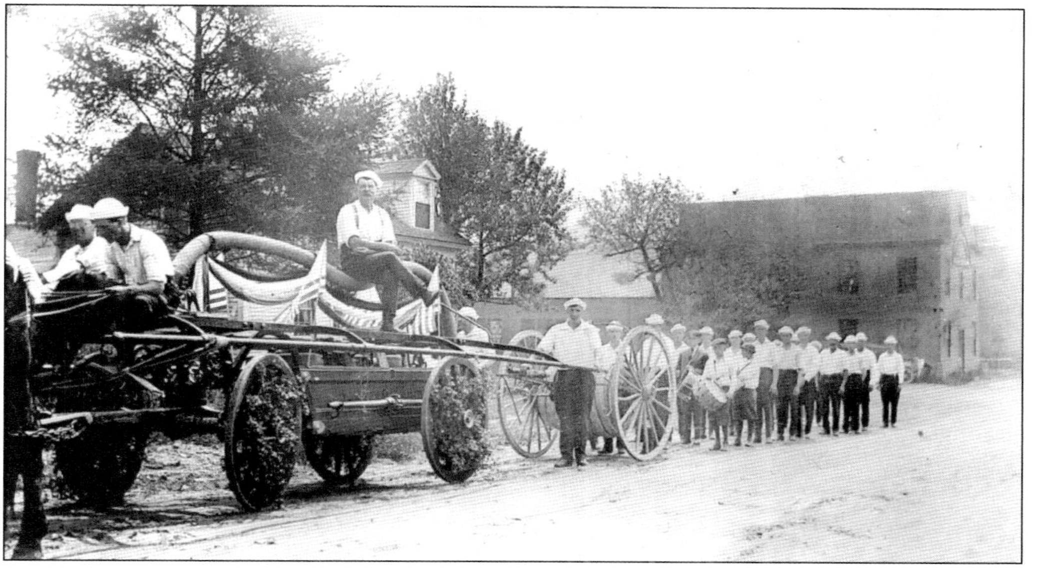

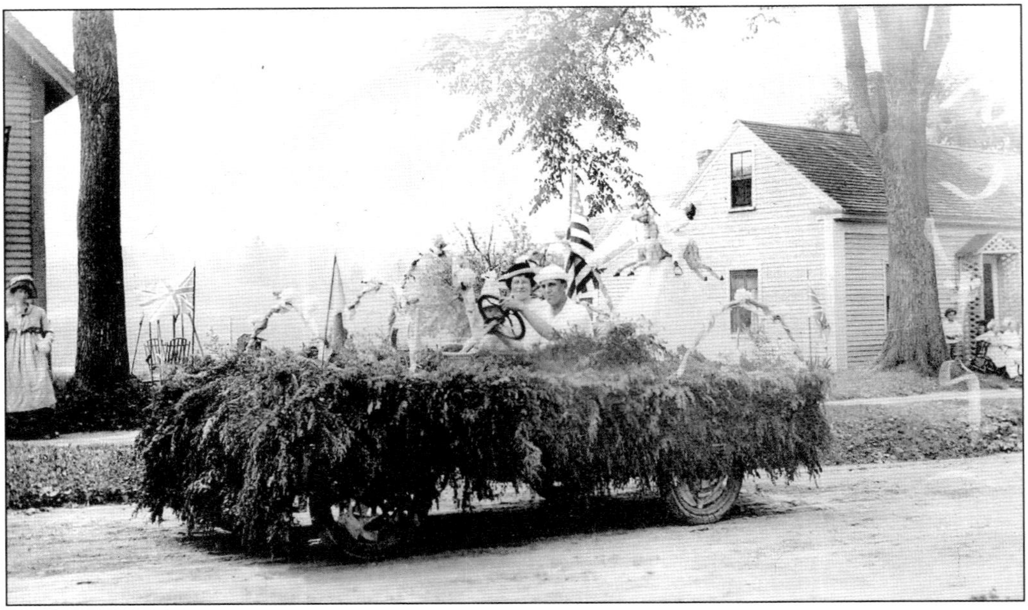

The Toy Theatre float had evergreens topped by a rocking horse and a large doll.

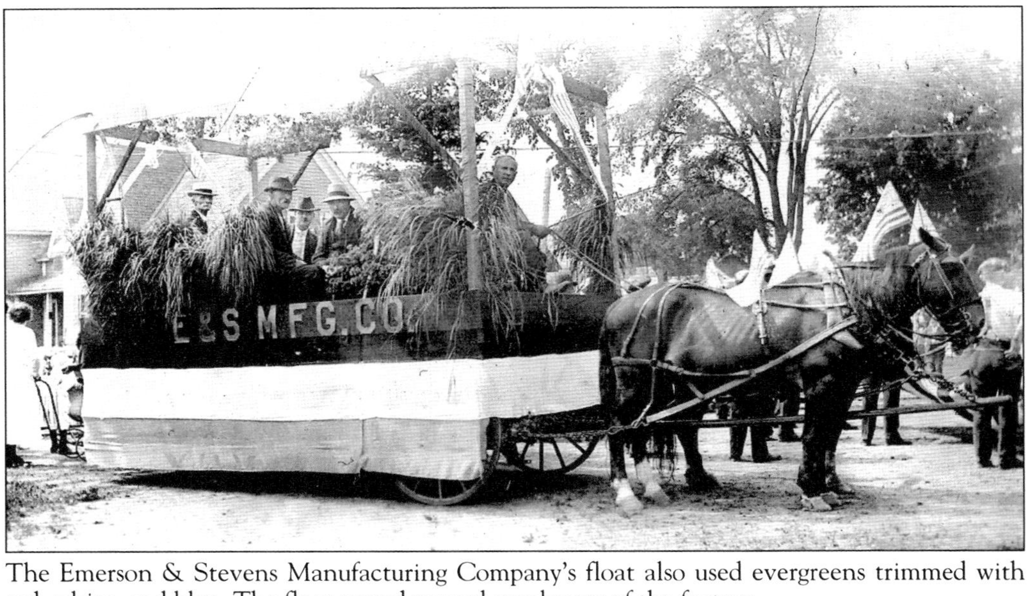

The Emerson & Stevens Manufacturing Company's float also used evergreens trimmed with red, white, and blue. The float seated several employees of the factory.

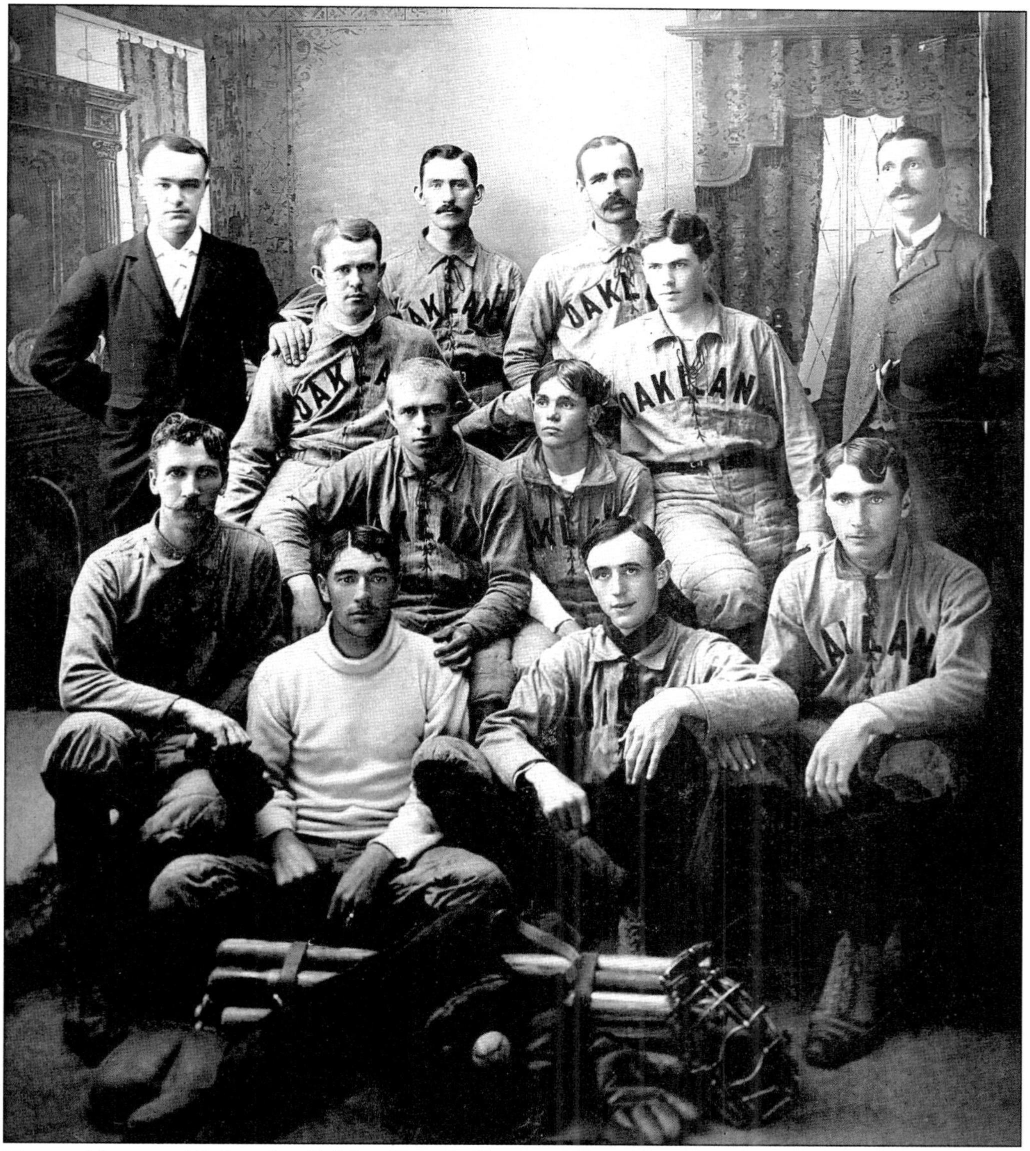

Pictured here c. 1900 is the Oakland baseball team. The official baseball field occupied the site of the Forster Manufacturing Company, now the site of Industrial Metal Recycling, between the railroad tracks and Fairfield Street.

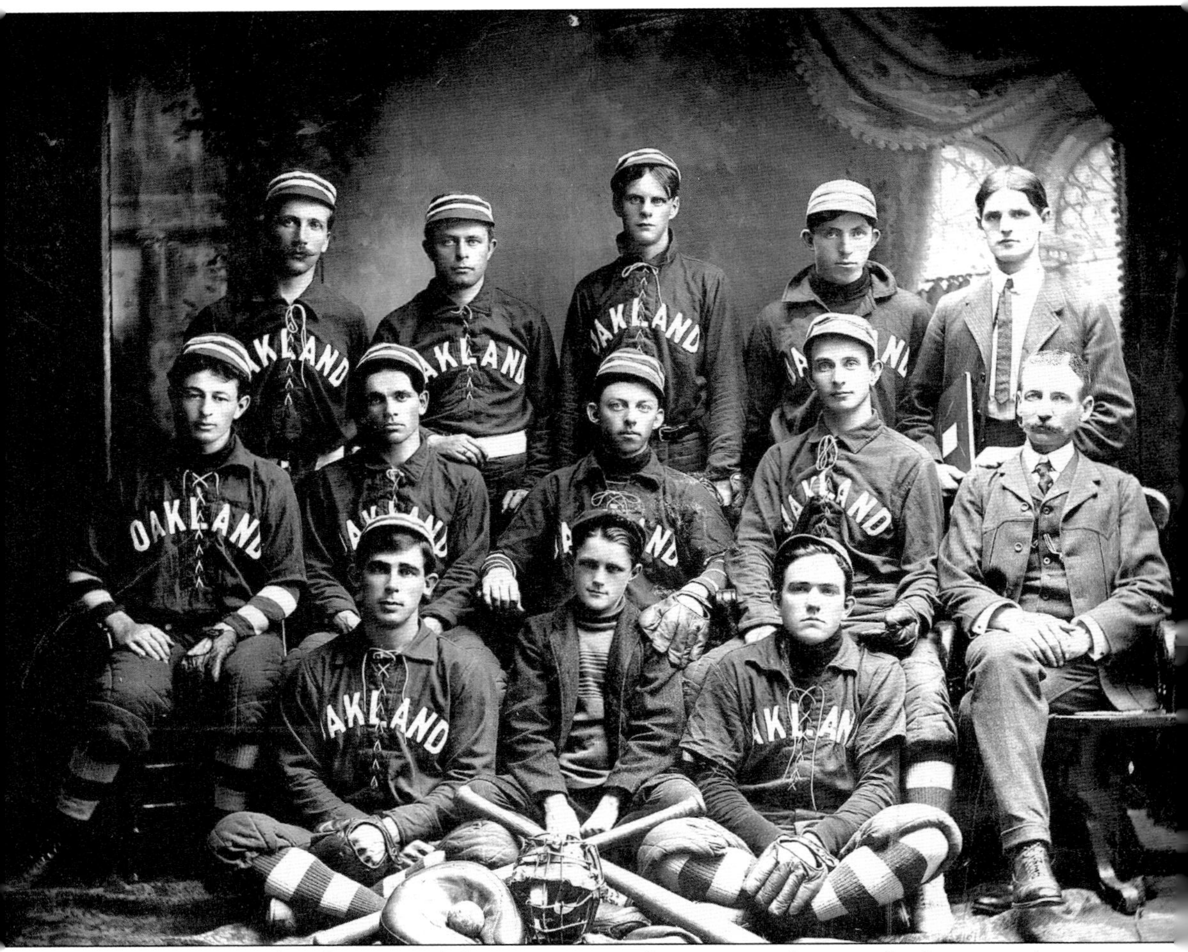

This photograph, taken around the same time as the previous photograph, shows another team of Oakland baseball players.

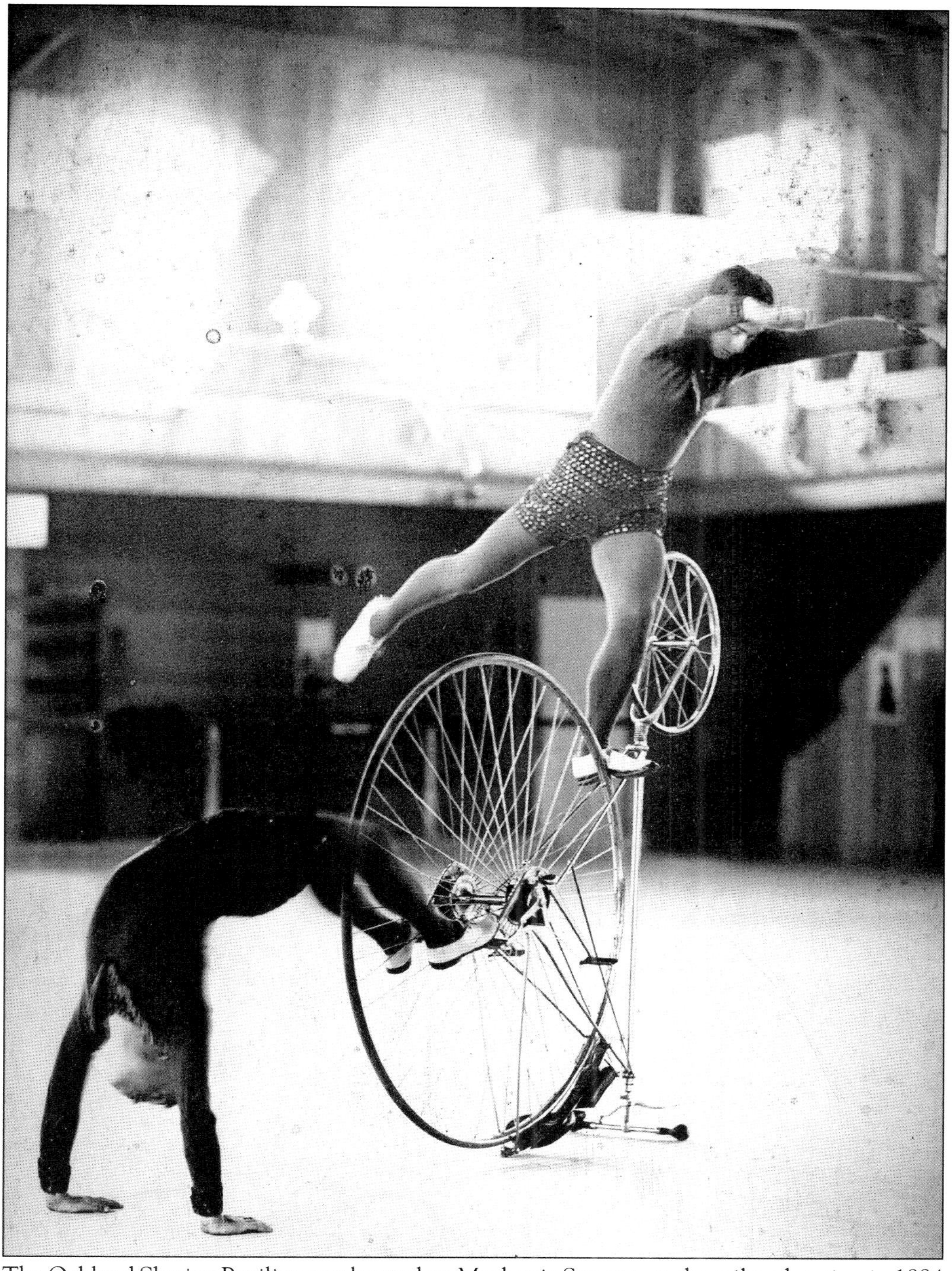

The Oakland Skating Pavilion was located on Mechanic Street near the railroad station in 1884 and 1885. The Oakland Roller Skating Company was located behind the Goulding Building on Mechanic Street near Main Street. George W. Goulding was the president of the company, and Orestes E. Crowell was the treasurer. Here we see Glen Blake on the wheel and Ernest Foster on the floor.

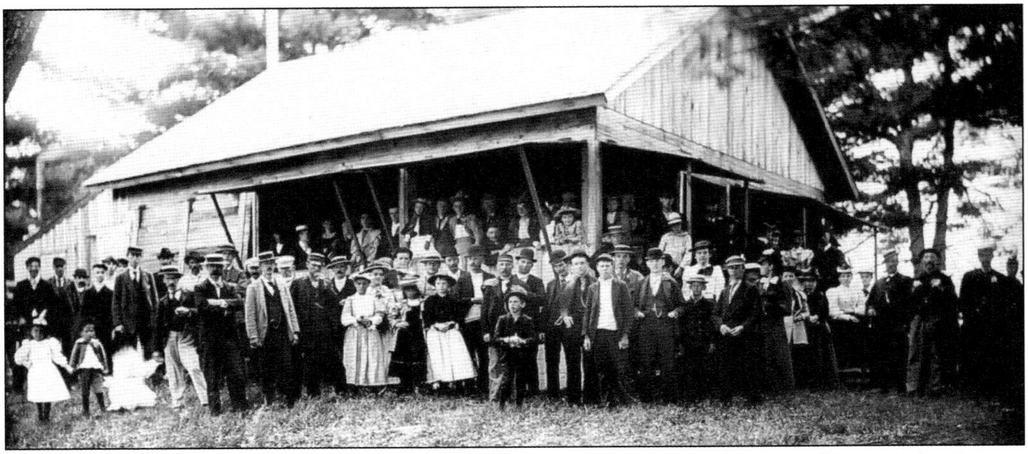

Seen here on Blake's Island are, according to the listing on the back of the photograph, George Soule, Henry Stevens, Clyde Stevens, Ed Hersom, Sylvia Soule, Bertha Crowell, Fred Hallett, Ada Hallett, George Wilson, Alfonzo Cook, Ella Penney, Joe Ryan, Tom White, George Hallett, Tom Johnson, John Damren, Jerome Damren, Jesse Blake, Milo Thomas, Ed Gallier, Will Hutchins, Salvato Principato, Lewis Lord, Tom White, Leon Batchelder, Arthur Gleason, Howard Gleason, Ella Penney (crossed out), Ada Hallett (repeated), Fred Hallett (repeated), John Johnson, George Johnson, George Wilson, Alfonzo Cook, Angie Osborne, George Shephard, Mrs. Shephard, Will Stowell, George Shephard (repeated), and Captain Stevens.

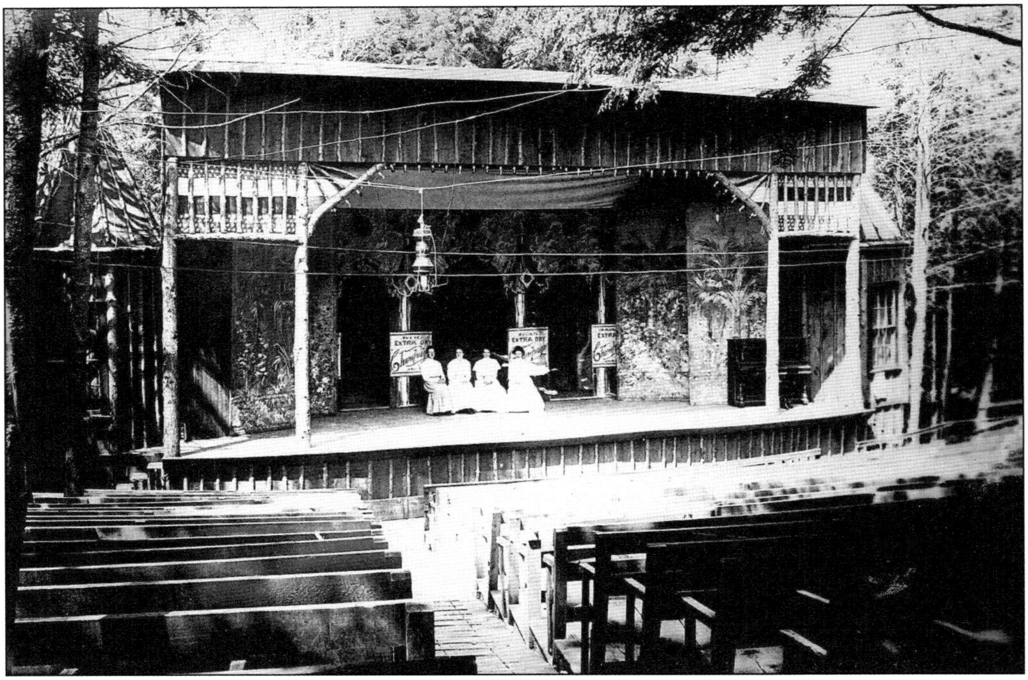

This photograph shows the theater at Cascade Park. The park was built as a summer recreation spot by the Waterville, Fairfield & Oakland Street Railway. If people had a destination in mind, the trolley could take them there. The park was located just north of Kennedy Memorial Drive, opposite the intersection of Country Club Road.

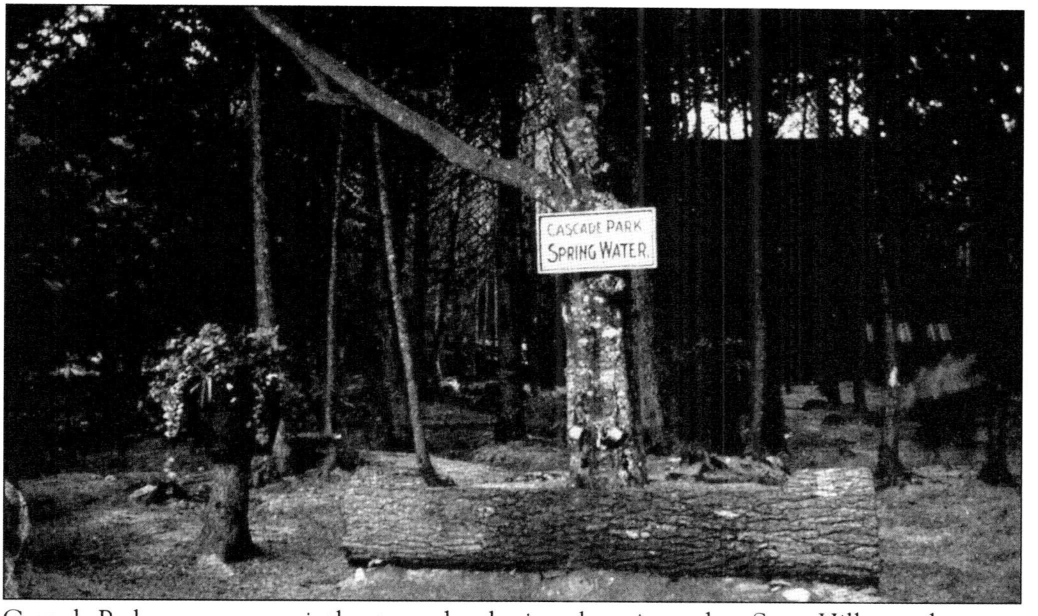

Cascade Park was an open-air theater and gathering place situated on Swan Hill near the curve in what has become the Old Waterville Road. It featured a fairgrounds and horse track, an open-air theater for concerts and plays, and a midway. Children also enjoyed a merry-go-round and swings. The park was open only during the summer months from 1903 to 1935. There were seats for 500 in its natural amphitheater, and 1,000 or more people came for vaudeville, music programs, the Ringling Brothers Circus, and Sunday band concerts. Admission was 10¢ for a reserved seat and 5¢ for open seating.

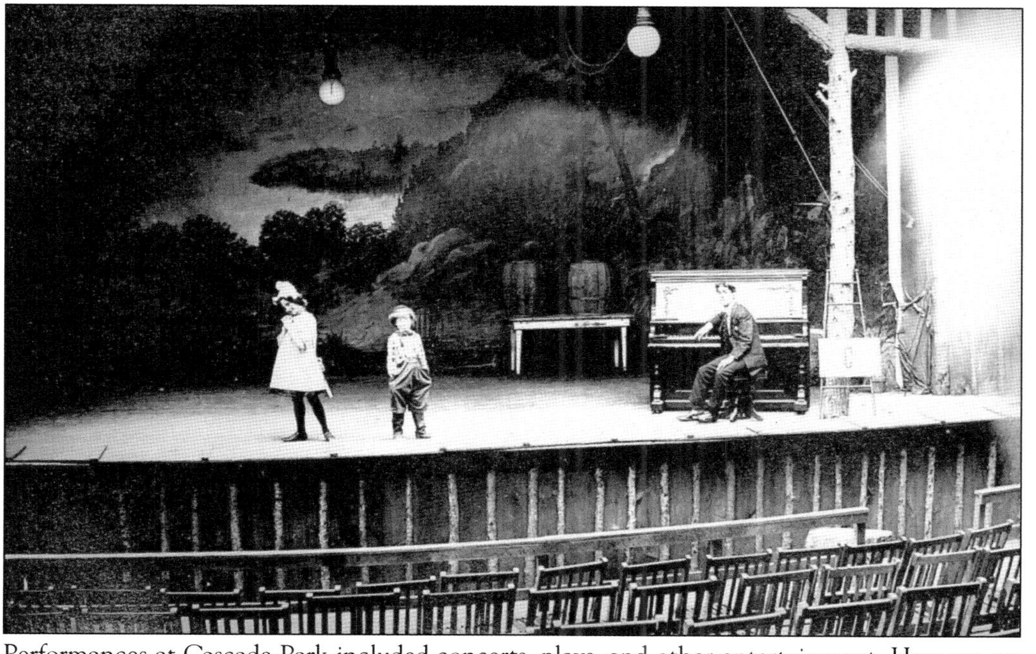

Performances at Cascade Park included concerts, plays, and other entertainment. Here we see two performers on the open-air stage.

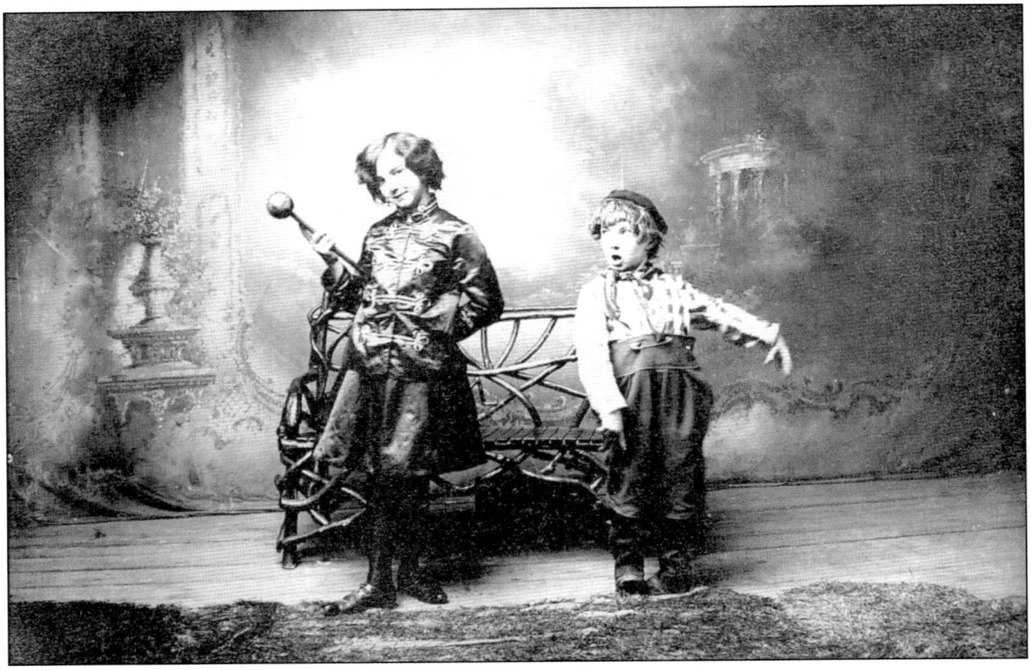

Cascade Park hosted musicians and actors of all ages during its time.

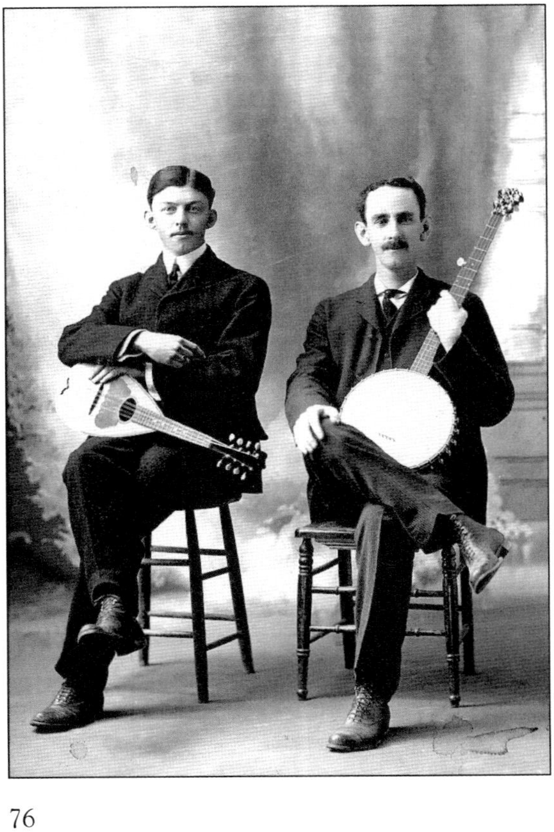

Pictured here in 1902 are banjo and mandolin artists Walter Sullivan and Dwight Macartney.

George W. Wilson was the town's barber for many years.

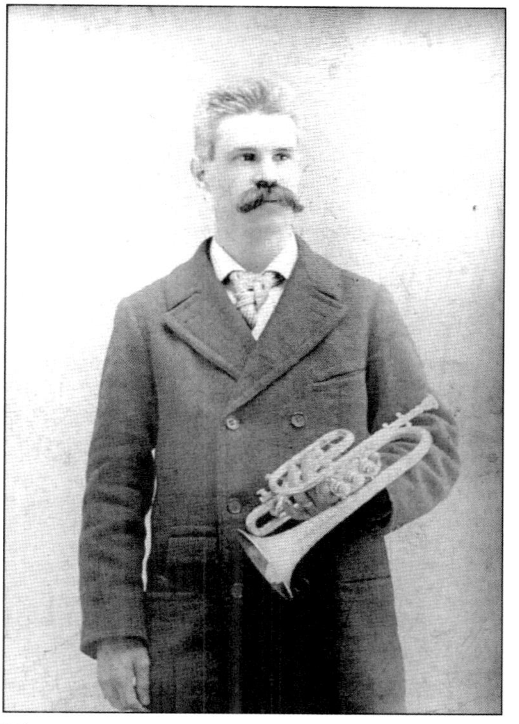

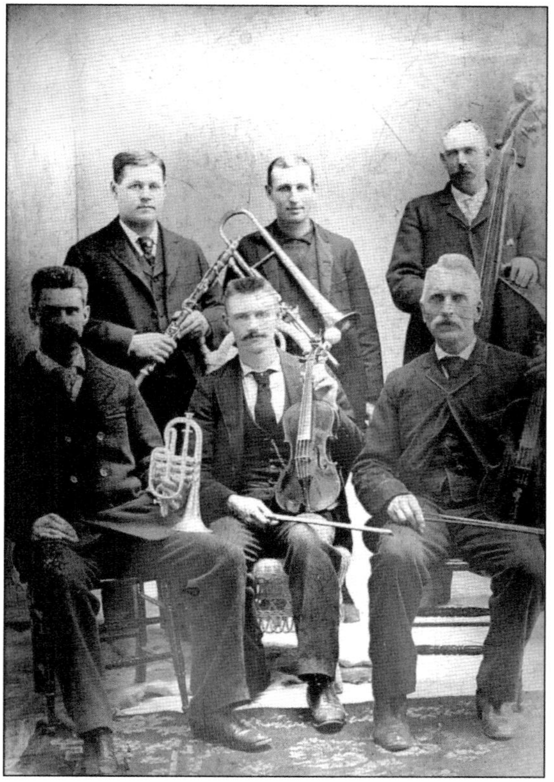

This photograph features more of Oakland's musicians. They are, from left to right, as follows: (first row) George Wilson, Bart Hallet, and Issac Dyer; (second row) Jess Blake, Will Blake, and Fred Pullen.

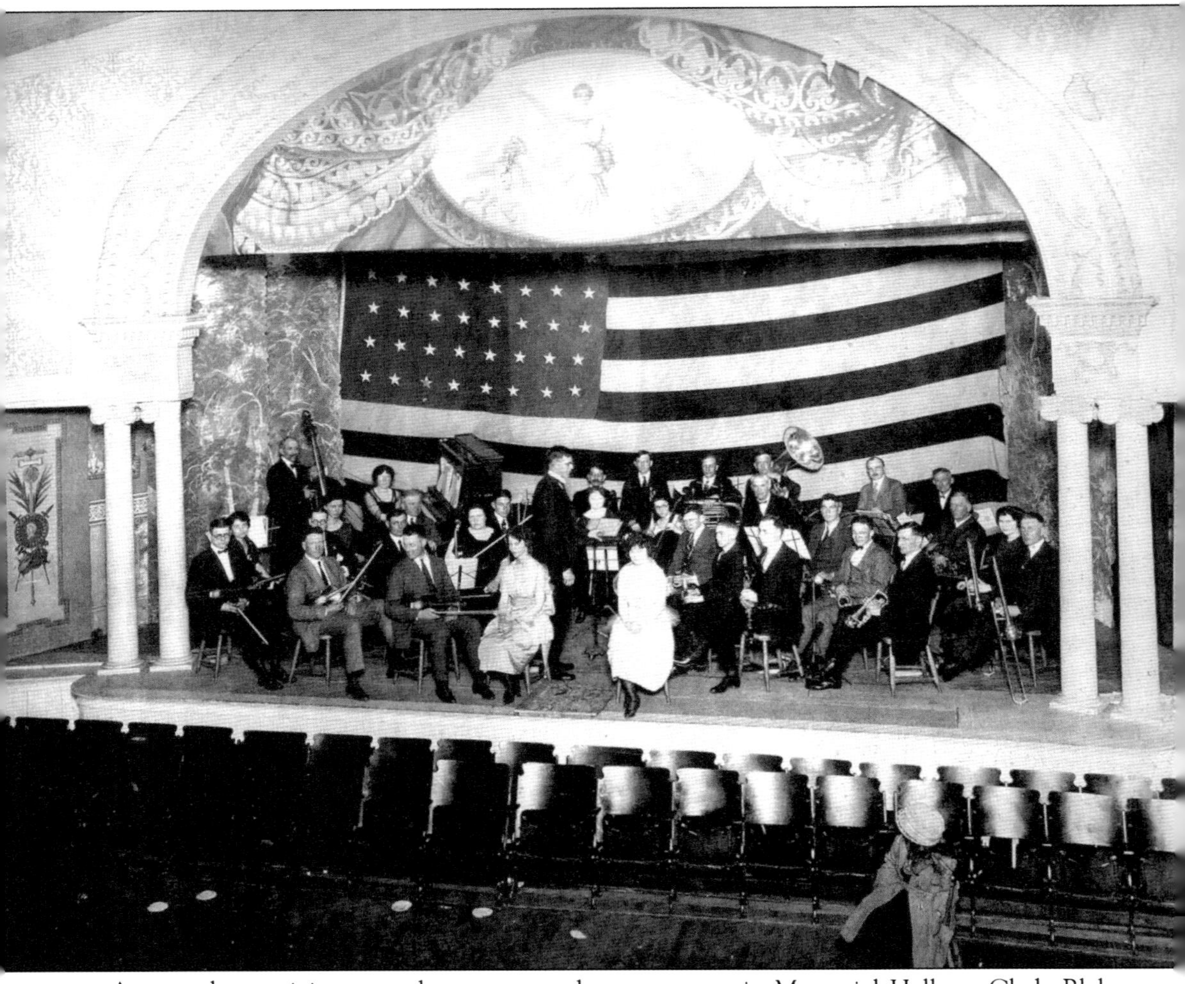

Among the musicians seen here at an orchestra concert in Memorial Hall are Clyde Blake, Franklin Marsh, Edgar Dean, George Bates, Ralph Martineau, Annie Folsom, Harry Drew, Gladys Manson, Carlton Towle, Harold Sawtelle, Helen Pullen (at the piano), Mrs. Ralph Martineau, Inez Stevens, Calvin Thompson, Eugene Savage, Salvatore Principato, Norman Spiller, Frank Anderson, Hallis Preble, and Dean Wheeler. A note with the photograph reads, "1994—This picture was sent to Carlton Towle (age 87) in Wakefield, RI, to help identify musicians. He played a clarinet in this orchestra. He died in 1995."

Five

SCHOOLS

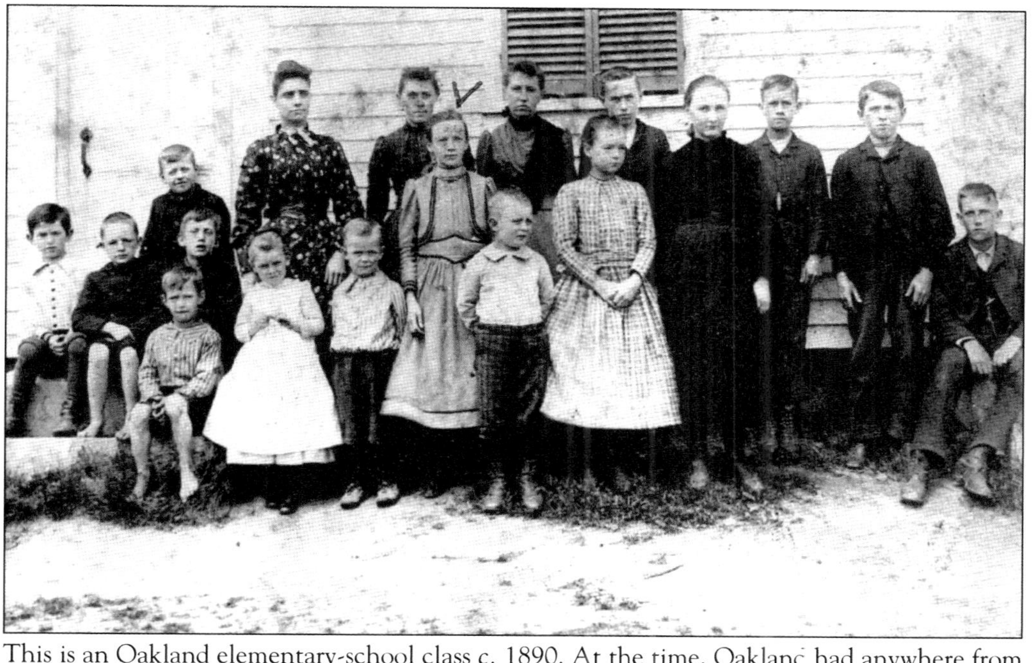

This is an Oakland elementary-school class c. 1890. At the time, Oakland had anywhere from 11 to 15 one-room schoolhouses located all over town. Where this one was located is unknown, but it could be the McGrath Pond School, the Fairfield Neck School, the Upper Primary School, the Lower Primary School, or any other for that matter.

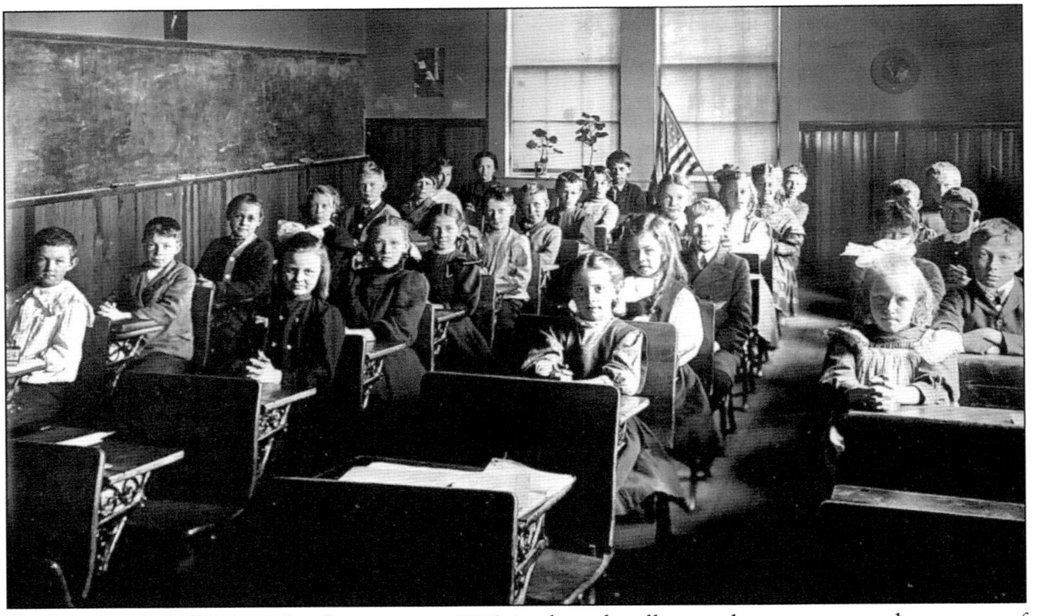

Students in this third-grade class pose *c.* 1910 in the schoolhouse that is now on the corner of School and Water Streets. Most of the primary schools had large round wood-burning stoves at the back for heat.

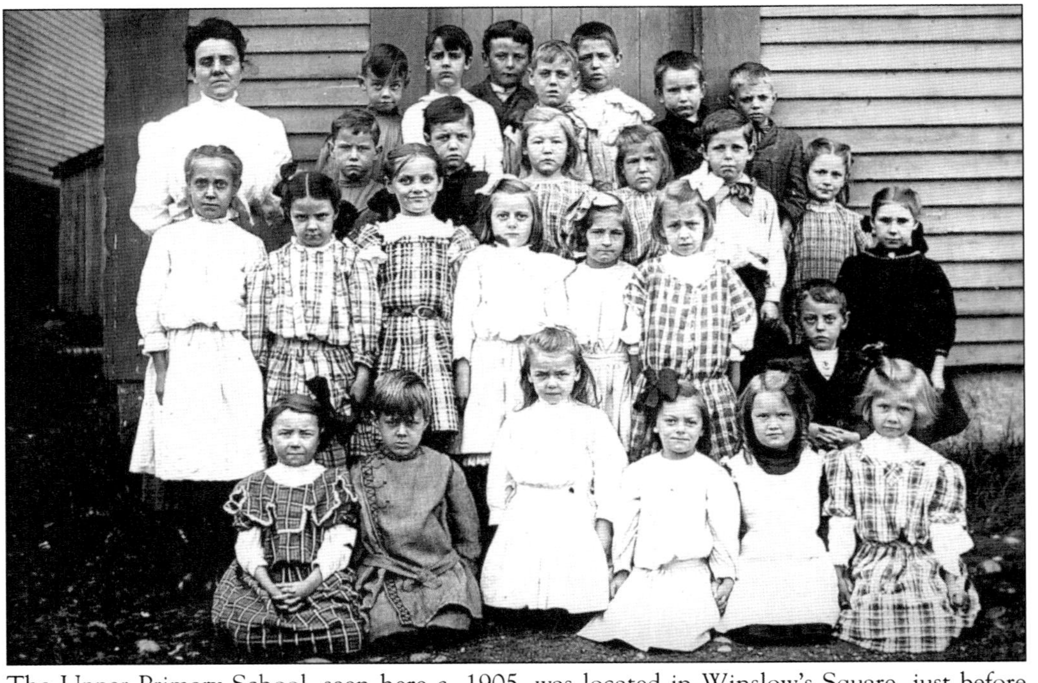

The Upper Primary School, seen here *c.* 1905, was located in Winslow's Square, just before Church Street turns right to become Summer Street. There were numerous small schoolhouses in Oakland. The Upper Primary School is still used by the town for storage. The Lower Primary School was located a short way down Fairfield Street; the site is now occupied by a basketball court.

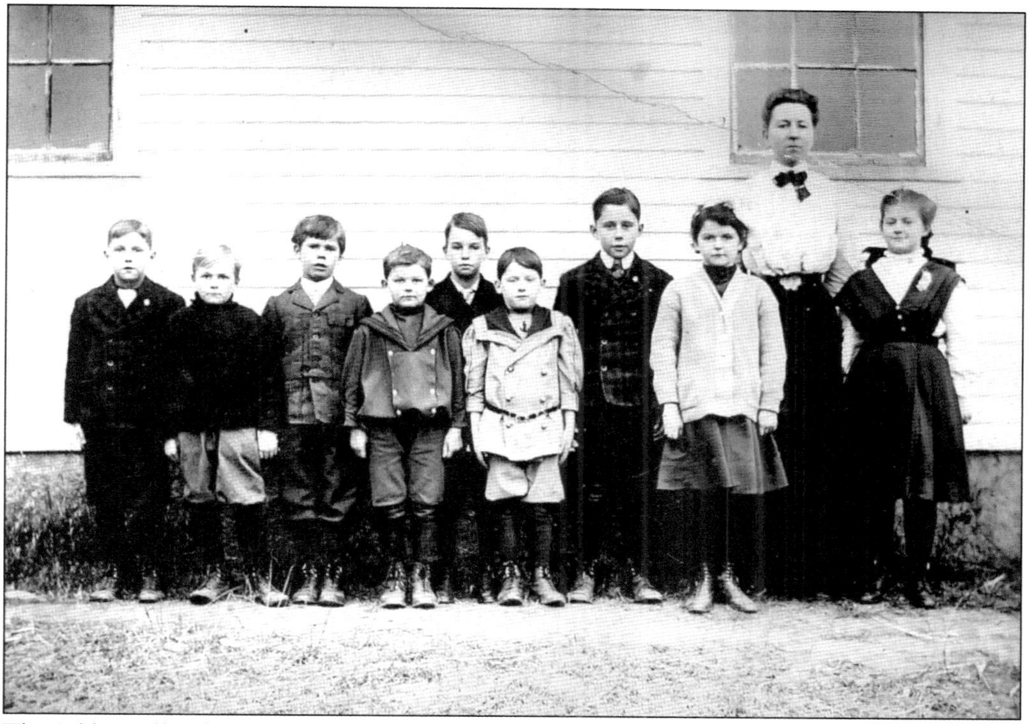

The Libby Hill School was on Webb Road. Clara Manter was the teacher. The building was moved to the corner of Gallagher and Middle Roads, where it is still located. It has been converted into a private home.

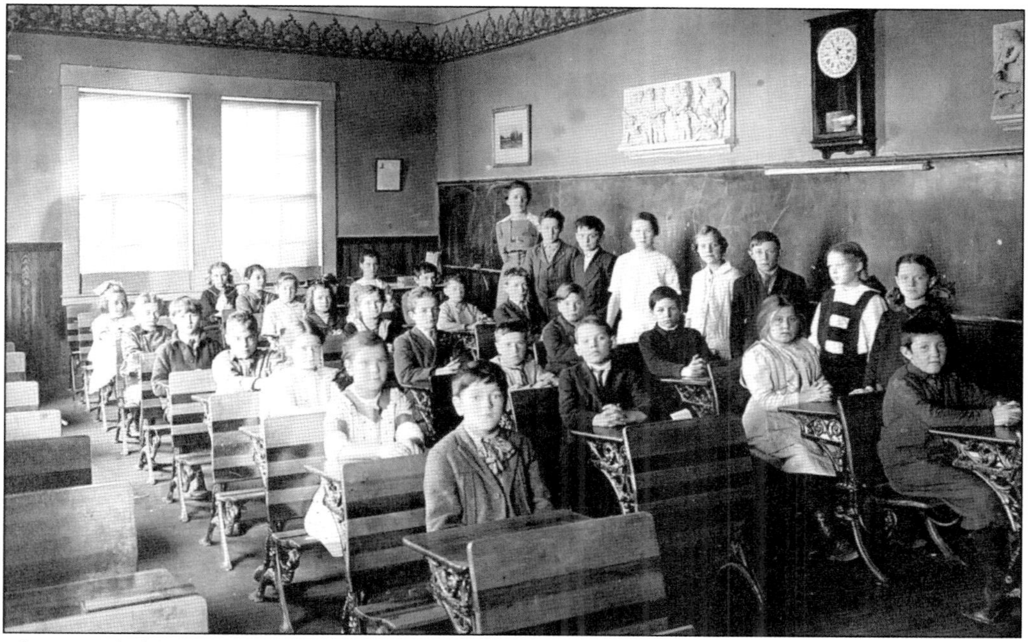

This is probably the fourth-grade class at the School Street School.

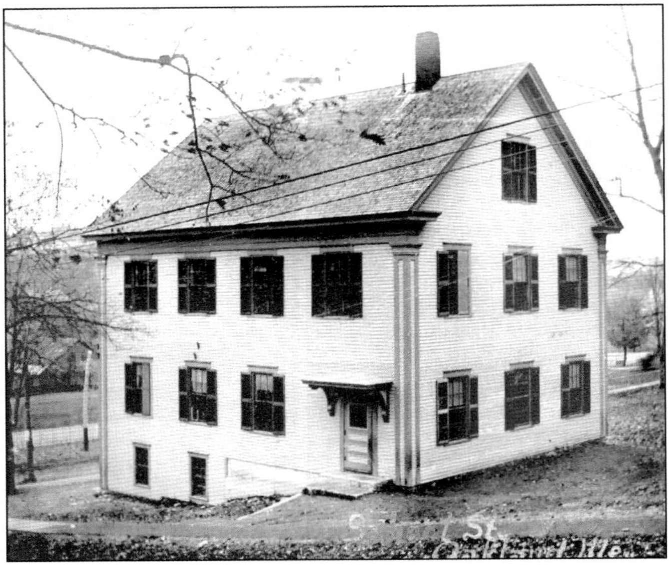

The Intermediate School originally stood higher up on the hill on School Street, closer to Oakland High School. It was moved to the corner of School and Water Streets in 1901, where it housed, at one time, grades 1–9; grades 10–13 were housed at Oakland High School. This was before kindergarten classes were introduced and the elementary schools were comprised of grades 1–8; high school was comprised of grades 9–12. In later years, grades 3–6 were housed here.

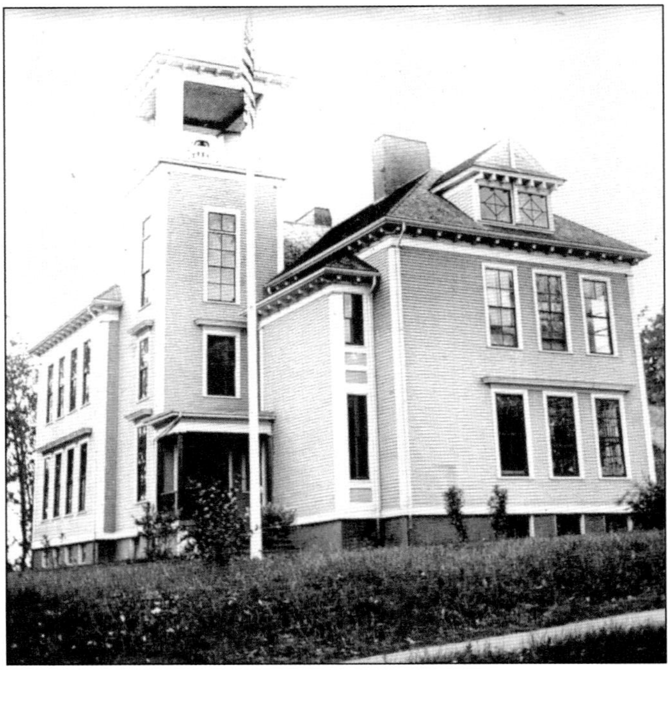

This photograph shows Oakland High School c. 1905. The first Oakland High School burned and was rebuilt in 1898; the second building burned in 1900 and was replaced with the building pictured here. When Williams High School opened in 1924, this building was used for the sixth and seventh grades. The eighth grade moved to two classrooms on the first floor of the new Williams High School building. Oakland High School burned in the late 1960s, and today the site is the parking lot for the Methodist Church next-door, although the cement walkway that led to the left front door is still there.

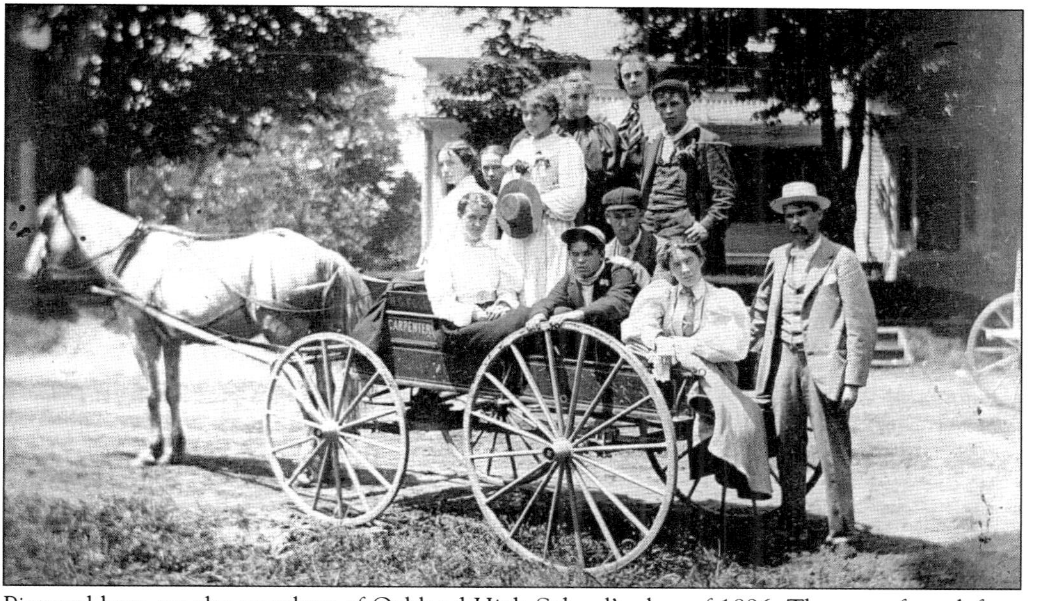

Pictured here are the members of Oakland High School's class of 1896. They are, from left to right, as follows: (in the driver's seat) Gertrude Sturtevant and Marguerite Smith; (sitting) Alice Field, Hiram York, Frank Farr, and Bertha C. Jackson (assistant); (standing) Vivian Thomas, Agnes Hetherington, Argie Lord, Earl York, and Lyman K. Lee (principal). This photograph was taken in front of Memorial Hall when the class was decorating for graduation.

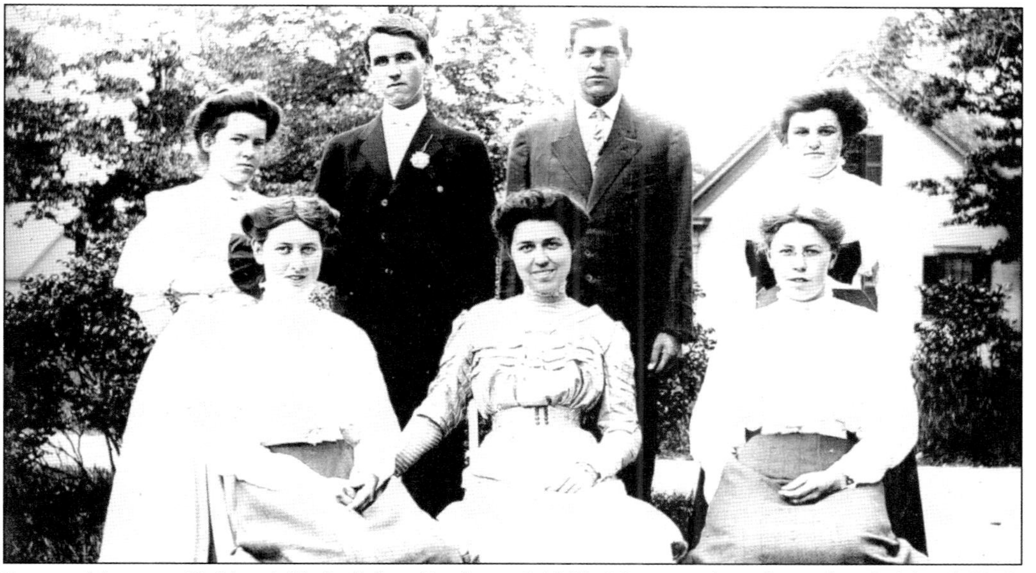

Pictured here is Oakland High School's class of 1909. Names taken from the Oakland High School yearbook, the *Messalonskee Ripple*, from 1920 and 1923 include Marion Hersom (Mrs. J. B. Smith) of Winslow; Charles I. Bates of Oakland; Marion Mithee of Oakland; Leonard Skillings; Edna L. Kerr (listed as Mrs. Frank Brown in the 1923 *Ripple*); and Lena Kerr. Kerr became a teacher in Oakland. This photograph shows seven graduates, whereas the 1920 and 1923 *Ripple* listed only six names.

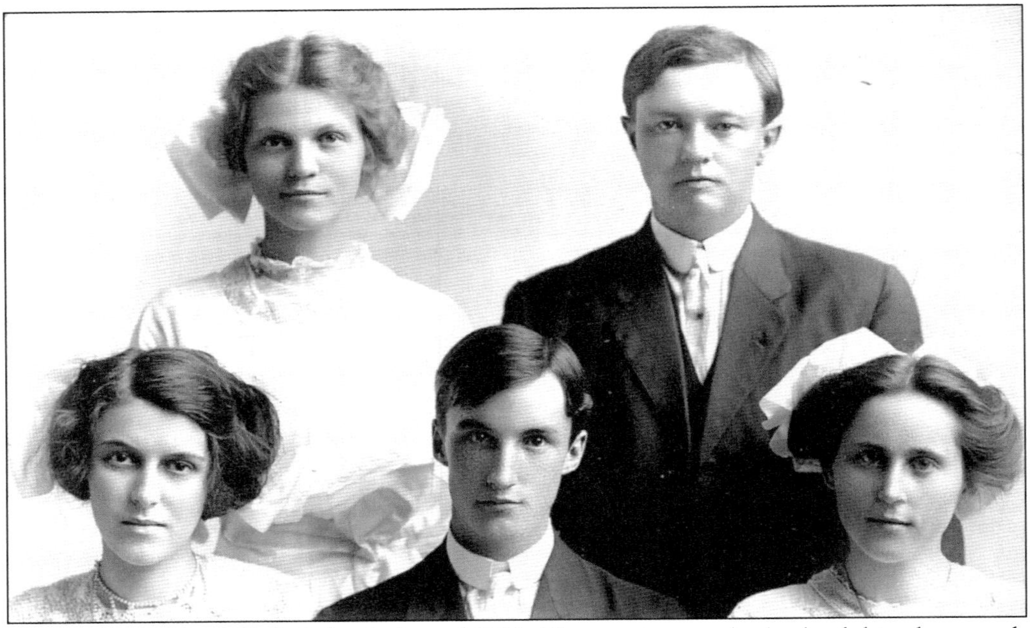

This is the Oakland High School class of 1912. The caption on the back of this photograph indicates that Lela Kelley is at the bottom left. The members of the class, as listed in the 1912 Town Report, were Lucretia Dingley, Gladys E. Gleason, Leda B. Kelley, Evan R. Perkins, and John Perry. Kelley's name is listed differently in various sources: Lela, Leda, and Lena.

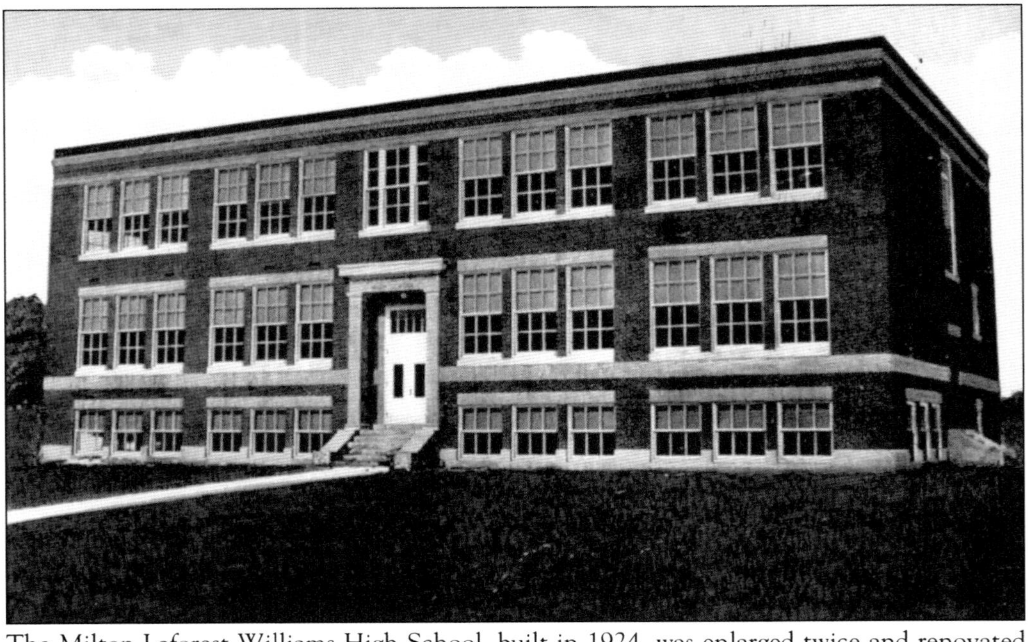

The Milton Laforest Williams High School, built in 1924, was enlarged twice and renovated twice. It continues to house Oakland's schoolchildren. It became Williams Junior High School in 1969 and Williams Elementary School in 2003.

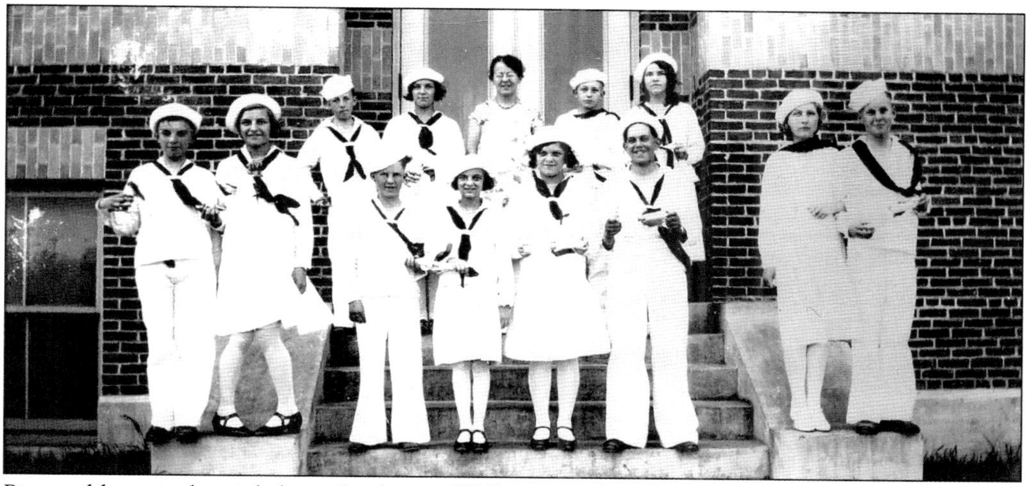

Pictured here is the eighth-grade class at Williams High School in 1930. Margaret Killman, a physical education teacher from 1925 to 1939, is the woman in the back row who is not in a sailor's suit. For many years, Williams High School housed some or all of grades 7 and 8, as well as high school grades 9–12.

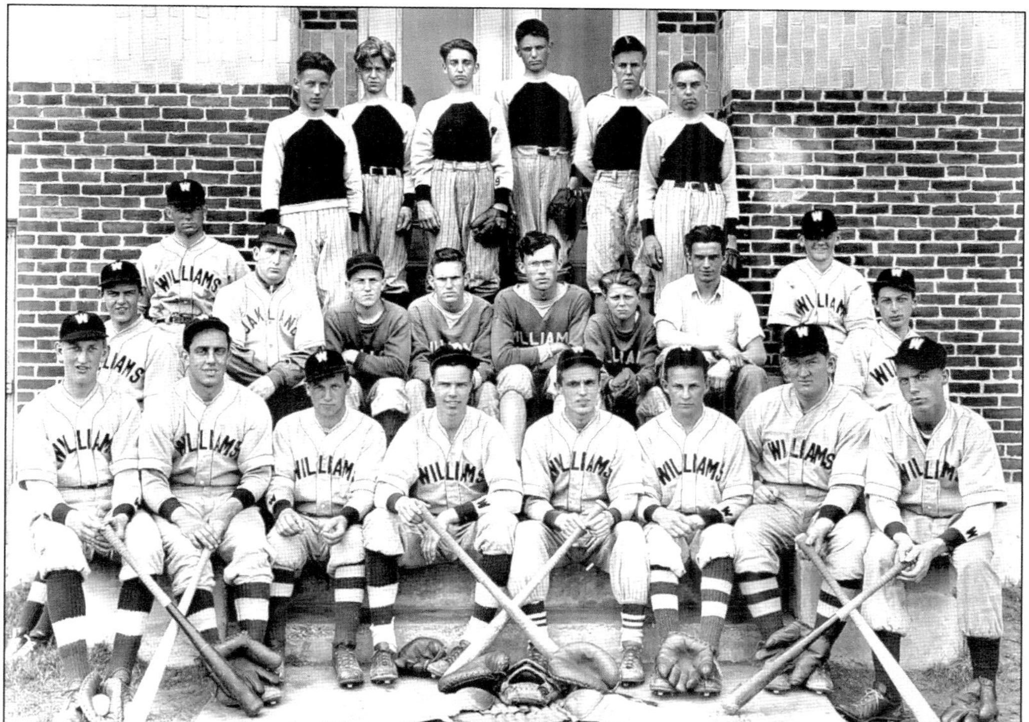

This is the 1937 Williams High School baseball team. The players are, from left to right, the following: (first row) Albert Spiller, Vernon York, ? Tibbetts, Gilbert Peters, Valton Wood, Otis Bacon, unidentified, and Arthur Noyes; (second row) two unidentified people, Clayton Cronkite (coach), Merle Tilton, Clarence Axtell, Ronald Handley, Floyd Kenniston, two unidentified people, and Carroll Richardson. The third row includes Lawrence Sedgeley, Elmo Lush, and Robert Beverage.

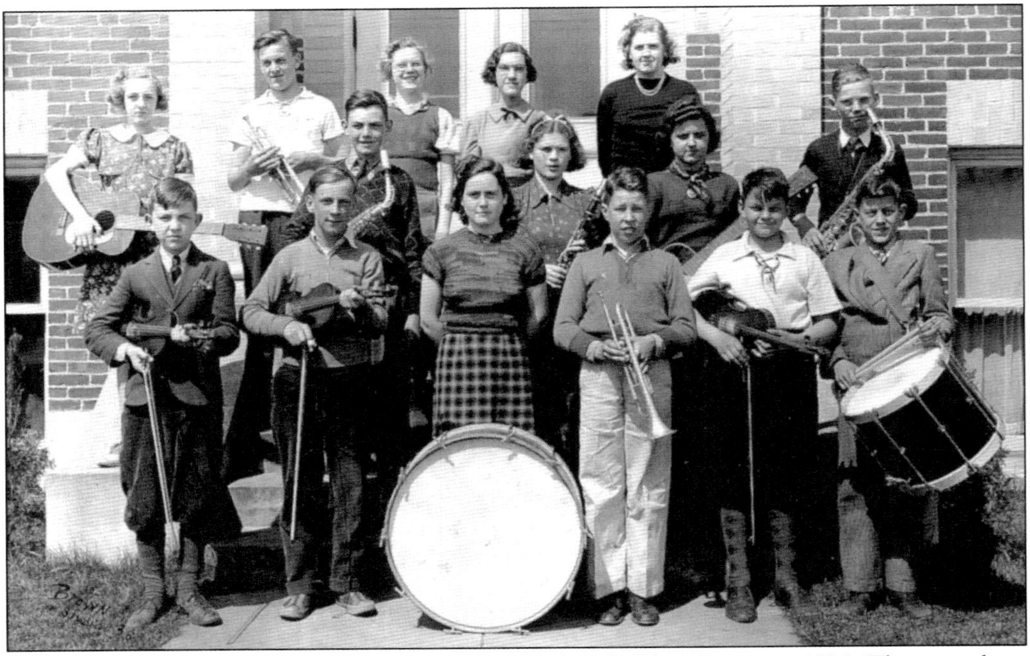

Pictured here are the members of the Williams High School orchestra in 1938. They are, from left to right, the following: (first row) Eugene Sturtevant, Everett Rockwell, Marion Dustin, Richard Norton, Neil Collar, and Merland O'Neal; (second row) Priscilla Landry, Richard Brillard, Ruth Wallace, Lois Wood, and Norman Sedgeley; (third row) Clifton Collar, Arlene Kennison, Edith Sturtevant, and Myrtle Bowlin.

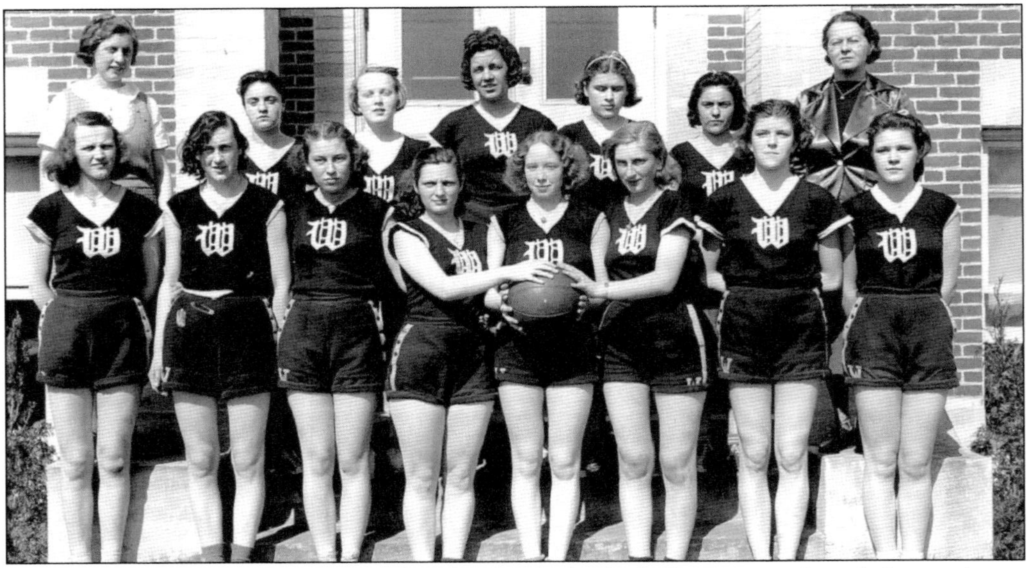

Members of the 1928 Williams High School girls' basketball team are, from left to right, as follows: (first row) Marguerite Tobin, Dorothy Hawes, June Marshall, Carmen Gagner, Muriel Carrell, Charlene Scott, Virginia Norton, and Mary Manson; (second row) Dorothy Randall, Delphine Perkins, Willa Richardson, Eva Gerrish, Ruth Wallace, Josephine Perkins, and Margaret Killman (coach).

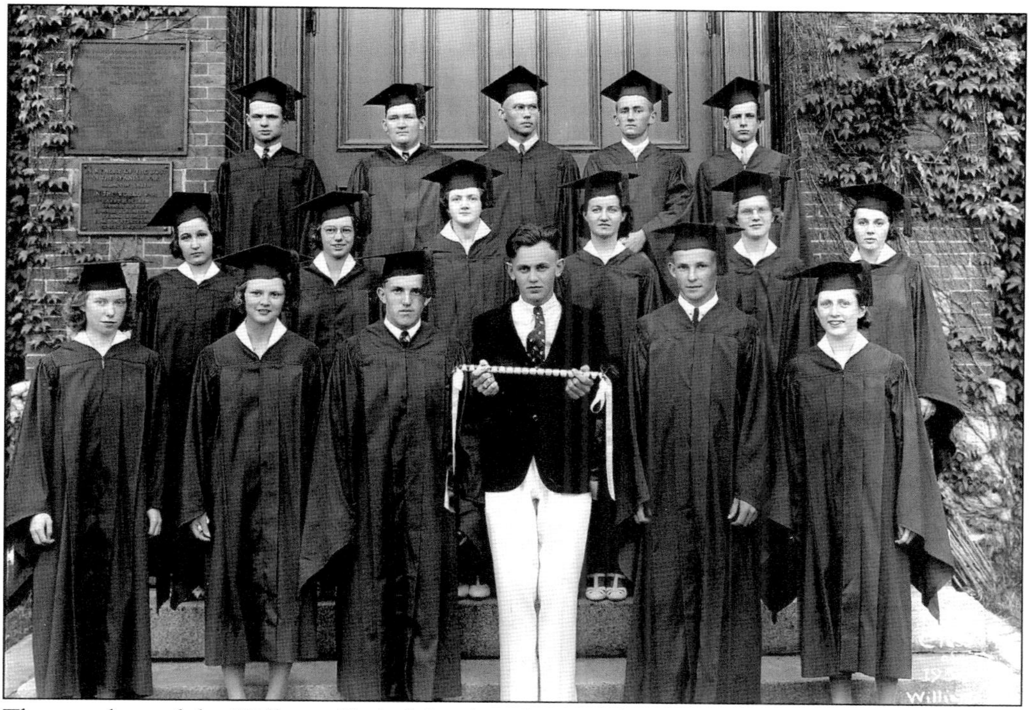

The members of the Williams High School graduating class of 1938 are, from left to right, as follows: (first row) Muriel Correll, Arlene Dyer, Merle Tilton, Roy Bacon, Otis Bacon, and Dorothy Randall; (second row) Marion Brewer, Pearl (York) Estes, Evangeline Giberson, Theo Mosher, Arlene Kennison, and Frances Forbes; (third row) William Blake. Alton Bates, Robert Lothrop, Max Leech, and Gerald Goodman.

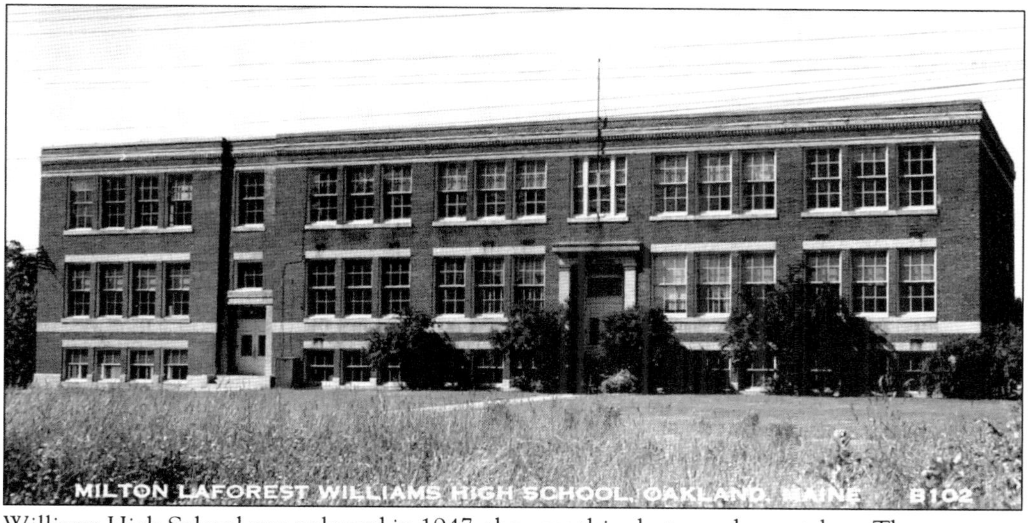

Williams High School was enlarged in 1947, the year this photograph was taken. The rooms on the left are new, as is a gymnasium addition on the rear of the building. The school was enlarged again in 1962 and was renovated and expanded once more in 1987. The Williams High School building is now Williams Elementary School, which houses Oakland's and Rome's grades three through five.

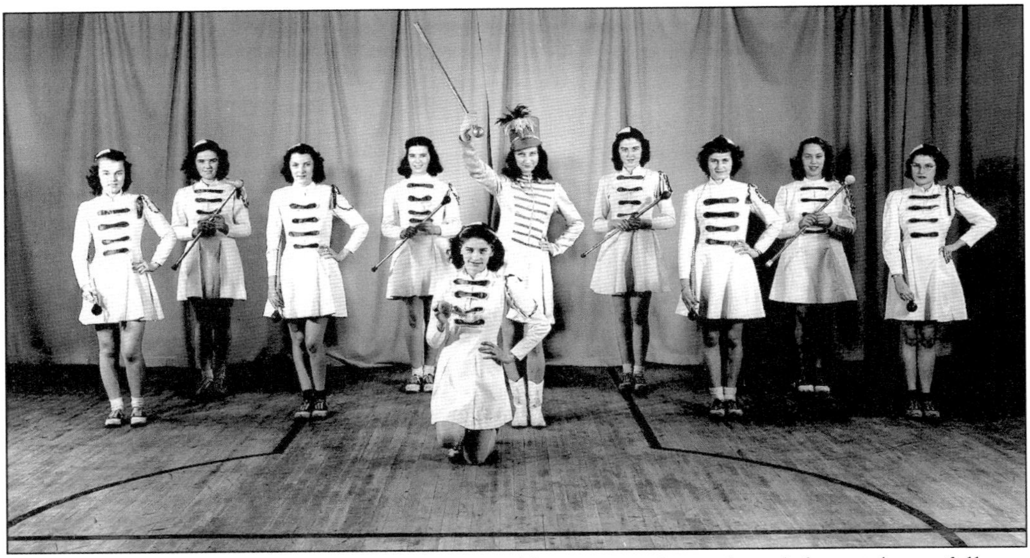

The Williams High School Majorettes, pictured here *c.* 1946, are, from left to right, as follows: (front) Carcline Smith; (standing) Arlene Furbush, Janet Pierce, Jean Hutchinson, Jean Clark, Coleen Smith, Leda Whitney, Betty Stowell, Sally Tuttle, and Doris LaCroix. This photograph was taken in the gymnasium, which was added to Williams High School in 1947.

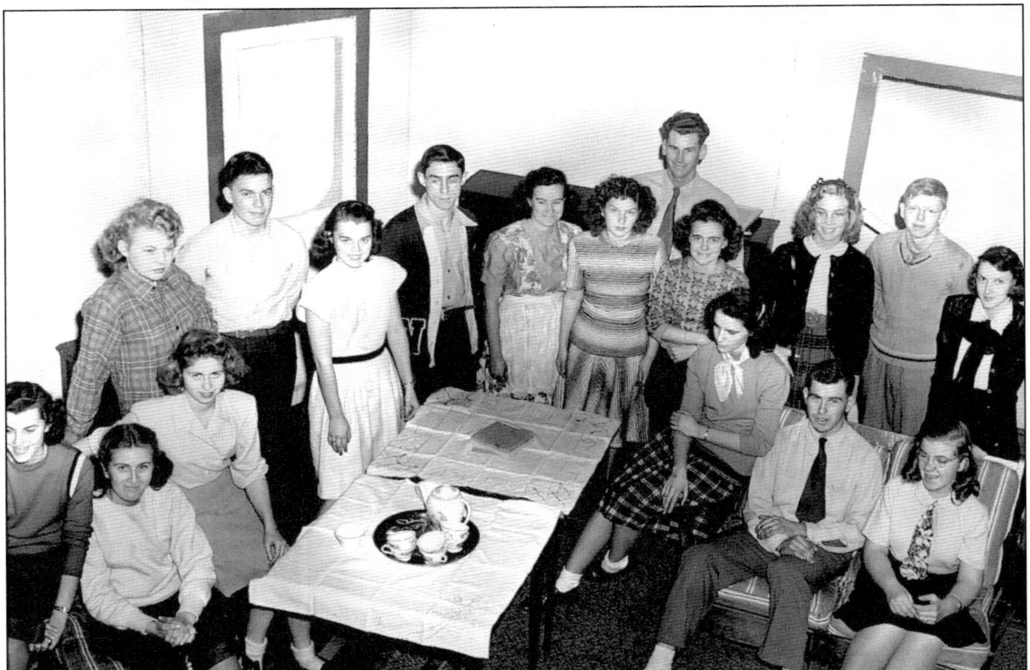

The students performing in the Williams High School senior play of 1948 are, from left to right, the following: (seated) Muriel Rossignol, Millie Ireland, Betty Stowell, Jean Clark, Eliot Chandler, and Carol Southard; (standing) Jacklyn Mosher, Robert McTaggart, Arlene Furbush, Robert Fotter, Ruth Benson, Lois Merrithew, Harvey Dolloff, Evelyn Warren, Carol ?, Warren Manter, and Jean Hutchinson.

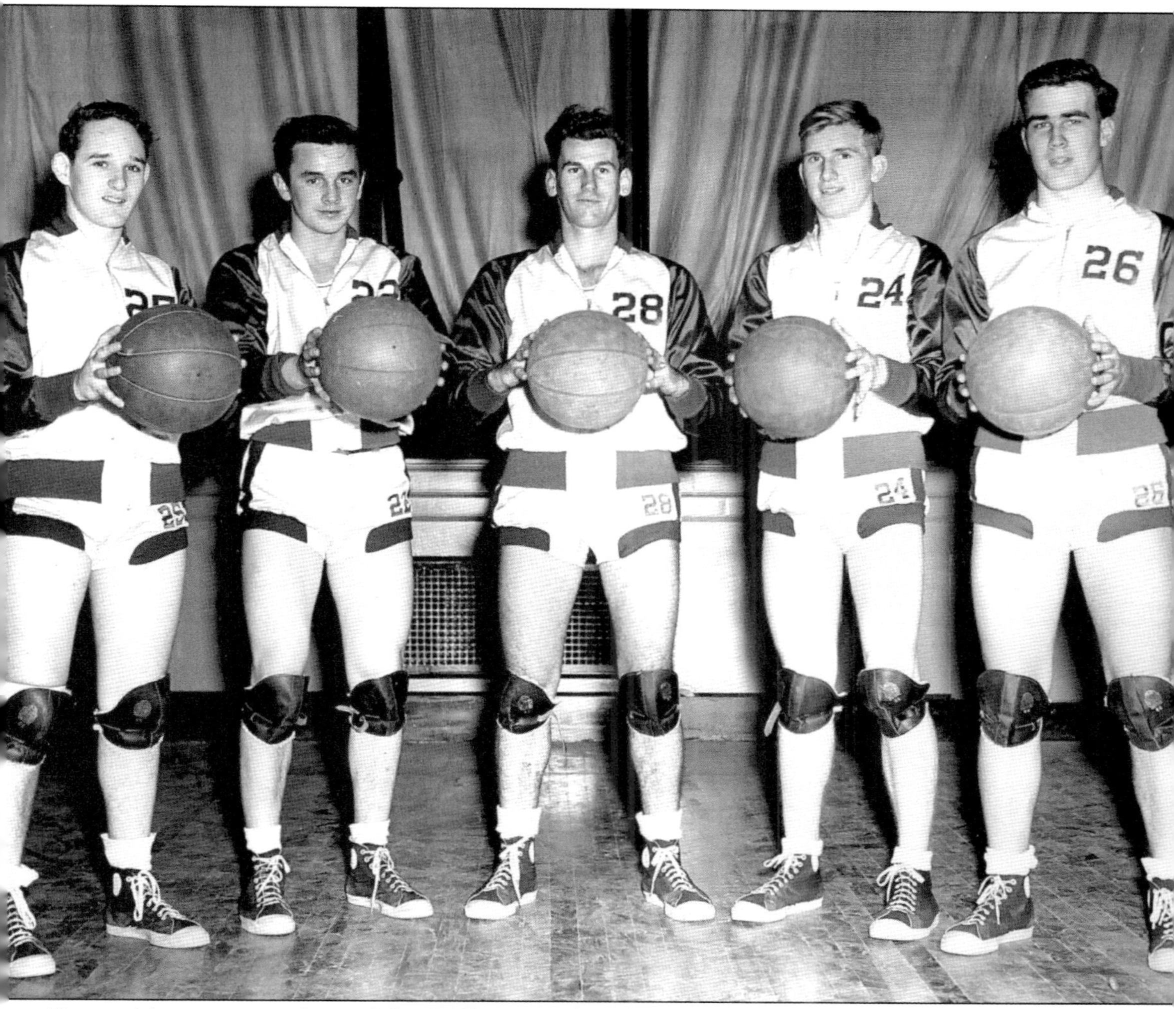

Pictured here are members of the Williams High School basketball team in 1948. They are, from left to right, as follows: Francis Monahan, Franklin Bickford, Harvey Dolloff, Clyde Luce, and Harvey Luce.

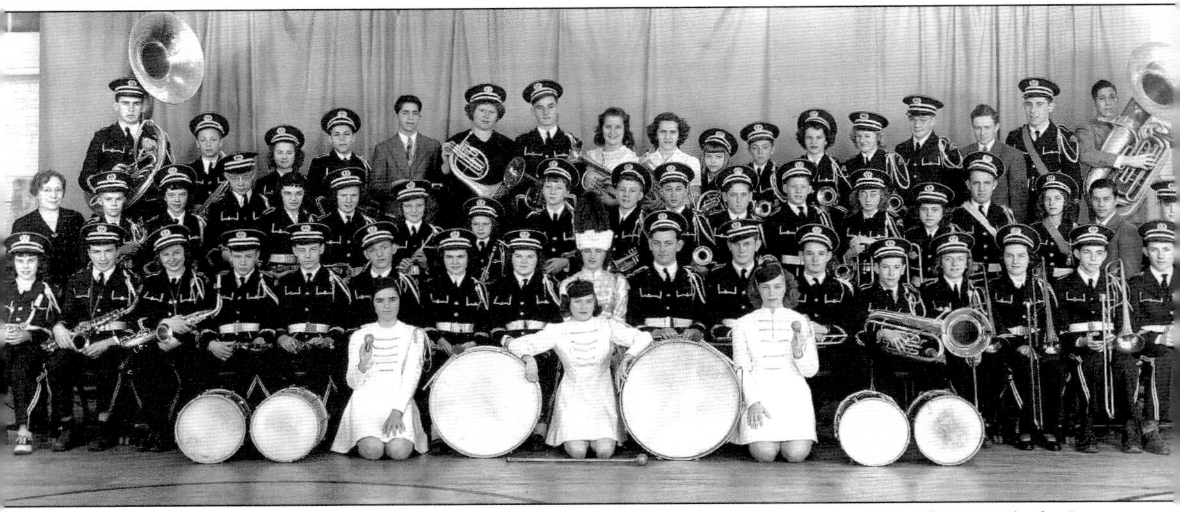

Members of the Williams High School band are pictured here in 1948. They include Janet Pierce, Doris LaCroix, Sally Tuttle, Natalie Gilbert, Noel Chandler, Margaret Oliver, Roger Luce, Mark Getchell, D. Bush, Louise Axtell, Ann Fuller, Carolyn Smith, Francis Vigue, Horace Pullen, Francis Monahan, Donald Mairs, Barbara Taylor, Patricia Nason, Robinson Whitney, Lilla Atherton, B. Fossett, Linda Walton, R. Stineford, S. Richardson, Roselmer Clark, Carol York, Geraldine Sawtelle, Elizabeth Hurd, Dale Collier, R. Principato, John Kerr, Thomas York, Jenny McCann, Gloria Gallagher, K. Southard, M. Smith, W. Romano, Thomas Pierce, Elliot Chandler, R. Fuller, J. Bickford, N. Stineford, B. Wentworth, Judy Allen, Joseph Ready, Hilda Baldic, Joan Berube, Charlene Gallagher, Peter Bastow, Marion Berube, and Geradine Rackleff.

Six

Scenes around Town

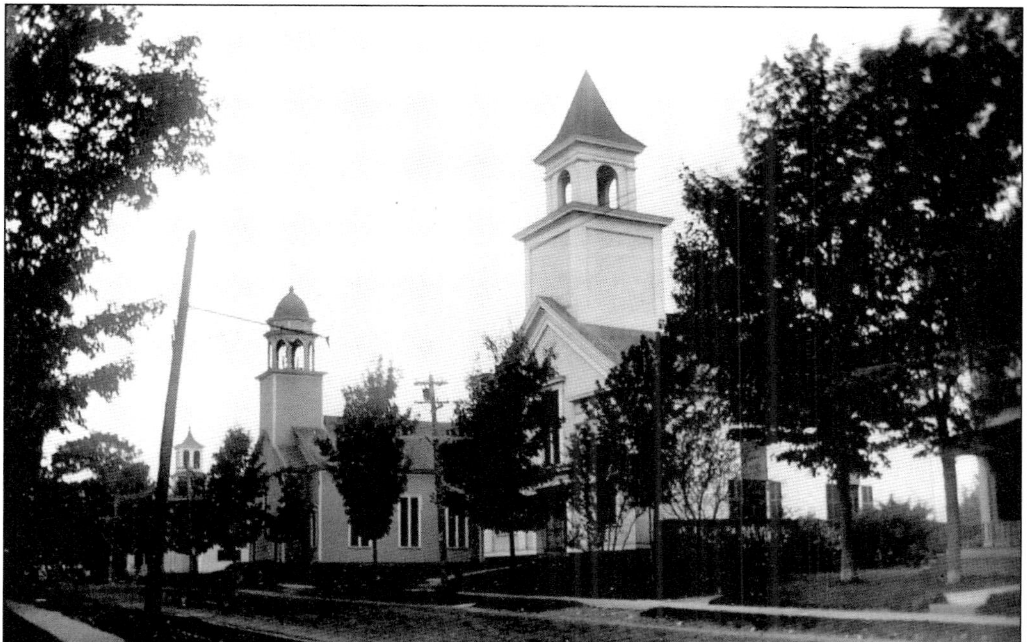

This is a view of Church Street *c.* 1910. The churches, from left to right, were the Calvinist Baptist, the Universalist, and the Free Will Baptist. Note the rails for the Waterville, Fairfield & Oakland Street Railway in the lower portion of the postcard.

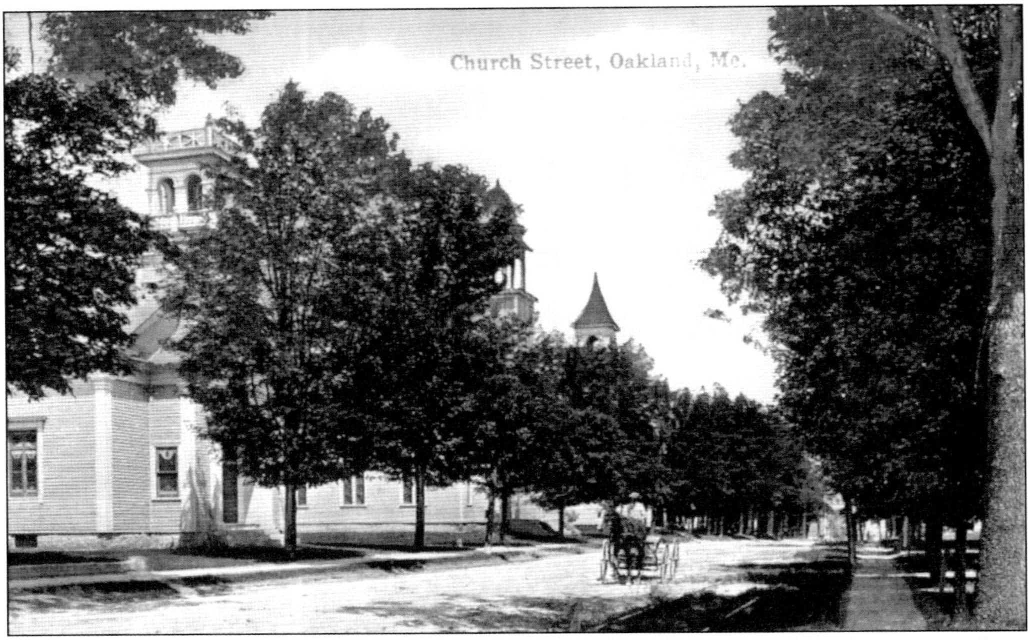

This postcard view of Church Street must have been taken after 1902, when the street railway came through town.

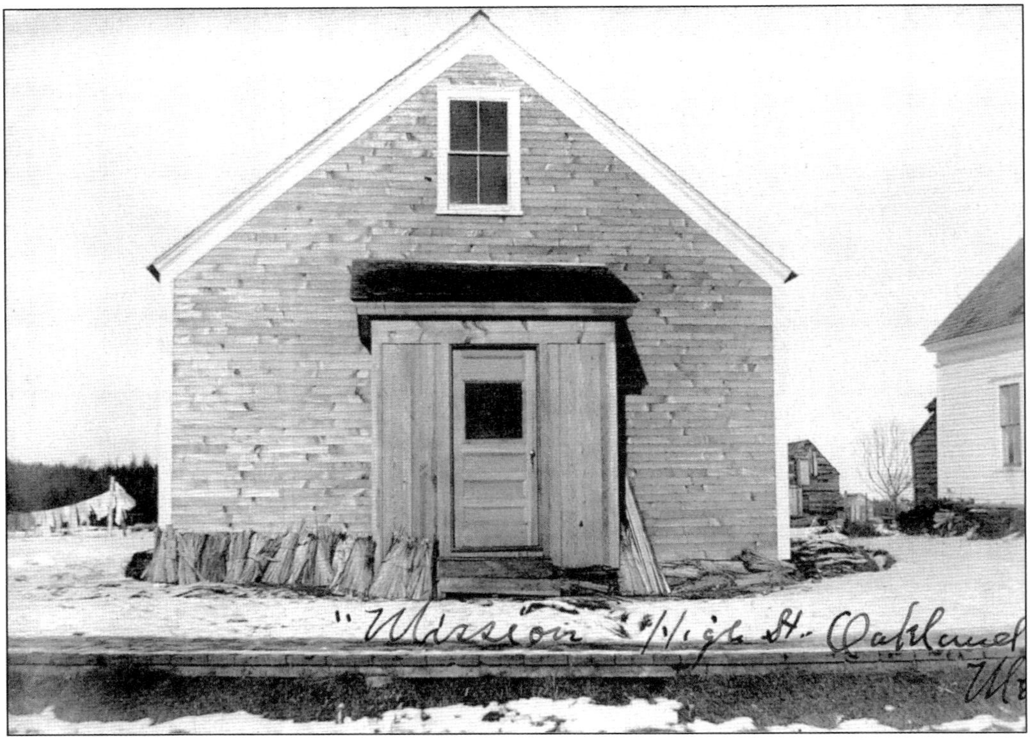

This small mission building was located on High Street. Its denomination is unknown.

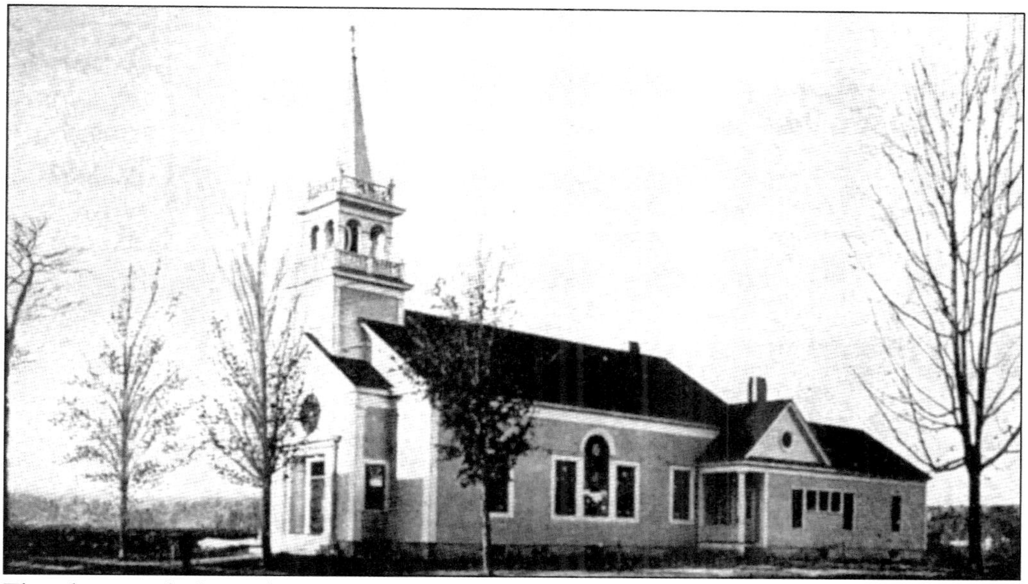

This photograph shows the Calvinist, or Second, Baptist Church of Oakland. It was an offshoot of the First Baptist Church of Waterville and was organized on September 12, 1844, with 45 members, mostly from the First Baptist Church of Waterville. They met in the Union Meeting House, which was located on the corner of present-day Church Street and Summer Street. In 1846, the church members voted to build a house of worship, and they bought a lot near the old meeting house for $45. The church was built in 1847 and has been enlarged since. In 1883, the church was renamed Oakland Baptist Church. The church bought a parsonage on Maple Street in 1884 or 1885. On May 26, 1921, the Free Will Baptists and the Calvinist Baptists merged, and the new church was renamed United Baptist Church of Oakland. They met in the former Calvinist Baptist Church, shown here. The Free Will Baptist Church building was sold to the Catholics of Oakland.

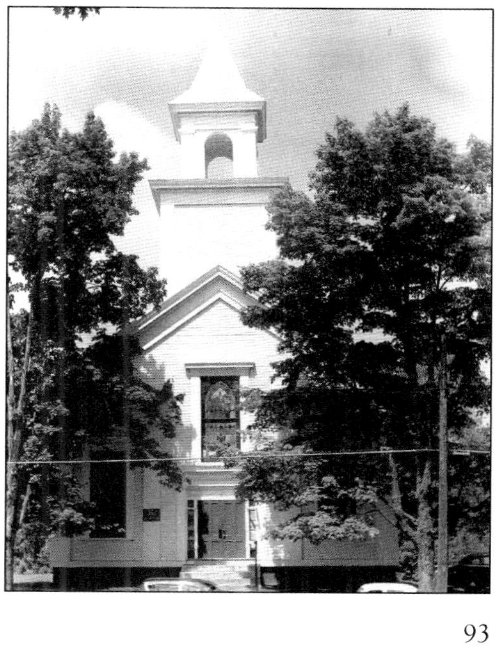

St. Theresa's Roman Catholic Church was formerly the Free Will Baptist Church, built in 1859. Oakland's Catholics first met in Memorial Hall c. 1880. They bought the Free Will Baptist Church building and organized their parish in 1928.

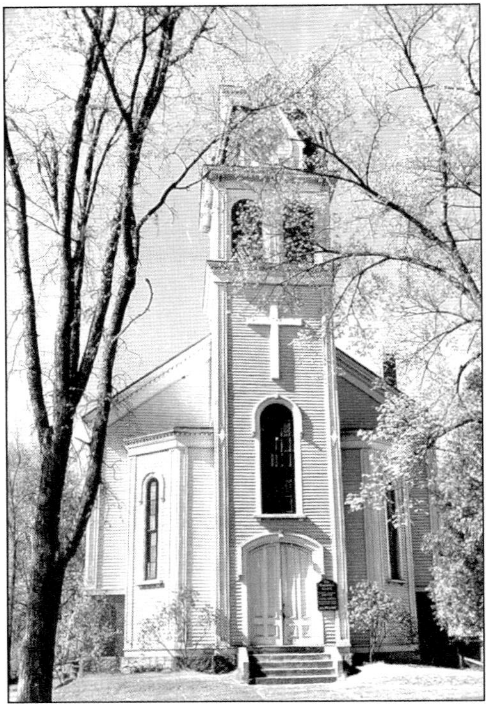

The Oakland-Sidney United Methodist Church, seen here, is located on present-day West School Street. In 1872, Sidney and Oakland began sharing the same pastor, N. C. Clifford. During his four years as pastor, he succeeded in building a $6,000 meetinghouse. R. B. Dunn gave $1,600 for the project. In 1872, the church sold the vestry on Church Street. The new building was dedicated in 1875, although the auditorium was not completed until 1884. Until 1967, it was known as the Dunn Memorial Methodist Church in memory of R. B. Dunn. In 1881, the Rev. M. C. King, who had inspired the completion of the Oakland Methodist Church, held a revival in Sidney that led to the construction of a chapel at Tiffany Hill. In 1967, the two churches voted to merge, forming the Oakland-Sidney United Methodist Church, where the primary worship is held. The Tiffany Hill Chapel is open for four worship services during the summer. In 1976, the Sunday school addition was built.

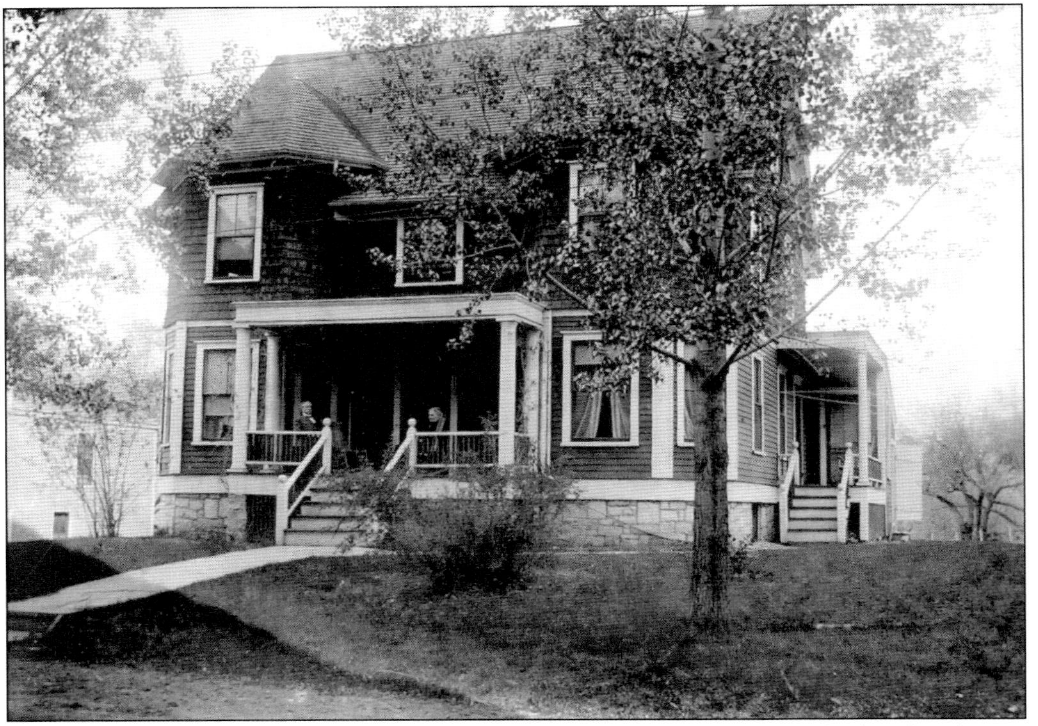

The Universalist parsonage was on West School Street across from the Methodist church. It is now a private residence.

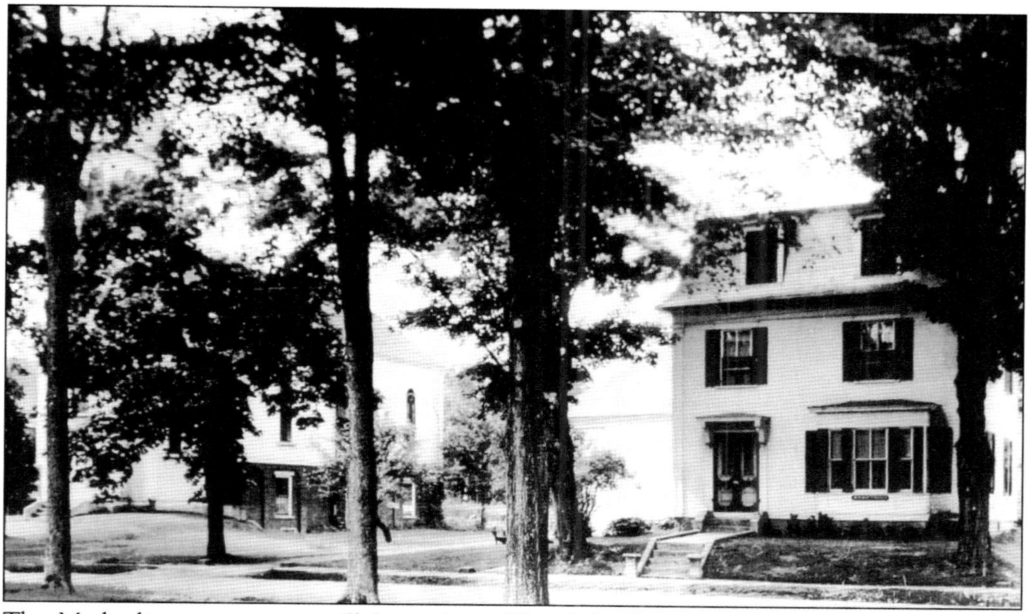

The Methodist parsonage is still located on West School Street just west of the Methodist church.

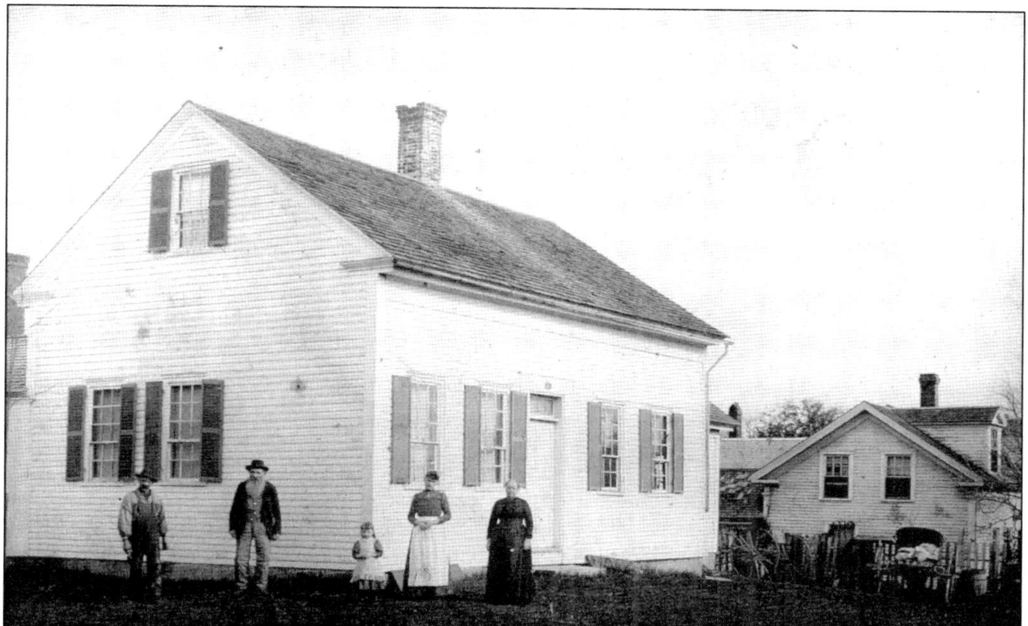

This photograph shows the Mathews home *c.* 1900. The caption on the back of the photograph reads, "Grandpa Mathews, Lettie Mathews, Carrie Maude Ellis."

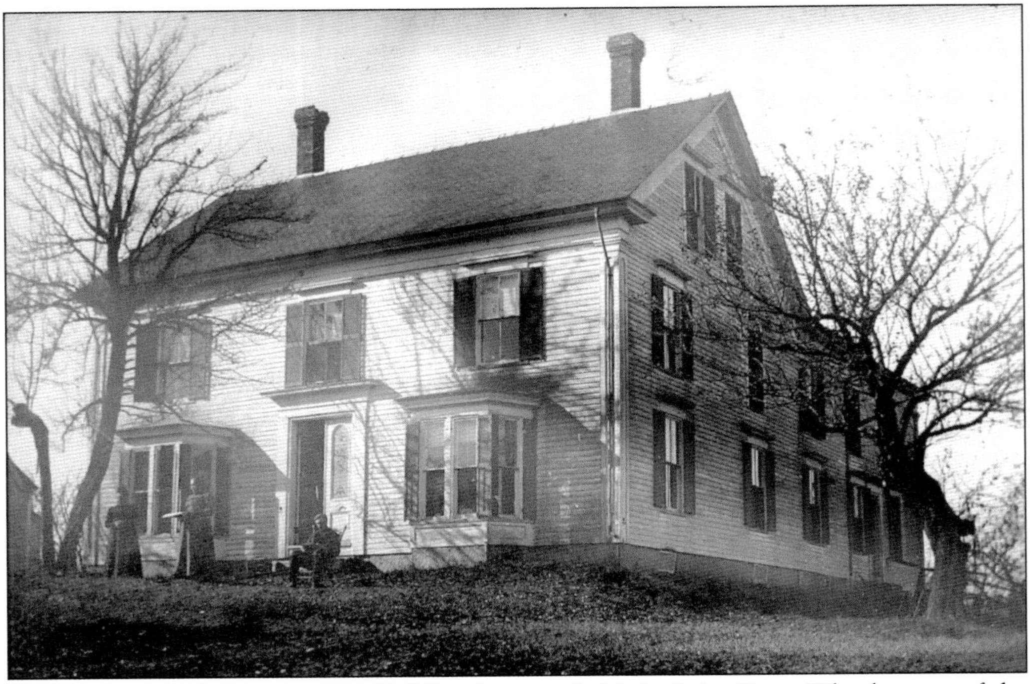

The Pullen Dyer house on Libby Hill Road was probably built by Cyrus Wheeler, one of the early settlers in the southern part of town.

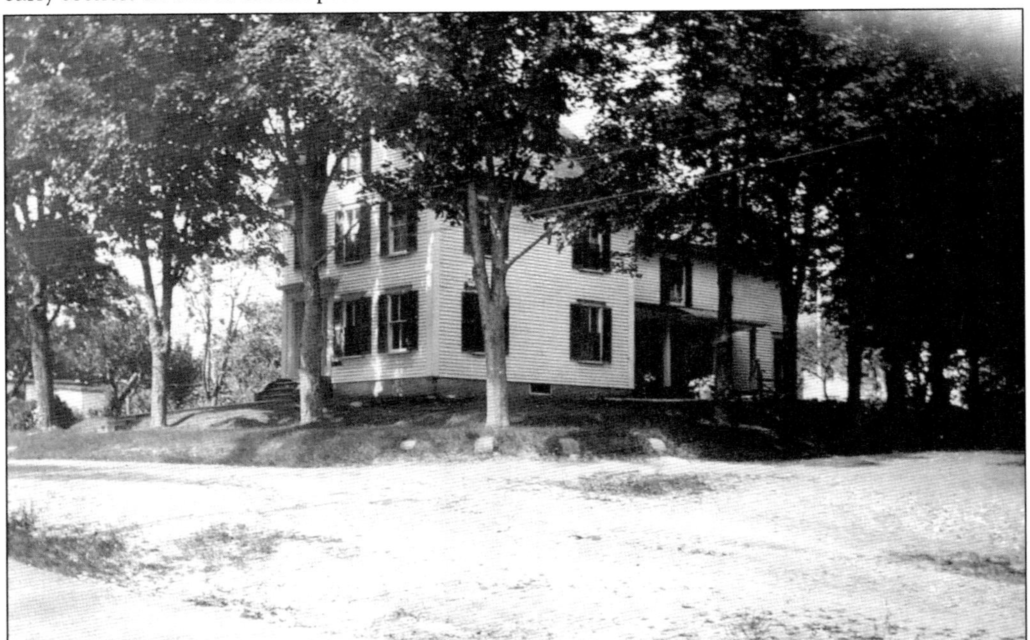

The Stowell House was located on the corner of School Street and Middle Street (now Center Street). Ralph Stowell ran Stowell's Pharmacy, a drugstore and lunch counter in the old True's building on Main Street until the 1950s. He was on the town council in 1950. His son Ralph Stowell Jr. was a dentist in the Dusty Block in the 1950s.

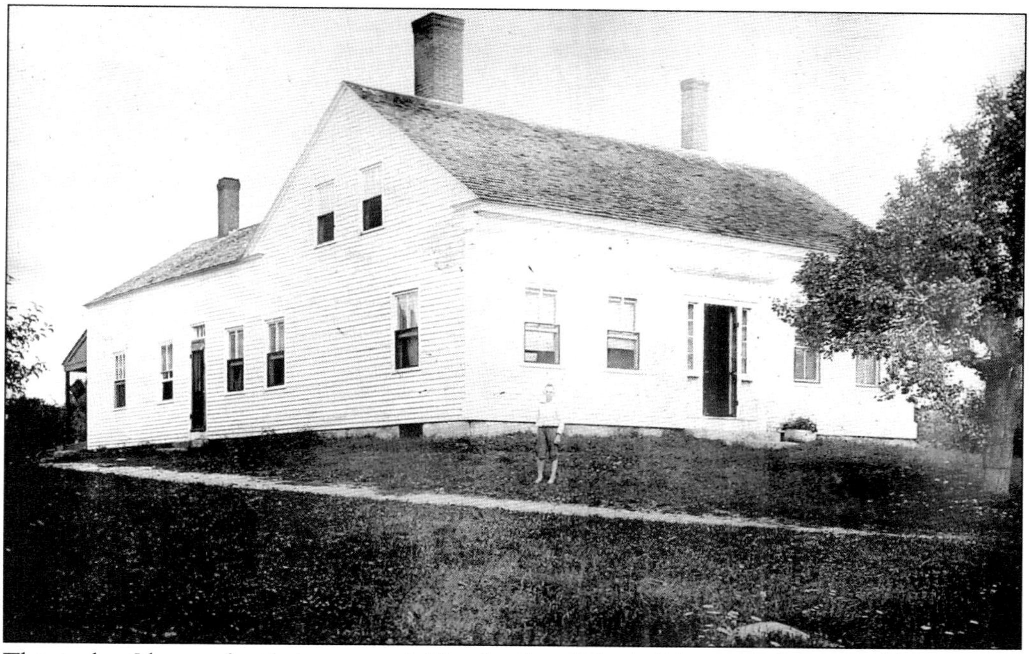

This is the Gleason family homestead. The family of Elijah Gleason (1767–1852) has been in Oakland since 1788. The photograph says "Arthur Gleason" on the back. Arthur Augustus Gleason was born in 1874 and was the son of Benjamin and Caroline (McIntyre) Gleason.

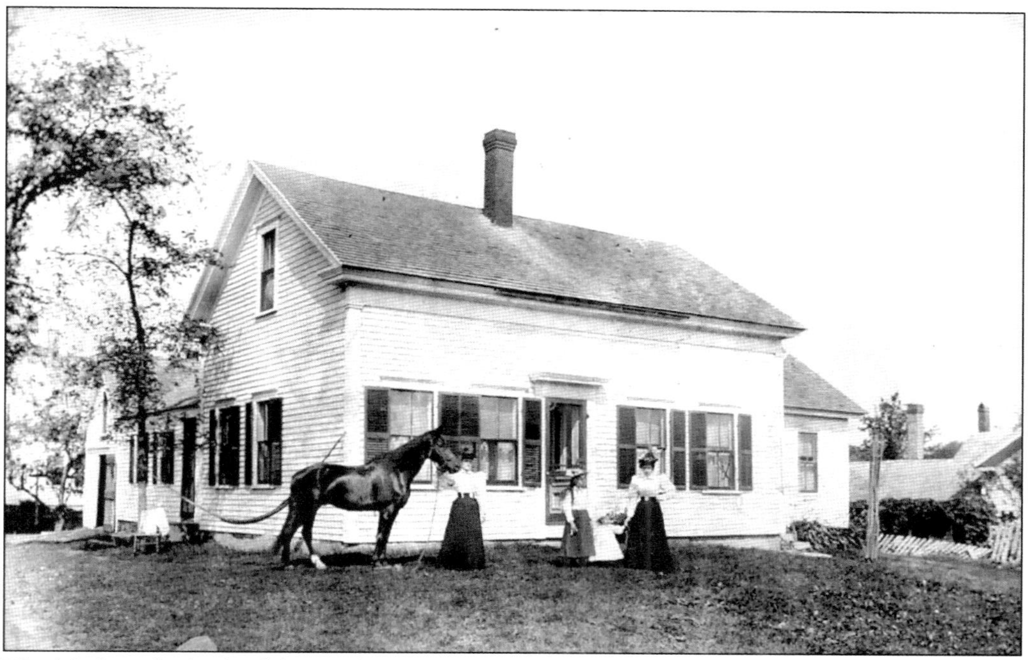

The label on the back of this card says, "Mrs. B. A. York, Mr. Burt Stevens and Mildred; Myrtie York; Doctor York; Mary is in the house." Lettie Mathews (widow of ? Lewis), the wife of Benjamin Otis York, was born in 1868; Myrtie York was born in 1884.

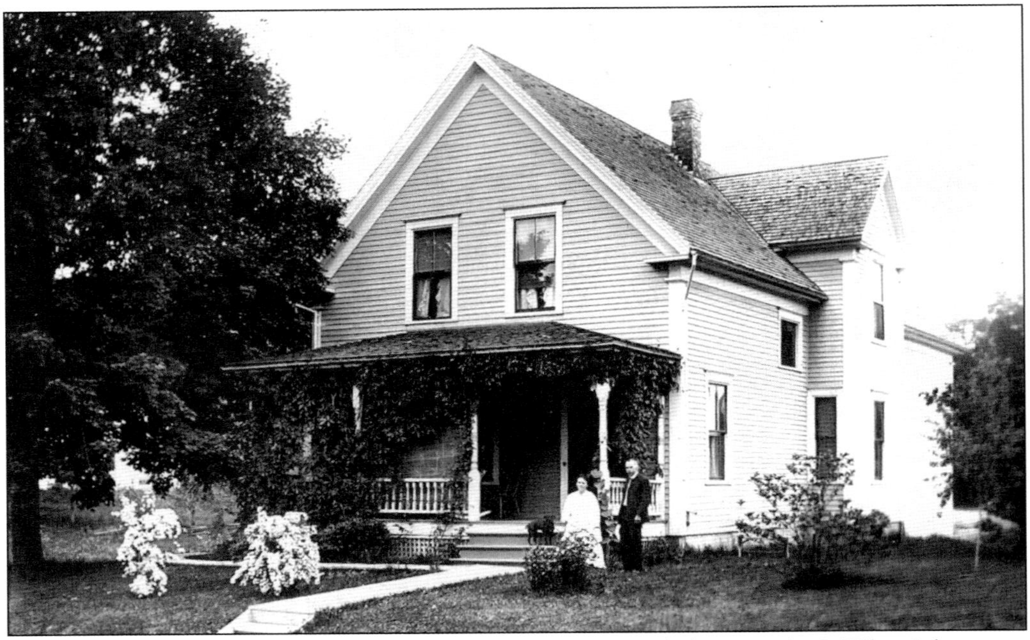

This is the G. W. Fields residence. In 1885, G. W. Fields boarded at Mrs. A. C. Tilton's home on Oak Street. By 1903, he had married Hattie Farnham. He had an office on Church Street near Main Street. He was a justice of the peace from 1885 to 1920, served on the school committee in 1886, and was the school supervisor from 1887 to 1890. He had a law practice and sold insurance from 1885 to 1920 and also dealt in real estate from 1903 to 1920.

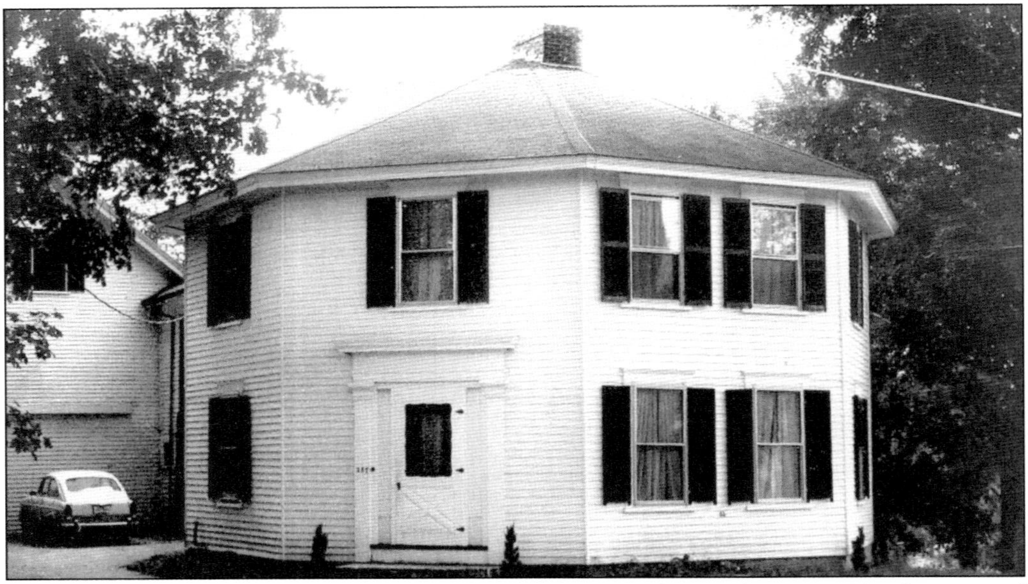

The Pressey House was built in 1855 by George Pressey, who was born *c.* 1801. Pressey and his wife, Tabitha, had eight children, all of whom were born before he built this house. The house is now listed in the National Register of Historic Places. Pressey died in 1861, only six years after building this home. Today, the Pressey House is a bed and breakfast, having been remodeled, restored, and enlarged substantially at the back.

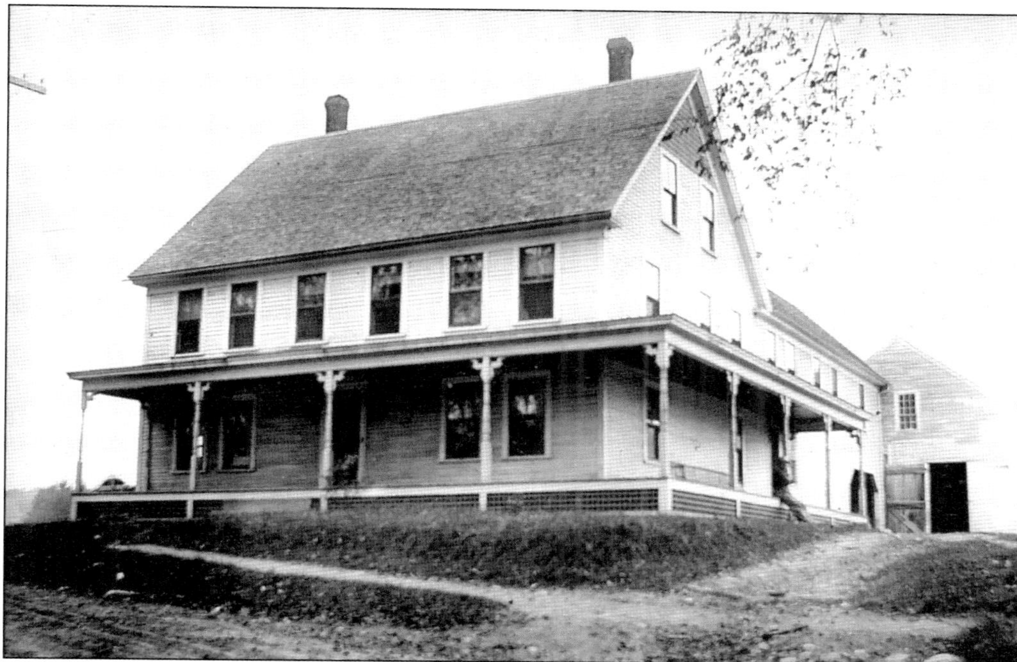

The Wentworth House, located on Summer Street, was owned at one time by Capt. Joseph Hitchings, who married Betsey Coombs, daughter of Jonathan Coombs. Hitching was captain of one of the militia companies of Waterville, and he was a one-sixth owner of the Coombs sawmill. His second wife, Keziah Wilbur (widow of Daniel Wilbur), had a daughter, also named Keziah, who owned the first piano in town. Charles Henry Wentworth owned and operated the Wentworth Vulcanizing and Battery Company from 1928 to 1930, and his wife, Nora Lorinda, ran a boardinghouse here from 1923 to 1926.

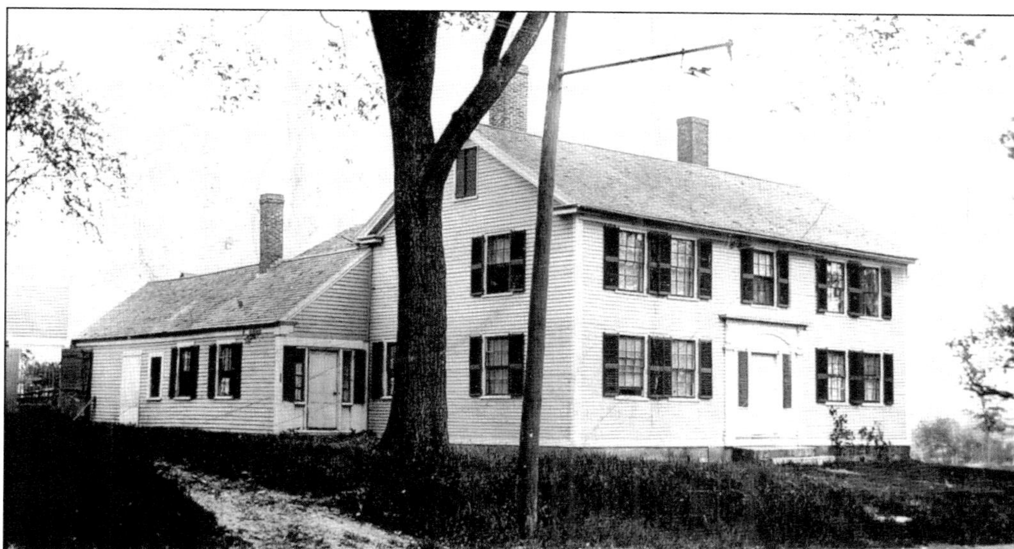

This house may be the one located on the site of today's Early Bird Restaurant on the north side of Main Street.

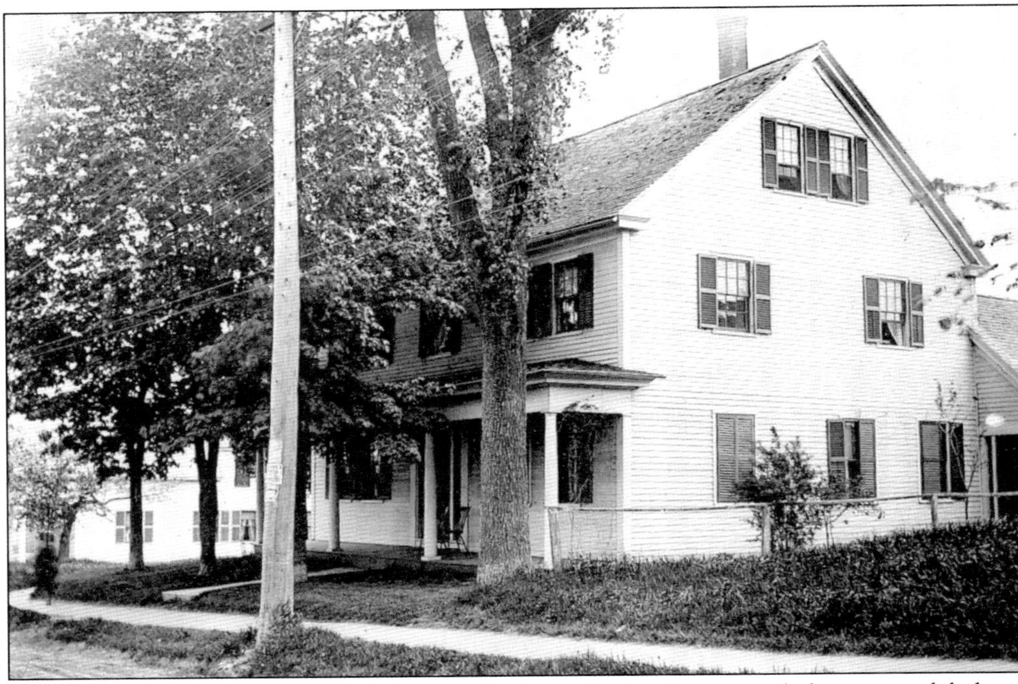

This building, located just east of the main business district, has recently been remodeled and serves as an apartment house.

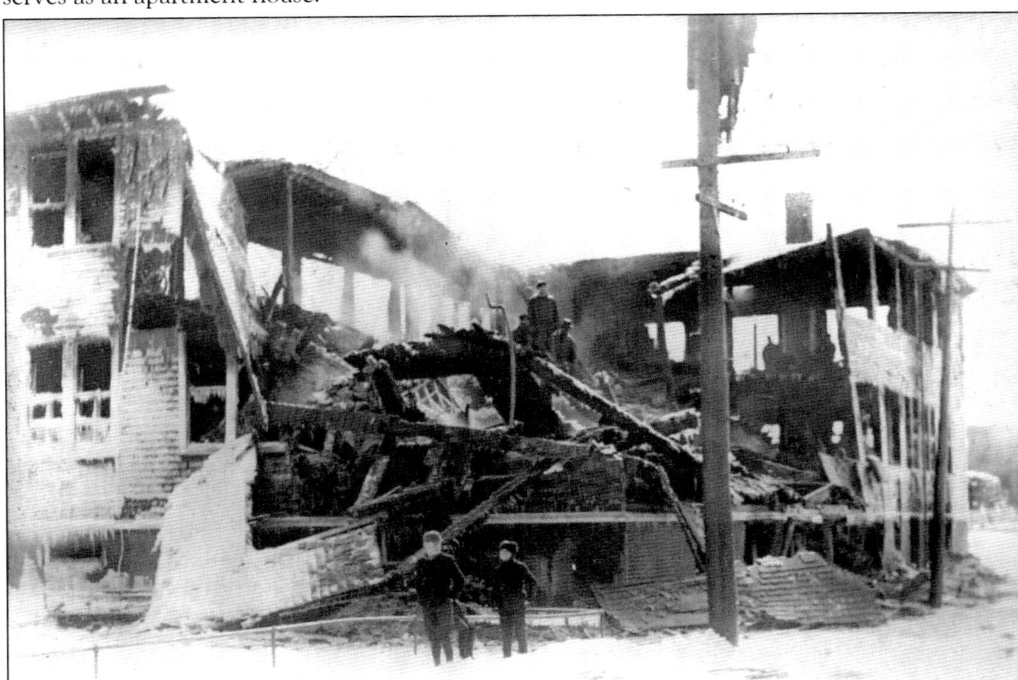

This photograph shows a January 1907 fire. Based on a list of fires in town reports, it probably occurred at a sawmill.

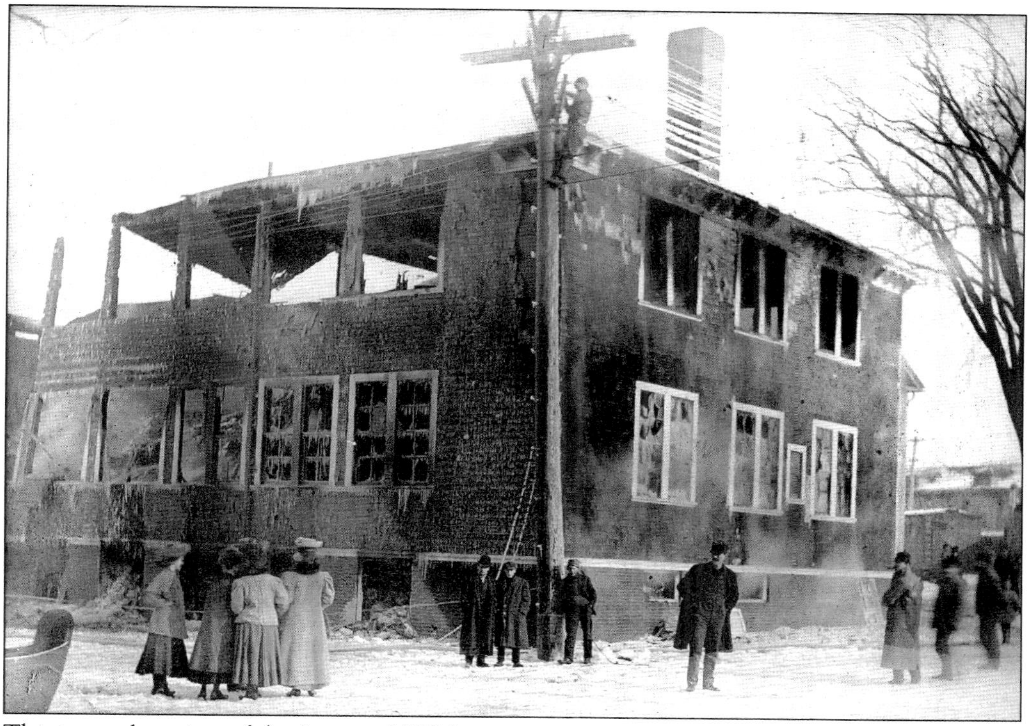

This is another view of the January 1907 fire.

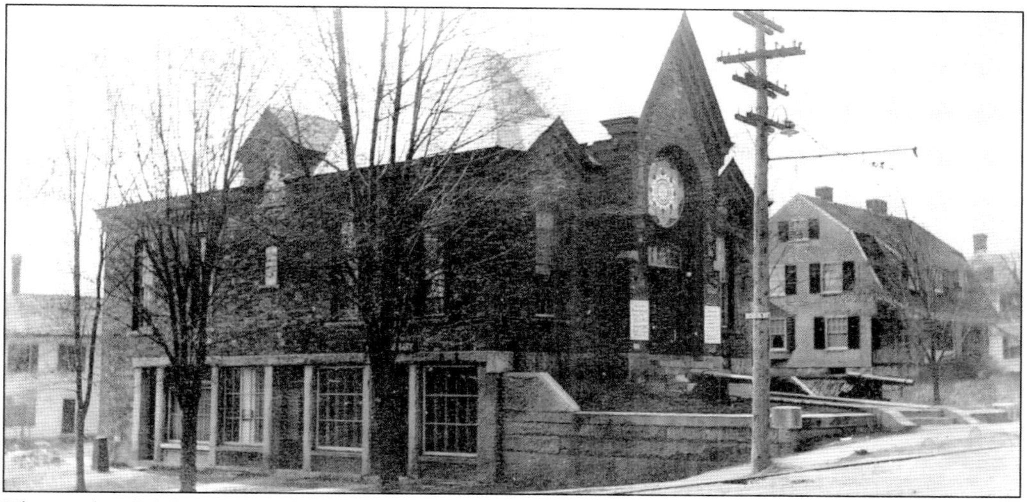

This is the GAR Memorial Hall. When West Waterville's Civil War veterans returned, John U. Hubbard was determined that the town would have a suitable memorial to its veterans, not the least of whom was Hubbard's brother, Andrew. It was said that what John Hubbard wanted, John Hubbard got, and so, by 1870, this beautiful hall was built. Located upstairs is an auditorium with a stage and a proscenium arch. The downstairs housed, at various times, a bank, the library, and the town offices; currently, the Messalonskee High School alternative-education program is located there. For years, the downstairs rooms were the town's polling place as well. On the building and on a tablet outside are listed Oakland's war veterans from 1861 to the present.

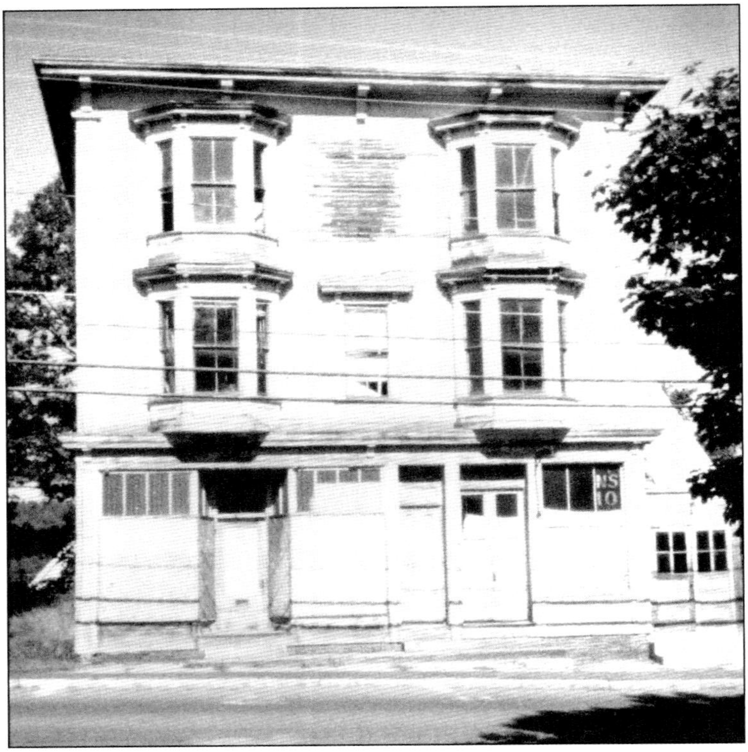

Located on Church Street across from the library, the Odd Fellows Hall building was demolished in the 1980s. The front left was the Toy Theatre, a movie theater for silent films, in the 1920s. The building also housed the Brown Studio (a photography studio) and Nellie B. Wilbur's dry-goods store.

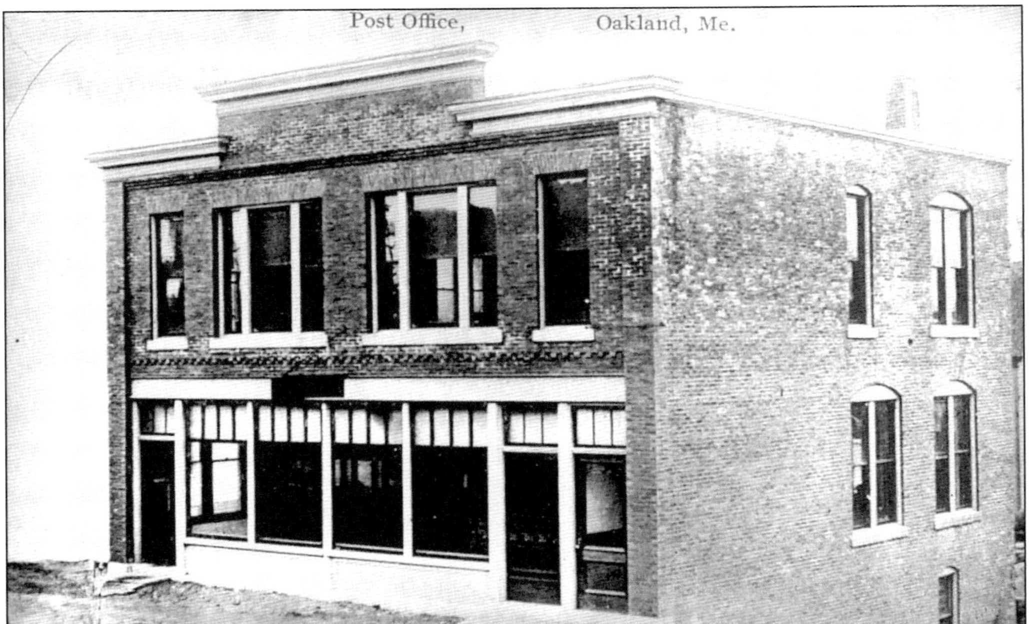

The new post office, built *c.* 1915, is located on Center Street (formerly Middle Street). Prior to the building of the post office, other small industries were located on this site, including a roller-skate factory. After another new post office was built on Main Street *c.* 1955, this building housed a church, a television repair shop, a restaurant, and a computer business.

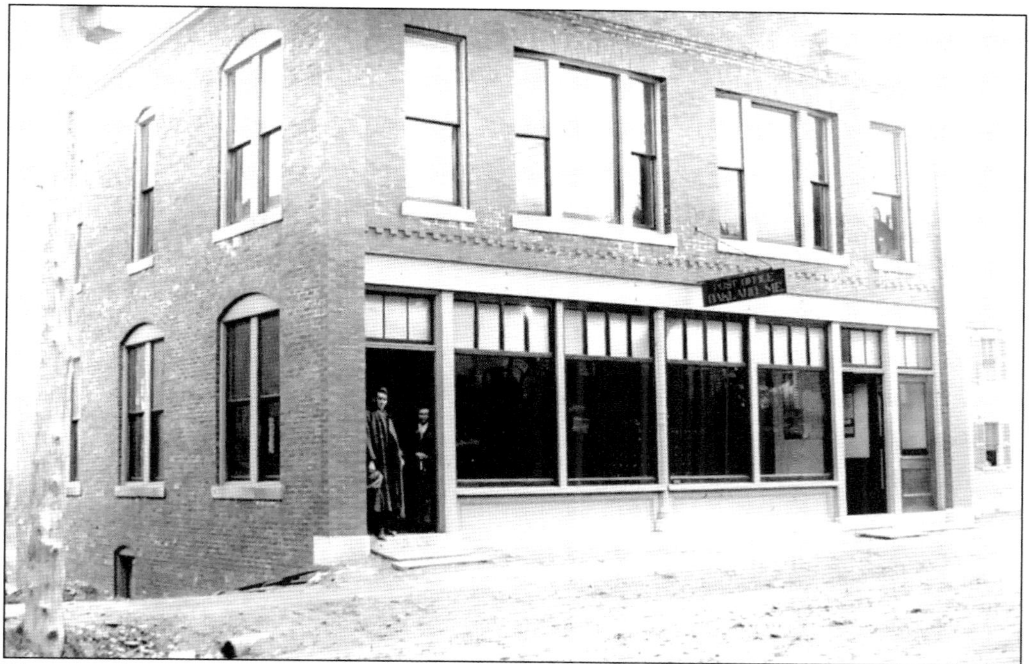

The post office building is currently being remodeled as a dentist's office.

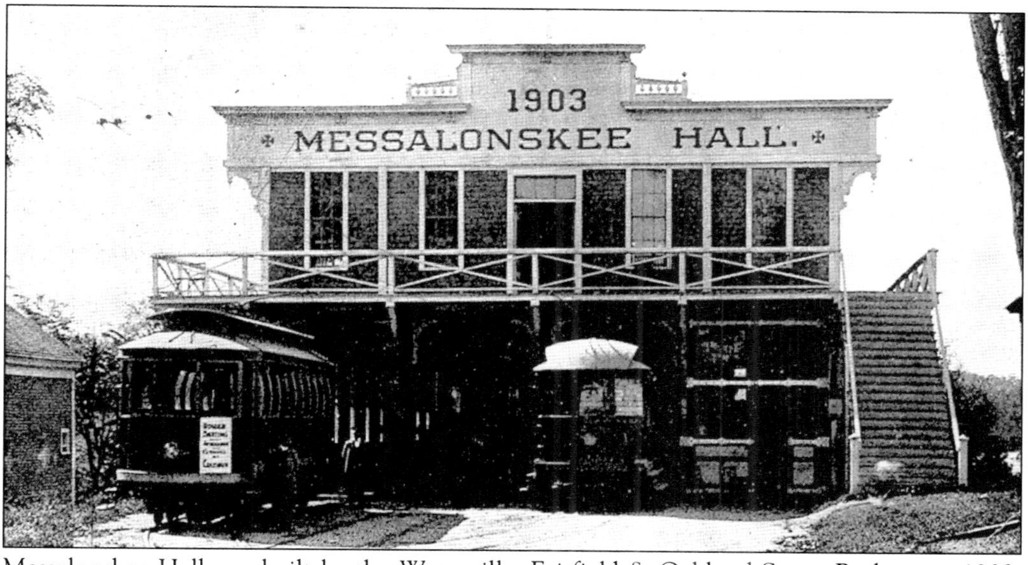

Messalonskee Hall was built by the Waterville, Fairfield & Oakland Street Railway in 1903. This building, located on Church Street at the lake, was the end of the line for the trolley cars. Upstairs was a dance hall; Oakland High School's basketball games were played there for many years. The wraparound porch was especially popular in the summertime, when young couples would stroll and look out at Messalonskee Lake. Below the car floor was a boathouse that rented small boats for lake excursions. The trolley cars ran back and forth to Main Street in Waterville continuously throughout the day. The run took about half an hour, with regular stops along the way. Messalonskee Hall was called the "car barn," and the car being used stayed outside until nighttime.

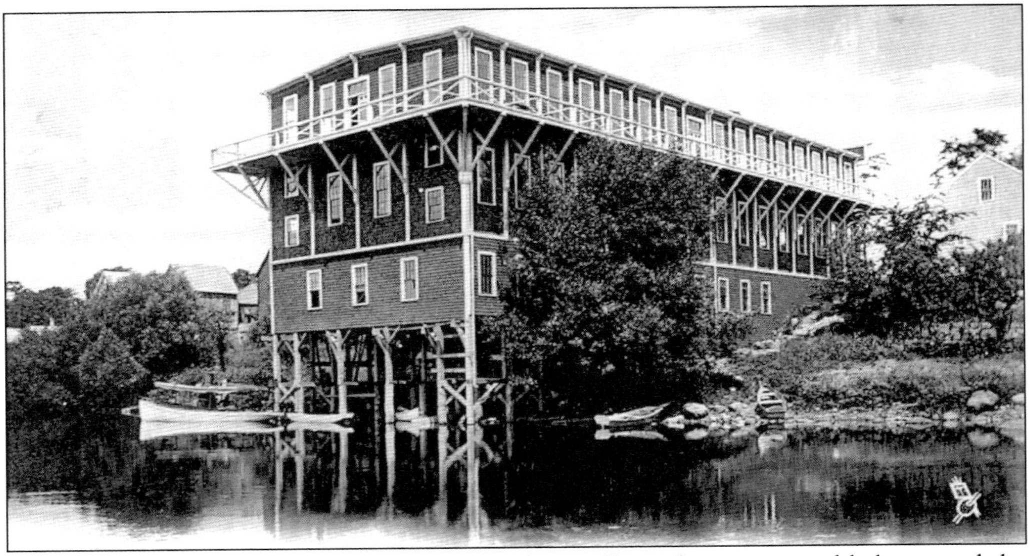

Clearly visible in this photograph of Messalonskee Hall are the wraparound balcony and the boathouse. By 1923, the building was declared unsafe; it was shortened and narrowed, the top floor was removed, and it was closed to public use. Today, the original cement floor can still be seen; it is used as a pad for a dog enclosure that is surrounded by a chain-link fence.

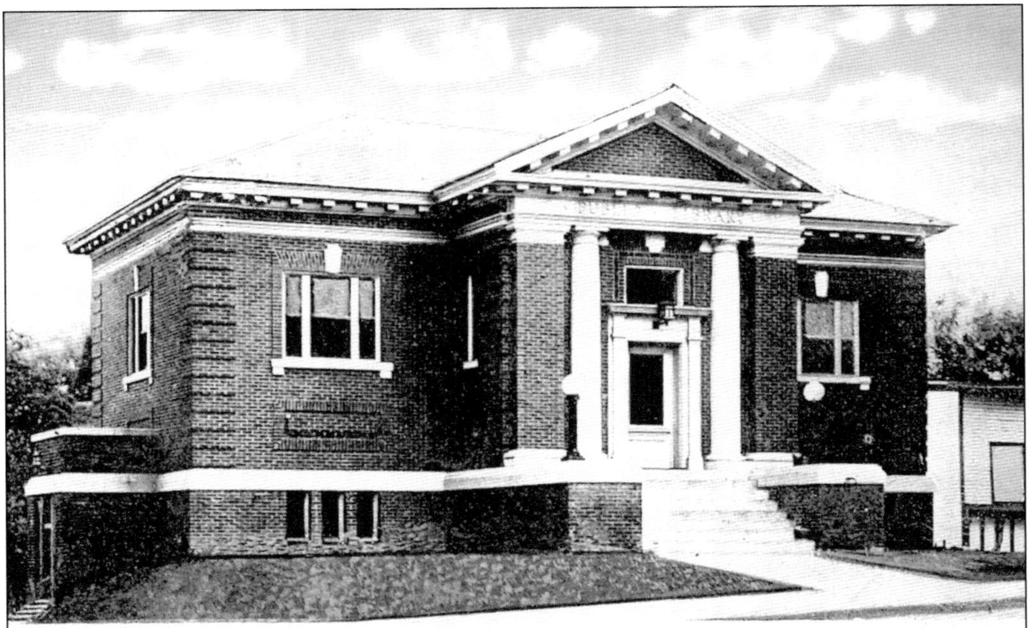

The Oakland Public Library was built in 1915 with a grant from the Carnegie Foundation on land donated by Alice Benjamin. The architect was H. S. Combs, and the builder was Horace Purington and Company. In 1895, there was a reading room over D. M. Marshall's store. Later, the reading room was located in the lower part of Memorial Hall after Cascade Savings Bank moved to Main Street. A 1903 map shows a public library in the back of a store between the hotel and the depot.

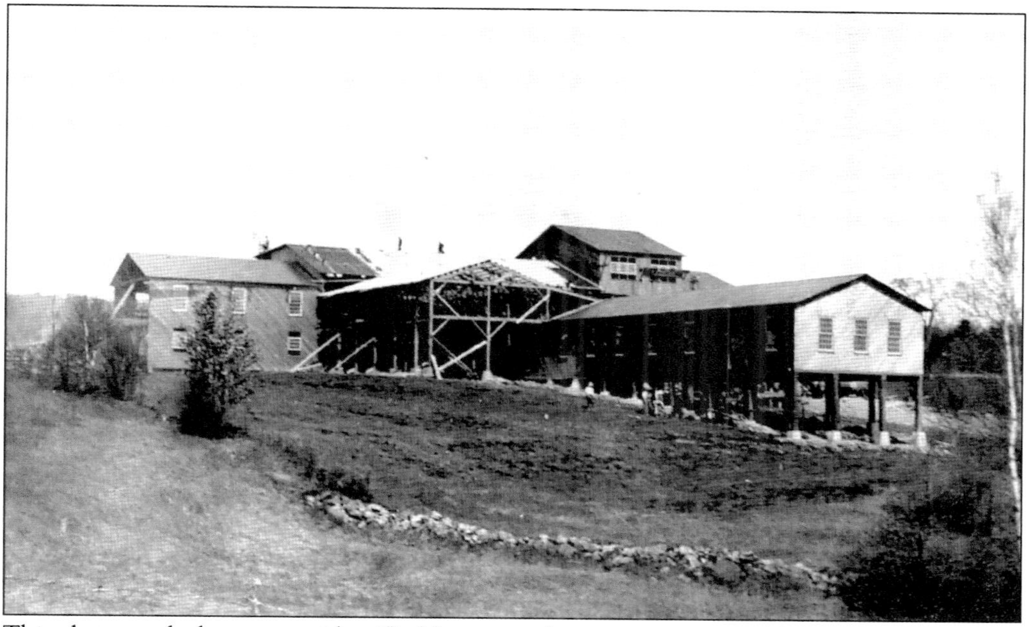

This photograph shows an unidentified factory under construction c. 1900.

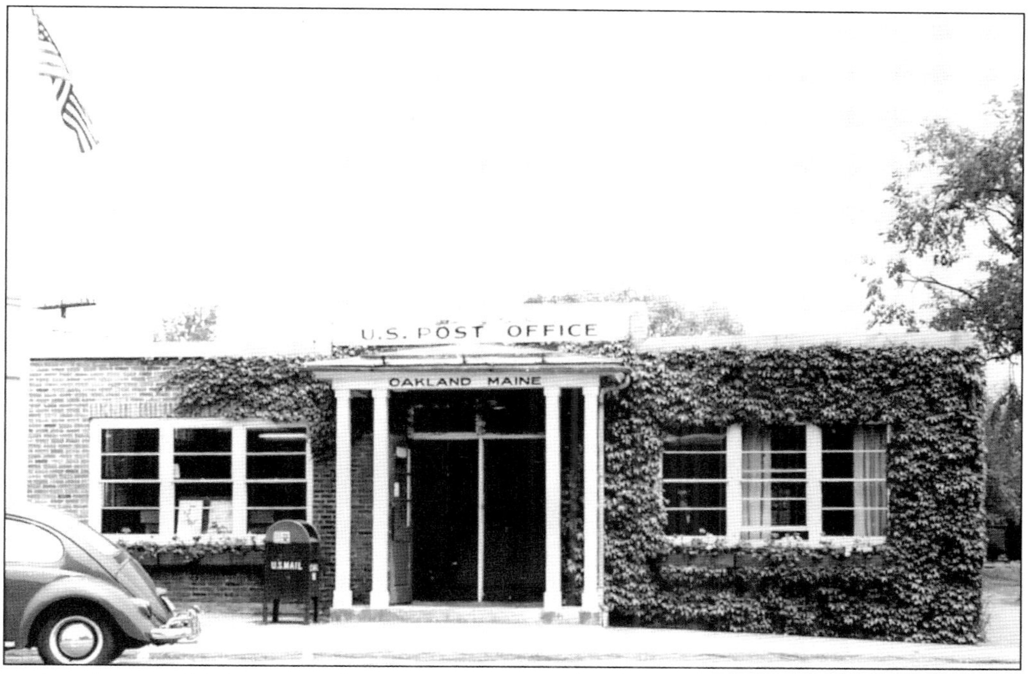

Built c. 1955 on Main Street, the former post office building is now a sports bar, having been replaced by an even newer post office on Water Street. The first post office in West Waterville, which opened on December 6, 1827, had only one mail delivery a week. Postmaster Elisha Hallett established rural free delivery routes in 1900. Until 1913, the post office was located on Church Street in the present-day Coughlin's Real Estate building.

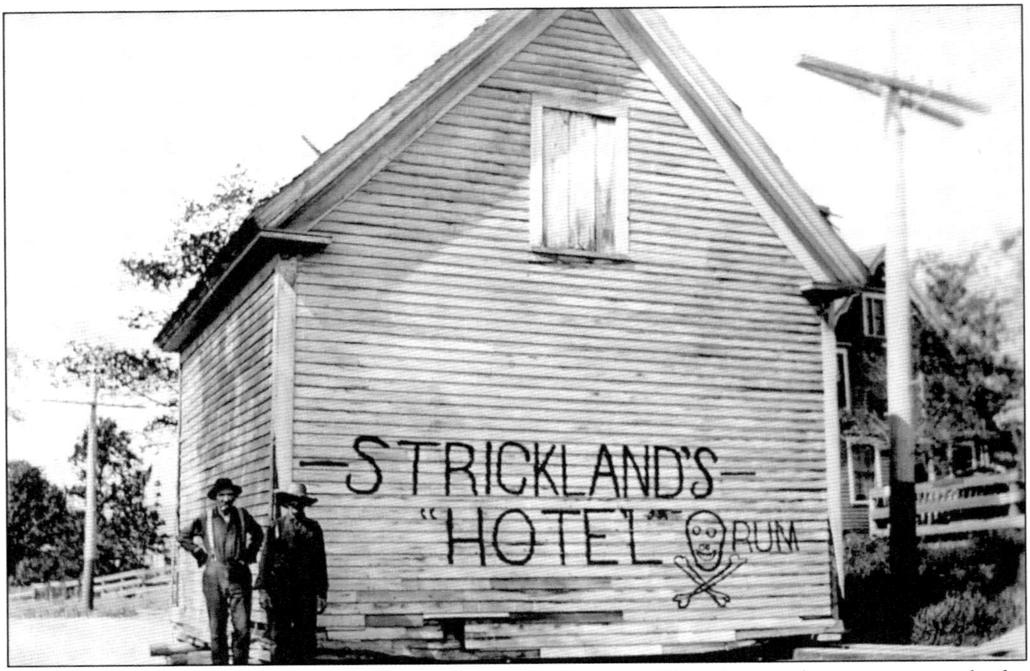

"Strickland's Hotel" was apparently a reference to a constable who used to arrest people for drinking and then housed them in the jail. The building was on the west side of Oak Street, where the new Fabian Oil building is located today.

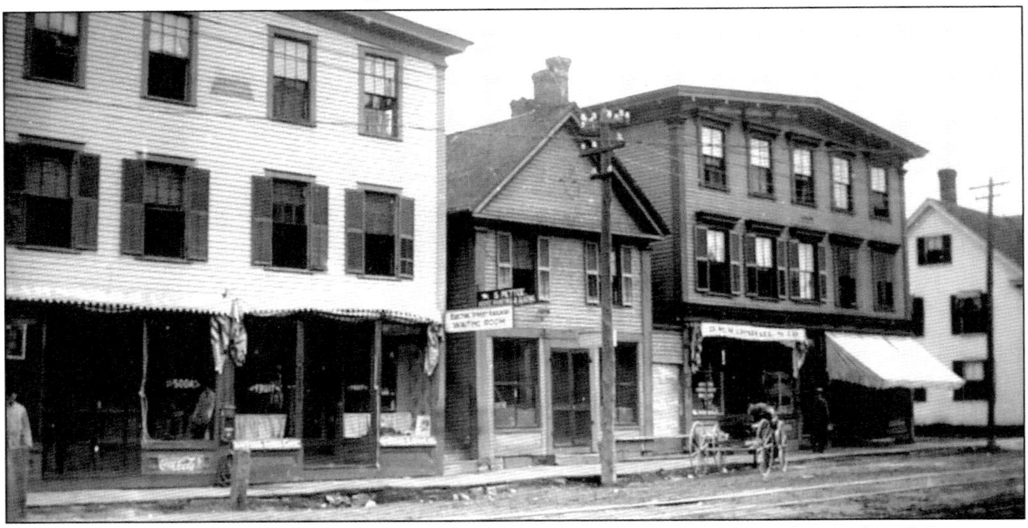

This is a view of the north side of Main Street *c.* 1900. Business on that side of the street included the Goulding building. The white sign in the center reads, "Electric Street Railway Waiting Room." Other businesses here included D. M. Marshall & Company; Goulding Book and Stationery; the Western Union telegraph office; a bank; George W. Wilson's barber shop; H. L. Hunton's insurance and law practice; A. W. Leonard, harnesses and groceries; J. E. Morrisette & Company, fruit and confectionery; J. B. Hodsdon, boots, shoes, and clothing; and Blake Brothers, glassware, groceries, and meats. The Dusty Block housed Morris L. Strickland, barber, and J. M. Field, retailer of watches and jewelry.

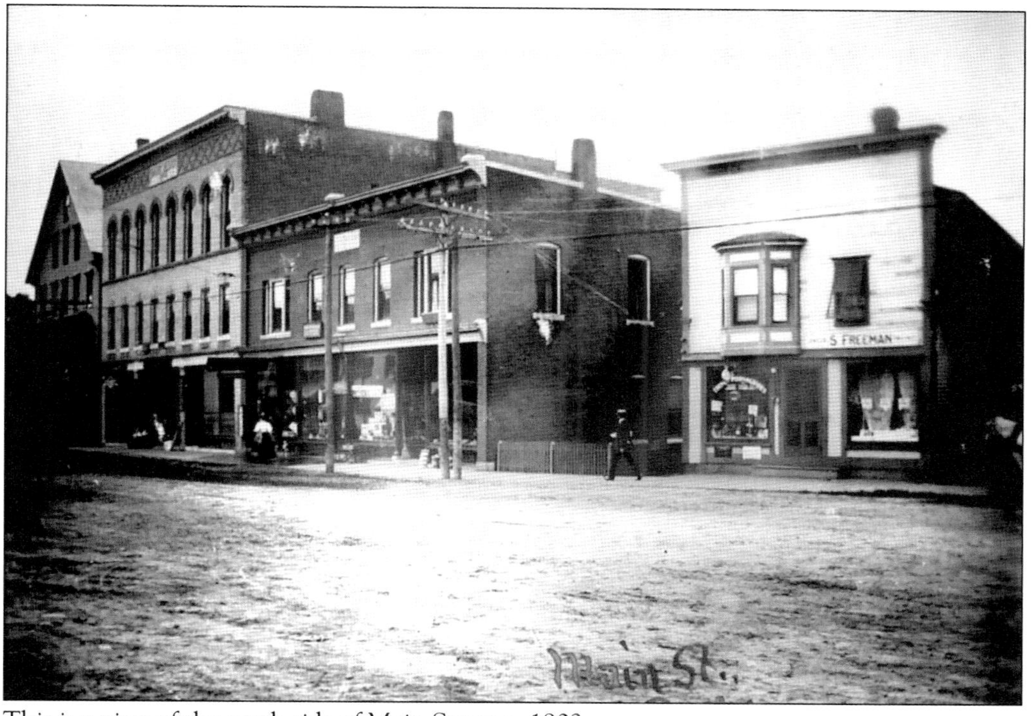

This is a view of the south side of Main Street *c.* 1903.

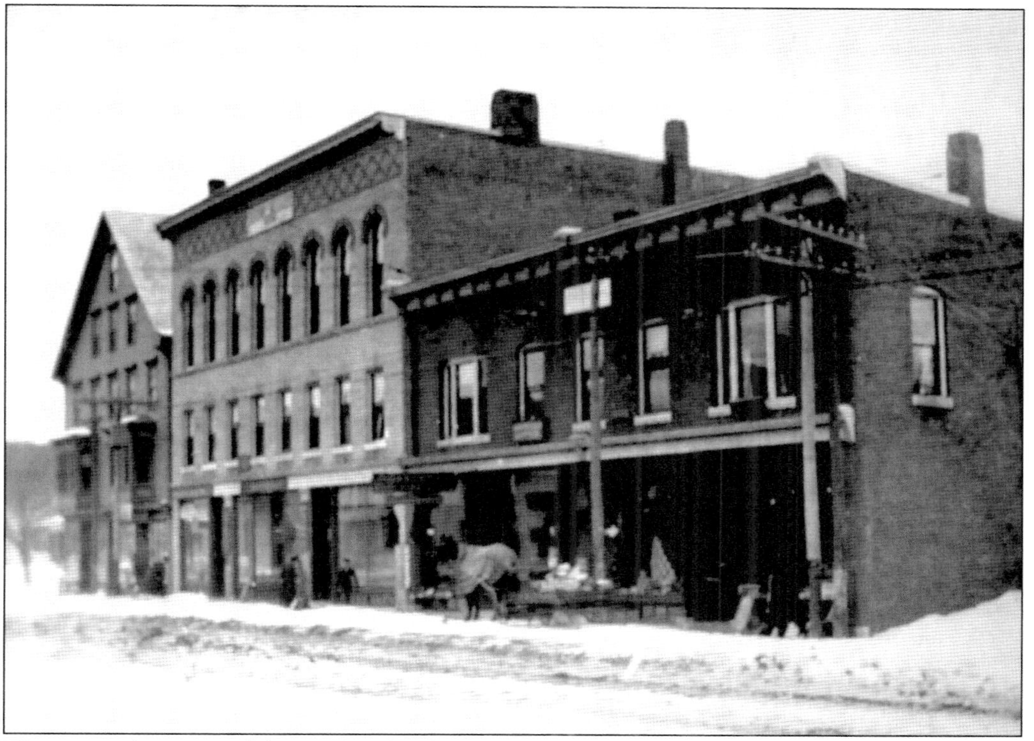

This is another view of the south side of Main Street, *c.* 1905.

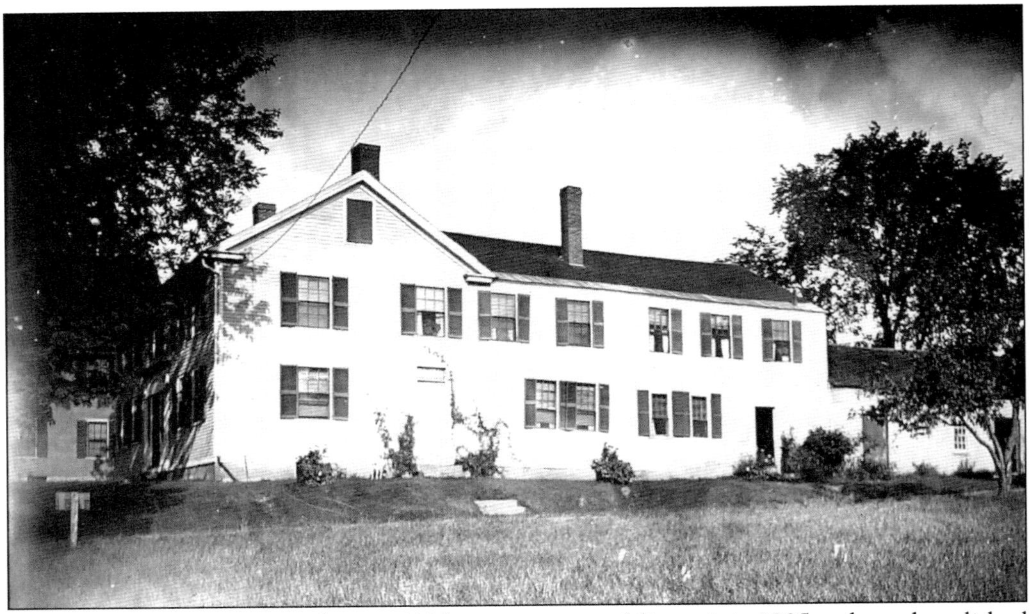

This Main Street home, seen here *c.* 1905, was in a state of disrepair in 1995 and was demolished in 1999. It is on the site of the present-day Early Bird Restaurant, next to Webber's Launderama. This is probably the same building pictured on page 99.

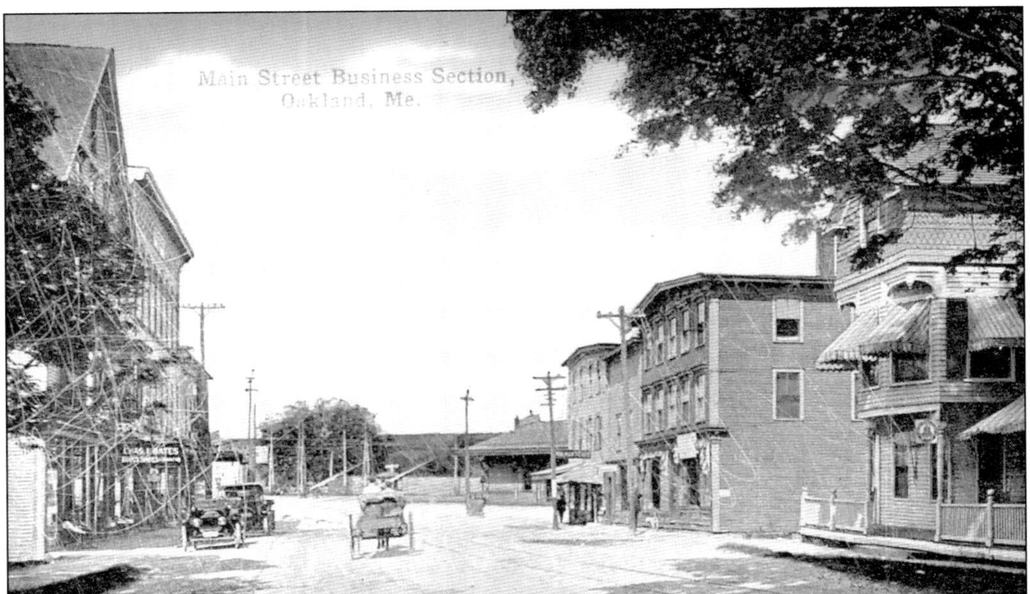

This is a view of Main Street, looking west, *c.* 1905. On the left, the Bank Block is still recognizable. None of the others are left, having either been demolished or replaced by other structures. The large building on the right with the awnings was the Oakland Hotel. There was a livery stable in the back. Other businesses included a meat and grocery store, the Cascade Laundry, a millinery and confectionery, and a billiards parlor. The public library was located behind the meat and grocery store.

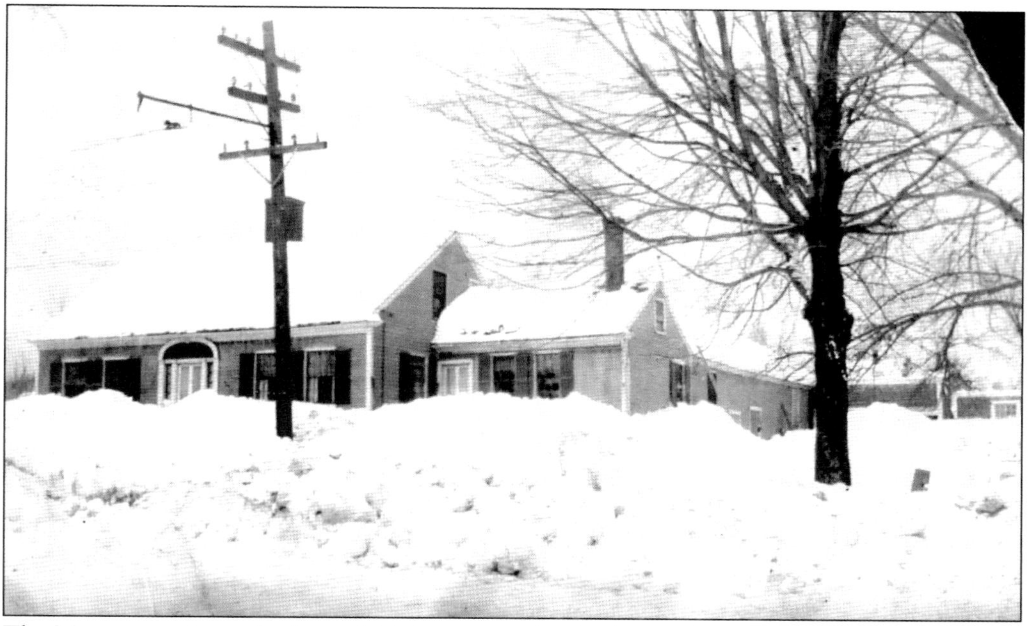

The Macartney House, built in 1815, is now the Oakland Area Historical Society's museum. It is shown here in the winter of 1920. The house has been moved north about 100 feet from its original foundation, and an ell on the rear has been removed, but otherwise it is substantially the same as seen here.

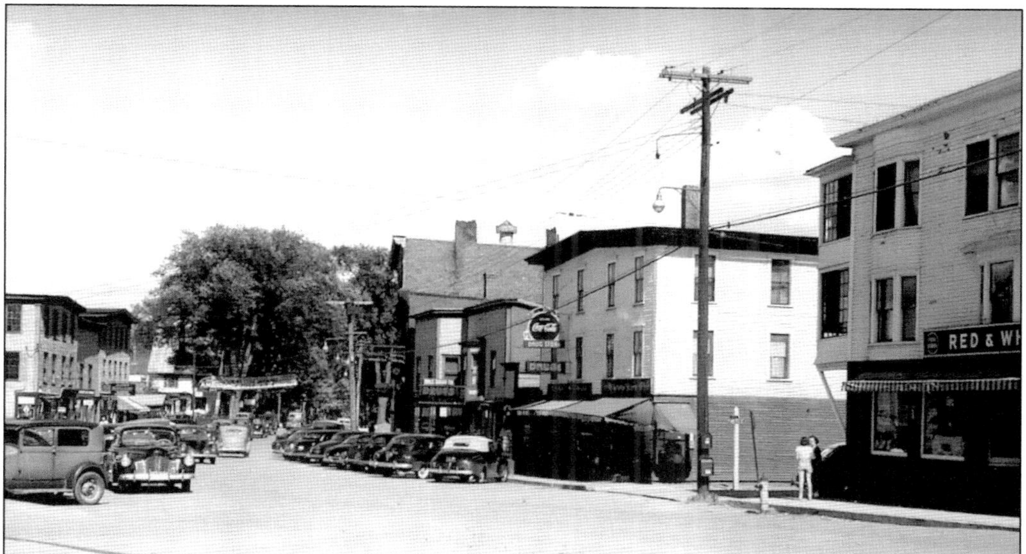

This is a view of Main Street, looking west, *c.* 1947. Many of the buildings here are still recognizable from earlier pictures, though the large building on the right and the Texaco station are no longer there. Businesses here included Samuel J. Foster's Drug Store and lunch counter in the Fossett Building; Blake's Hardware; M.B. Helms, barber; First National Grocers; Hal's Restaurant; Oakland Insurance Agency; H. L. Hunton, lawyer; Minnie L. Livingston Rowe's beauty shop; National Bank and Trust; Depositors Trust Company; Ralph Stowell Jr., dentist; and Rancourt's Cash Market.

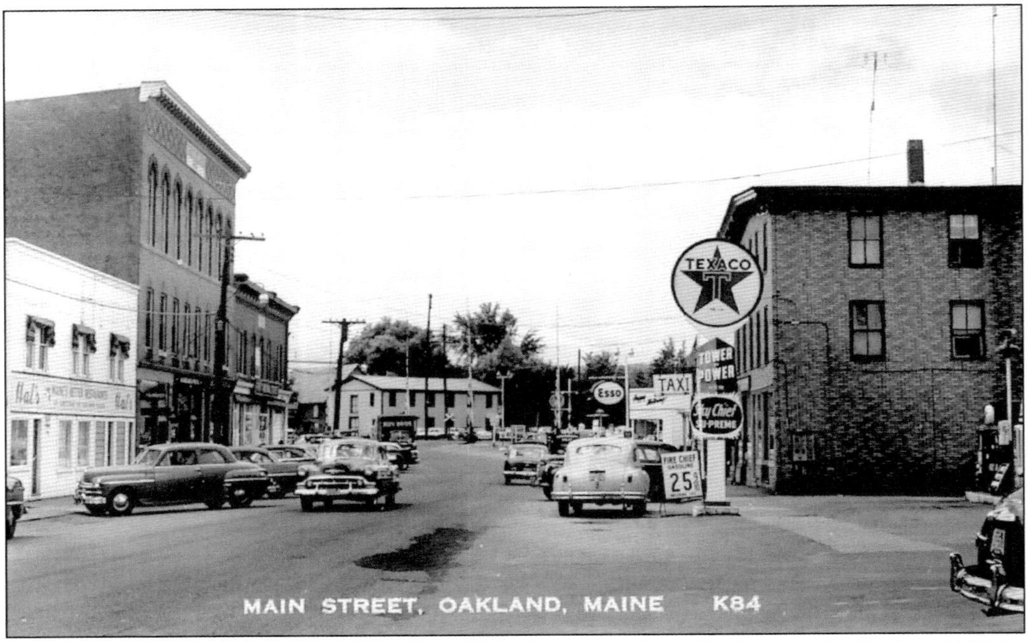

This *c.* 1947 photograph shows Main Street, looking east. Notable here is the Red and White store, owned by Bernice Michaud, which was later moved across the street and eastwards. The large white building left of center housed Fossett's Ben Franklin store for many years.

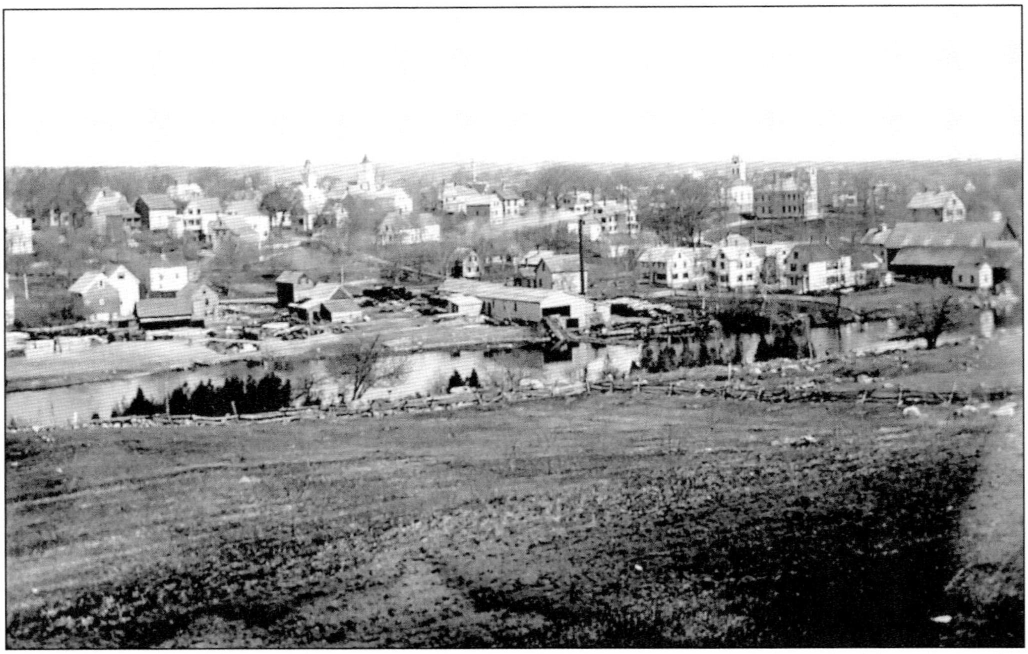

This is a view of Oakland from Alpine Street. The number of axe factory buildings near the School Street Bridge is very evident here. The churches and Oakland High School are also visible. Showing much open land and few trees, this photograph depicts a scene very different from the way the town looks today.

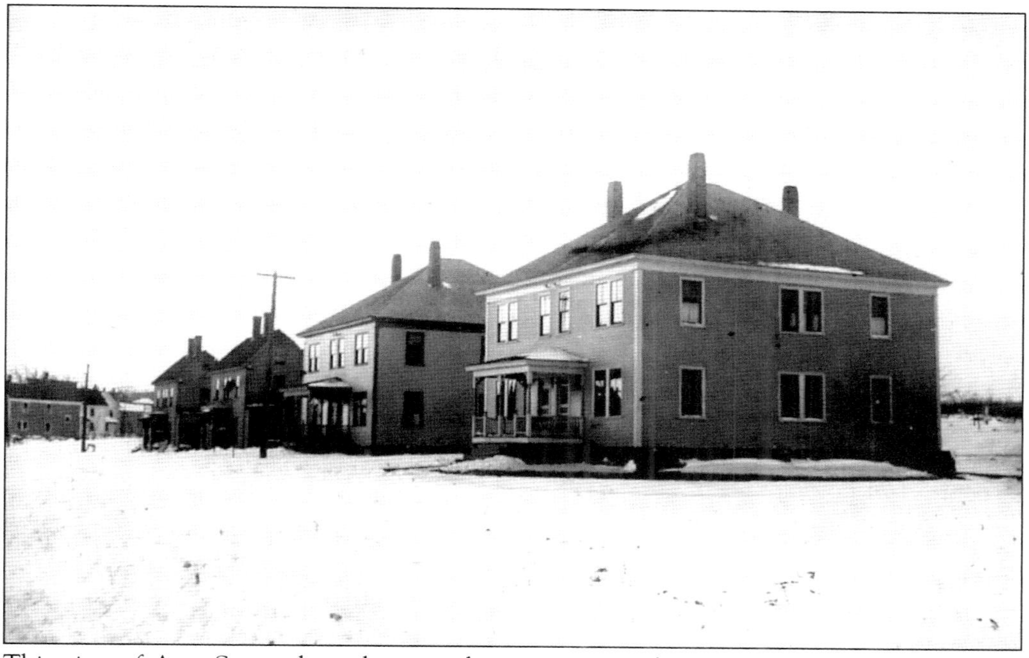

This view of Ayer Street shows housing that was apparently erected by one of the mills for workers. Many of the houses are still here today. Also shown are the offices for what became the Diamond Match Company.

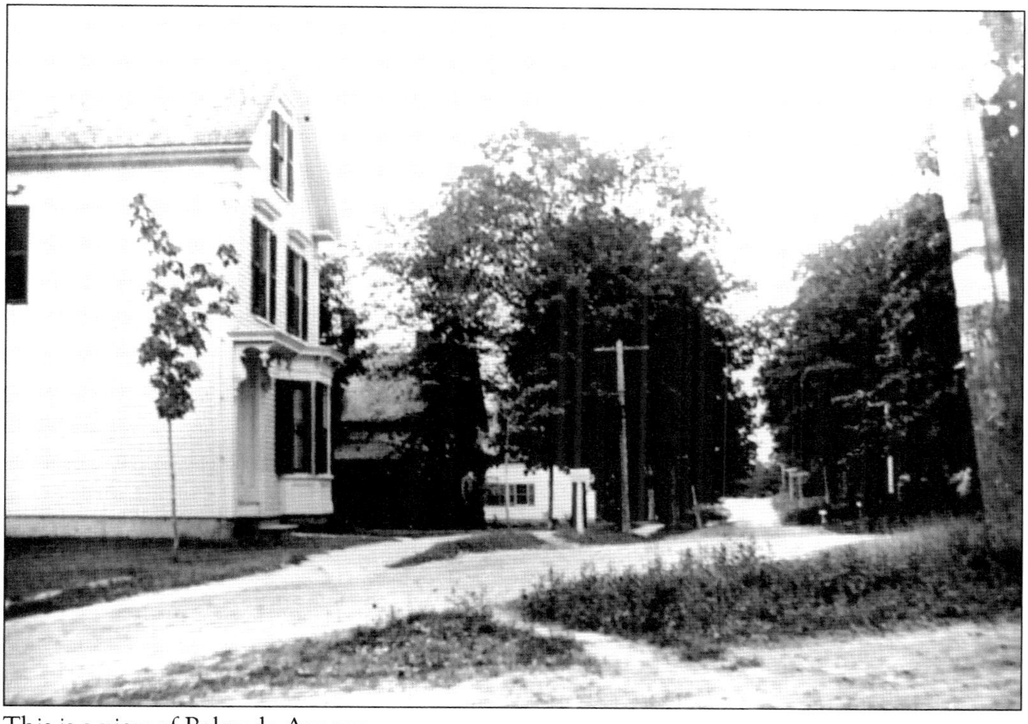

This is a view of Belgrade Avenue.

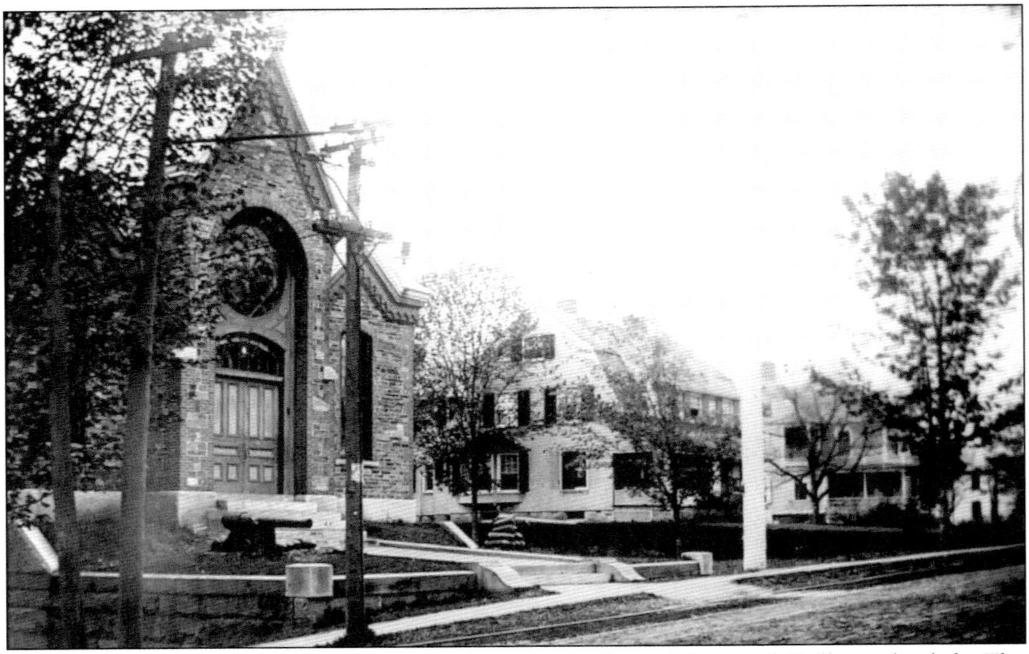

This view of Church Street, taken on July 6, 1909, shows Memorial Hall on the left. The Memorial Hall Soldiers Monument Association was incorporated on February 12, 1869, to build a hall dedicated to the brave men of the Civil War. Guy Hubbard donated the land for the building. He had lost a son in the war. The building cost $12,000 and was built of stone with brick trimmings. The basement has been used as a post office, the West Waterville Savings Bank, the town office, the library, the food bank, and a temporary Catholic church. Currently, the downstairs is used as an alternative-education school by the Messalonskee School District. The upstairs housed social events, plays, high school graduations, minstrel shows, and recitals

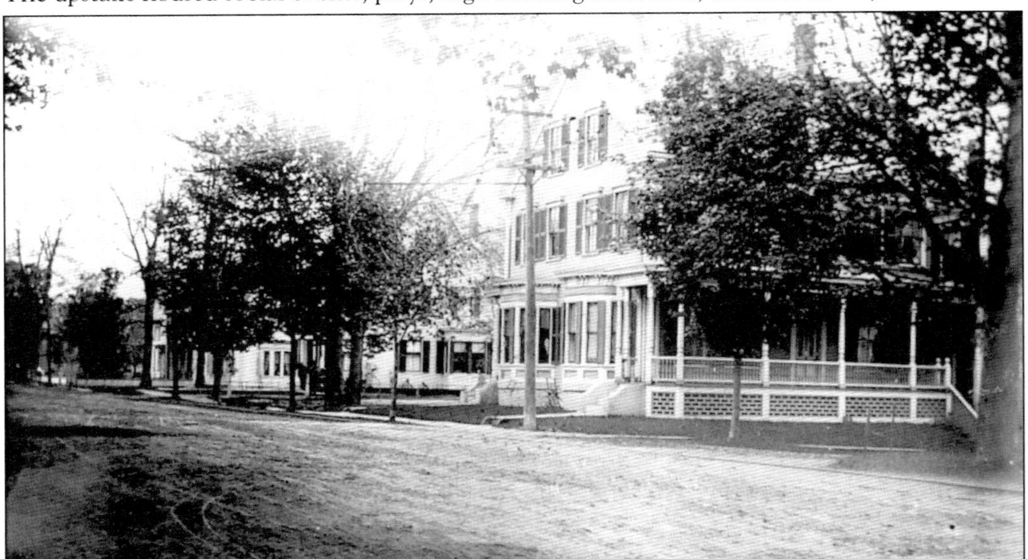

This postcard shows the east side of Church Street, looking toward downtown. The large house pictured is still located on the corner of Church and Maple Streets.

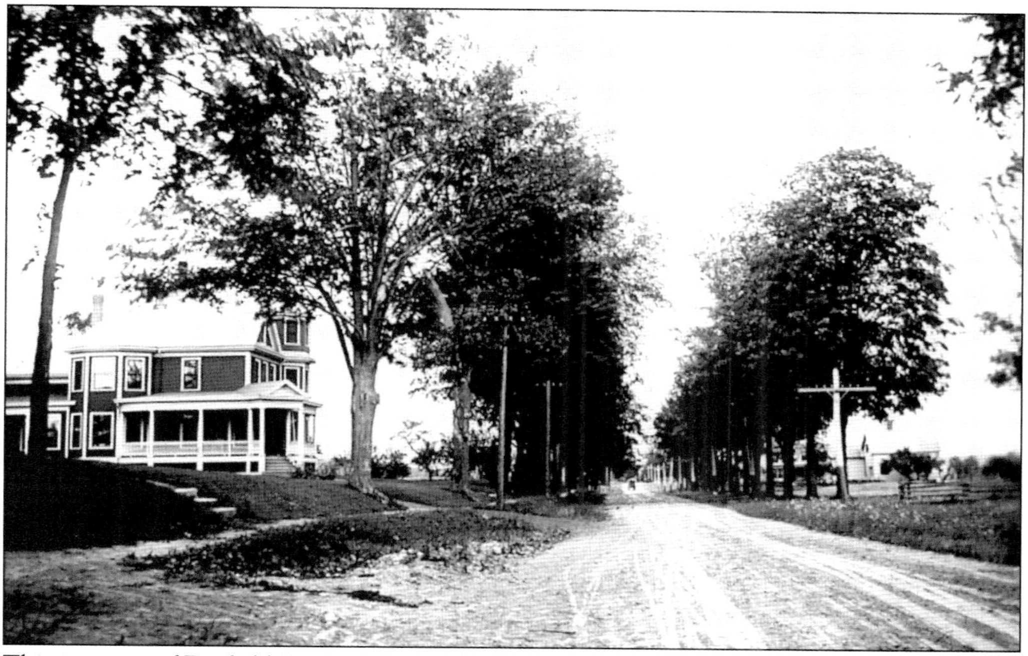

This is a view of Fairfield Street c. 1910. The house on the left was the residence of John Ayer, who in 1883 was one of the owners of the Cascade Woolen Mill. Today, the house is the Johann Sebastian B. restaurant.

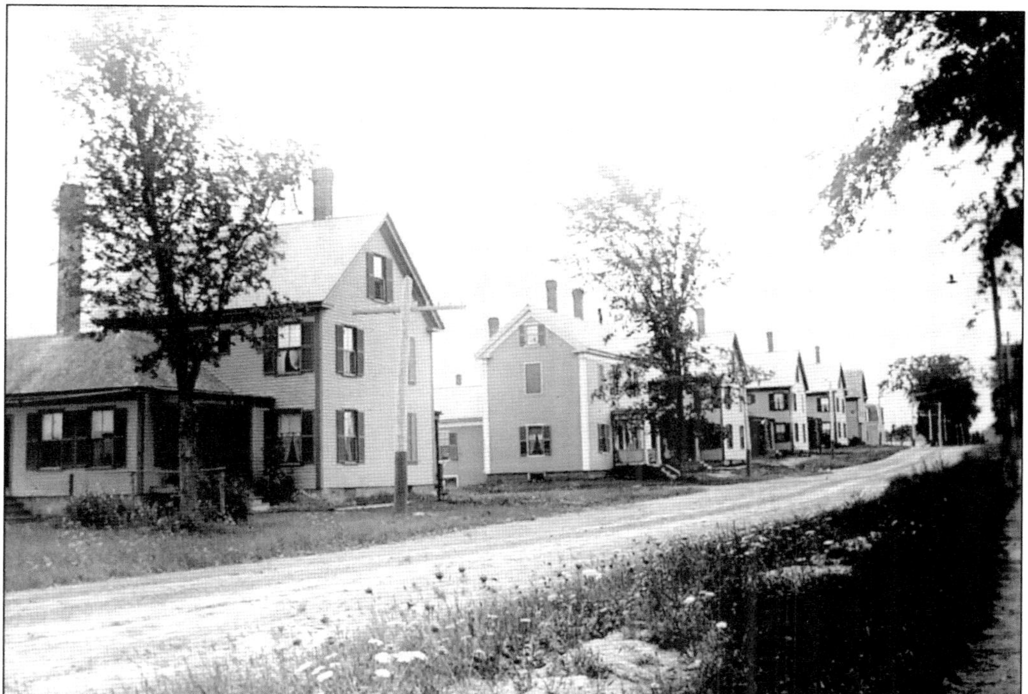

This is another view of Fairfield Street, looking south toward town. Most of the houses here were erected by the Cascade Woolen Mill for its workers.

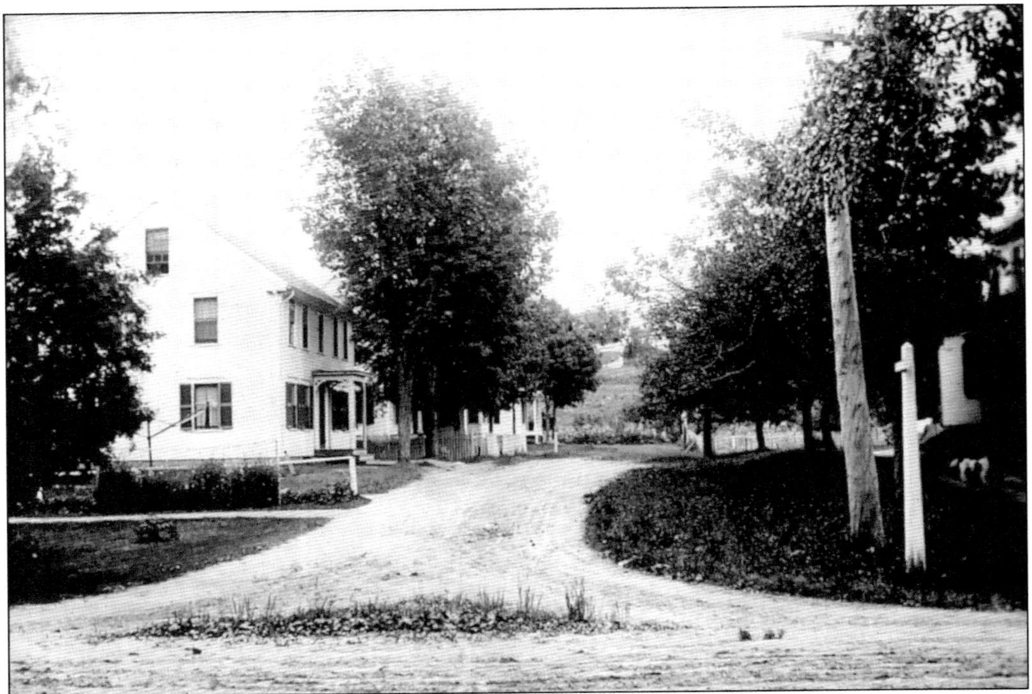

This view of Goodwin Street is looking east, just off Water Street. The Spiller family, of Spiller Axe Company fame, lived on Goodwin Street. It was at the end of the street that Walter Wyman leased waterpower from Benjamin and Allen Machine Works to create the Oakland Electric Light Company, which eventually became Central Maine Power Company.

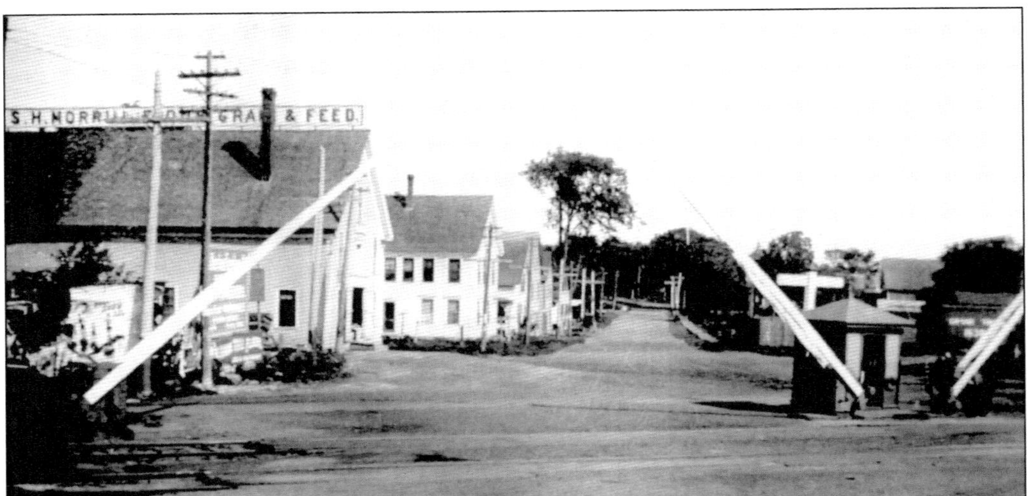

This is a view of Oak Street at the tracks, looking north toward High Street. An attendant lowered and raised the railroad gates until they were mechanized. Businesses here included the following: S. H. Morrill and Sons, which operated a grist mill from 1895 to 1903, sold lumber from 1899 to 1907, and sold fertilizers, flour, and grain from 1896 to 1904; and H. W. Greeley Company, which sold coal and wood from 1908 to 1931 and feed and flour in 1924. Across the street, Ayer & Greeley were in business from 1883 to 1920.

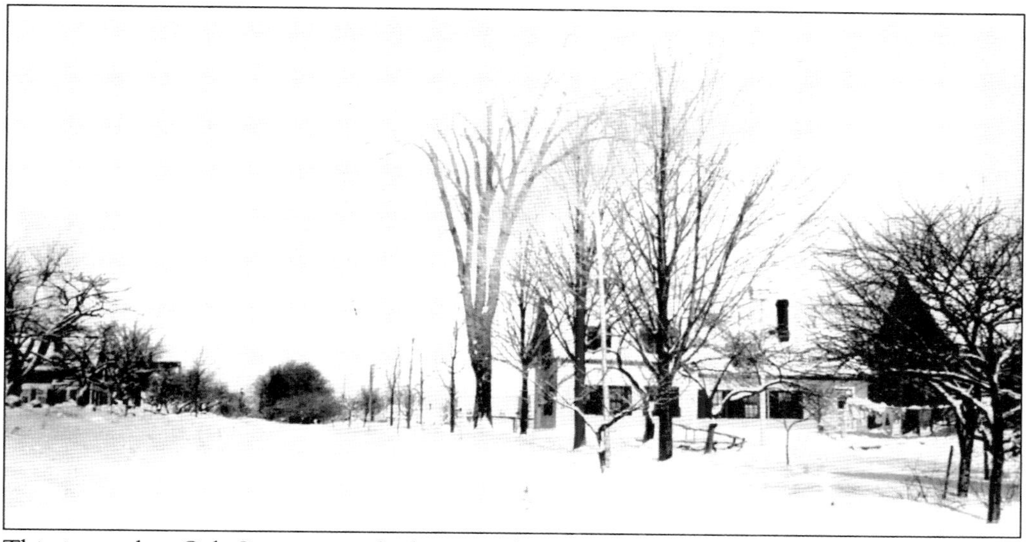

This is another Oak Street view, looking north. Today, the main driveway to Messalonskee High School is on the left just after the white house.

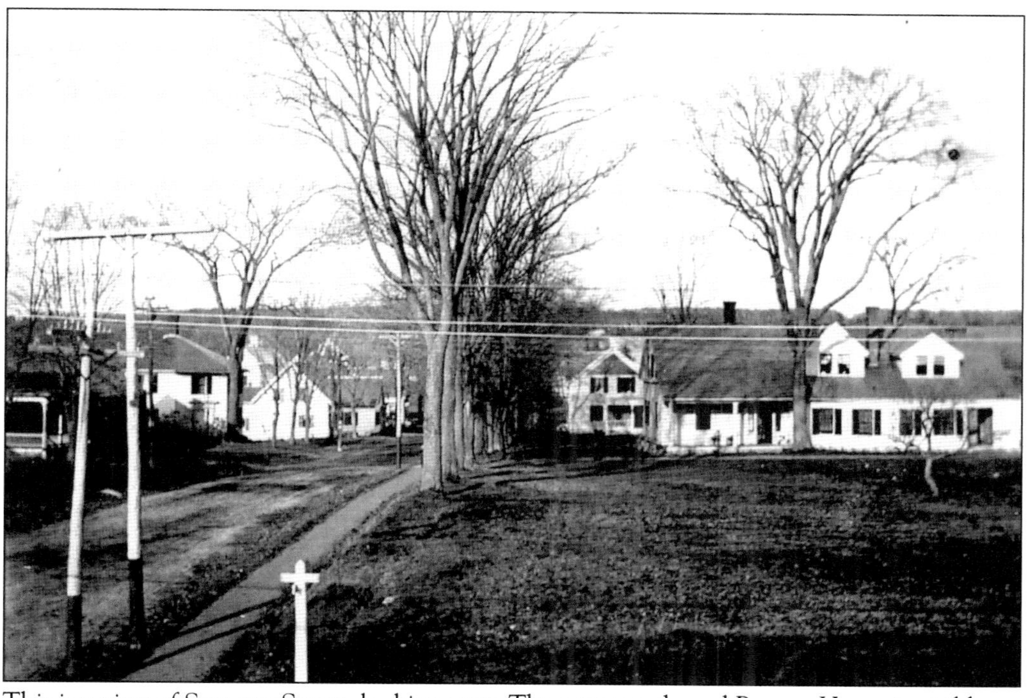

This is a view of Summer Street, looking west. The octagon-shaped Pressey House is visible on the left.

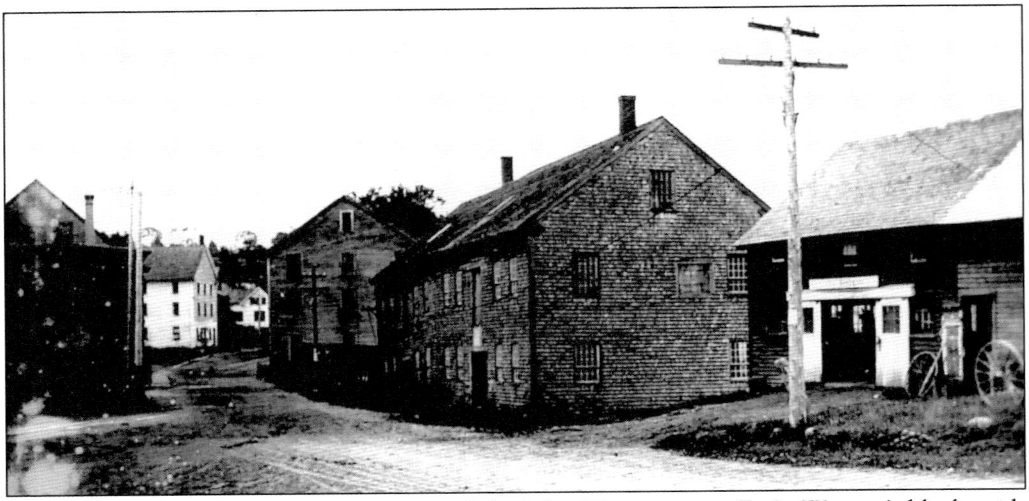

This is Summer Street, looking east toward the lake. The sign over E. A. Watson's blacksmith shop reads, "Horseshoeing." He was in business from 1892 to 1918. J. C. Holmes ran a blacksmith shop here from 1867 to 1886. Cyrus Wheeler told Louise Benson in 1918 that there were two bowling alleys, one down in the mill yards and one behind Holmes's shop. E. A. Watson's blacksmith business ran from 1892 to 1918. The third building was J. Bachelder & Son's Chair Factory from 1872 to 1903. The white building was Liberty Hall, built in 1850 by Cyrus Wheeler as a meeting place for pre–Civil War abolitionists. From c. 1870 to 1875, the building was a shirt factory under various names, including Farr's Shirt Factory. The Grange was organized in the building by Hiram Cornforth in 1875. On the left side was A. J. Libby's store, which opened in 1886 and sold flour and meal. It was later owned by Morrison Libby from 1896 to 1924 and sold fertilizers, hardware, and groceries.

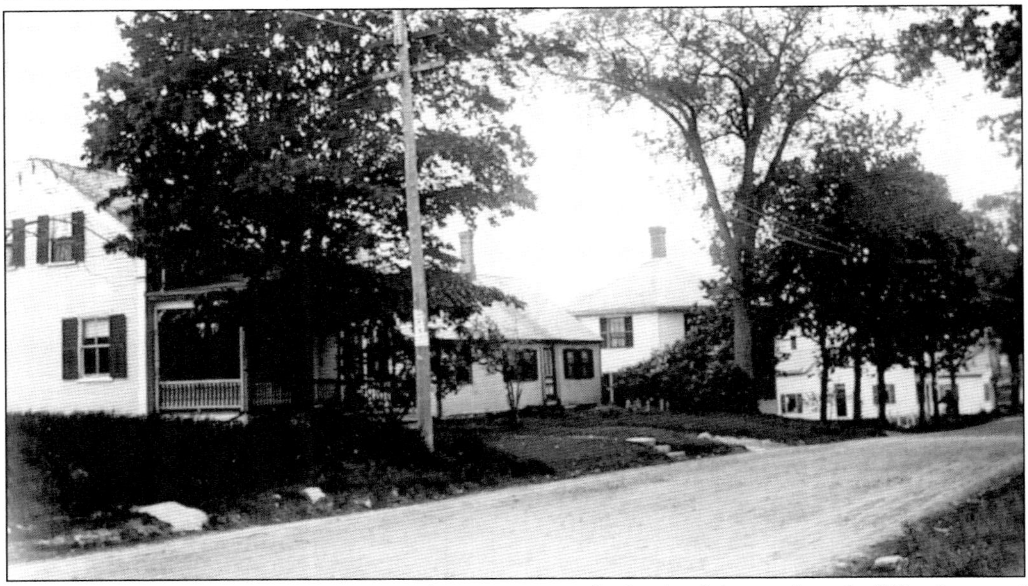

This is another Summer Street view. The caption on the back of the card reads, "The home of my dear friend Mabel (Mrs. C. A. Stevens) and her mother Mrs. Olive Bragg, is shown in this view—the pretty low house in the centre. And I think the oldest home in Oakland village. M.E.C." Also note the Pressey House in this view.

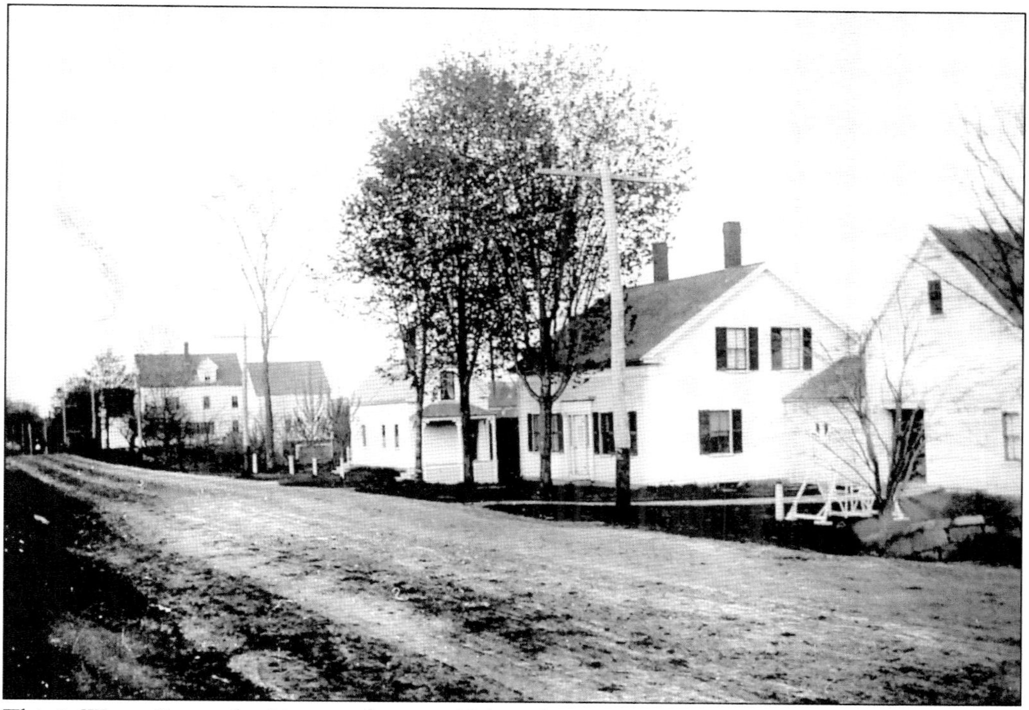

This is Water Street, looking north toward Main Street.

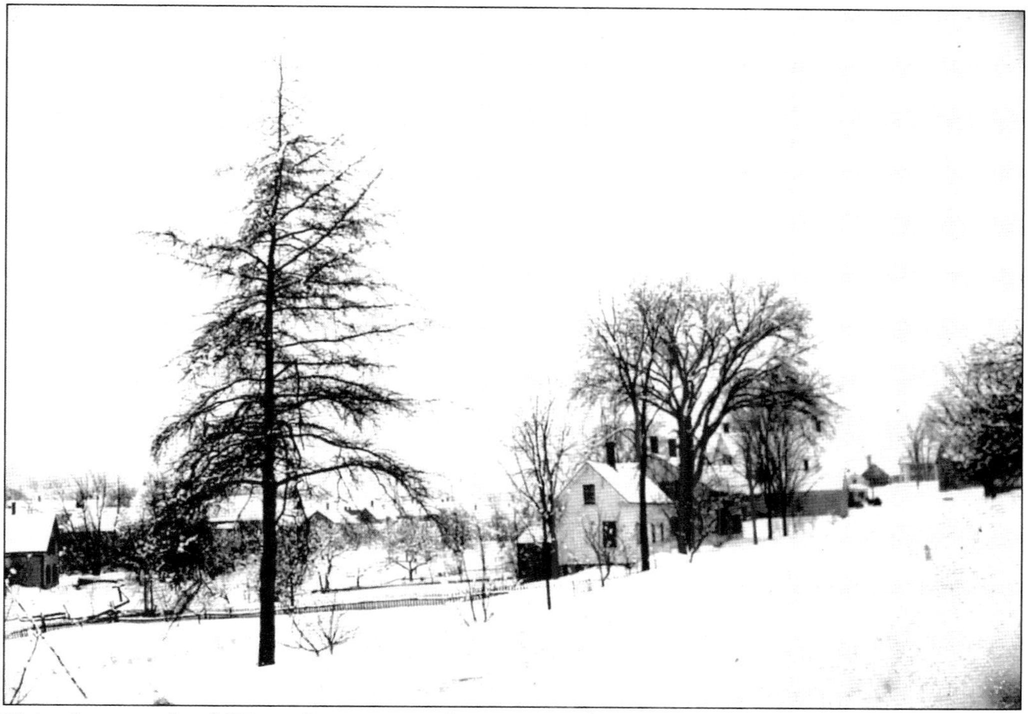

This photograph of Water Street was taken on March 4, 1901, and is looking south toward the lake.

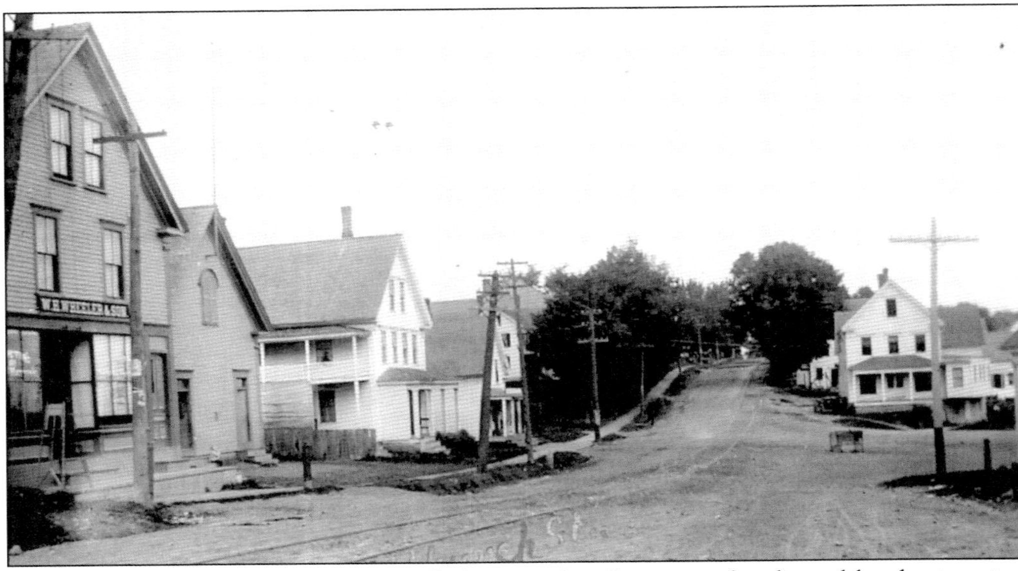

Winslow Square, seen here, is now called Haymarket Square, and is formed by the junction of Upper Church and Water Streets. Seen here, from left to right, are Wheeler's Furniture Store, the Upper Primary School, and George W. Boynton's house and store. The building on the right in the photograph (also seen on the left in the photograph below) was at the intersection of Water and Church Streets; it was the store of C. W. Folsom from 1876 to 1899. He sold hardware, stoves, and tinware, which was made on site. The building later housed the Messalonskee Clothing Company, which produced pants from 1903 to 1907.

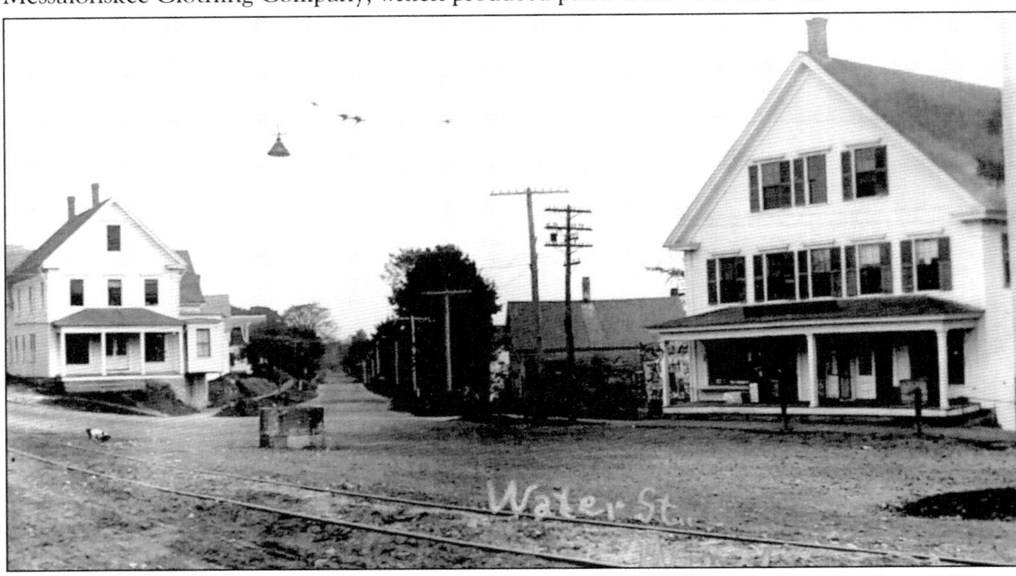

This is another view of Winslow Square. The caption reads, "This was taken in Oct. 1906 and shows a little of our street. Alice." Church Street is off to the left of the photograph, with Water Street going off in the distance, left of center. The horse watering trough is in the center of the square; though the trough is no longer there, a dip in the road indicates where it was, no matter how often the road is paved! The large white building on the right was Winslow's Store. A store has been on this site since *c.* 1820.

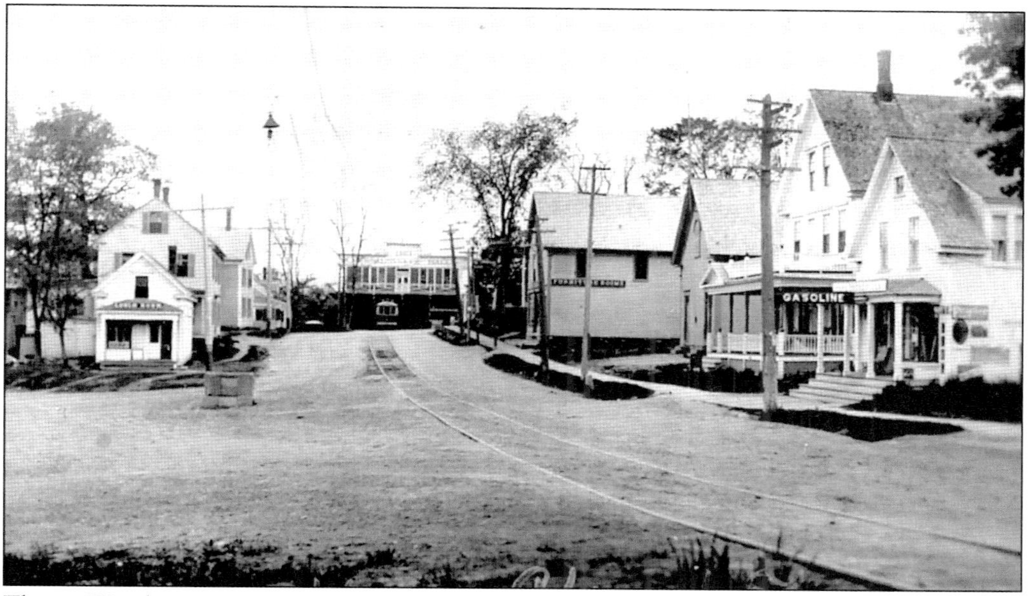

This is Winslow Square at Upper Church Street. Messalonskee Hall is in the distance, with Wheeler's, the Upper Primary School, and Boynton's to the right.

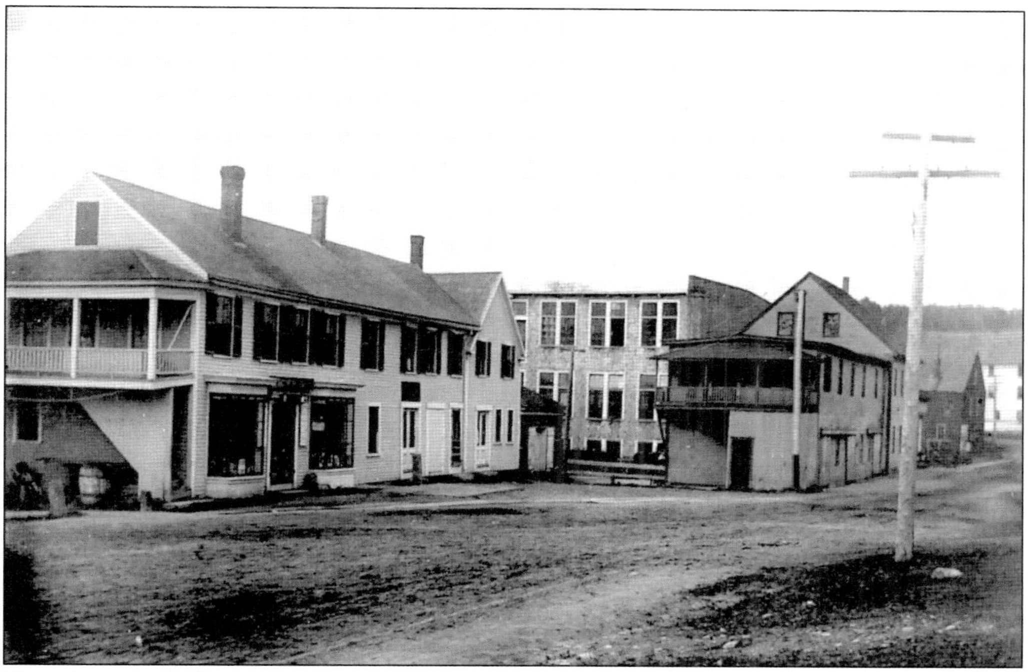

This photograph shows the Upper Mills. Manter's caption reads, "This is quite a good view but think I will try again some time." On the left is Morrison Libby's store and the Oakland Woolen Mill (the tall-windowed building). The white building in the distance across Messalonskee Stream was a shirt factory. Today, the Oakland Water Company and the Veterans of Foreign Wars post are located here, at the junction of Summer Street and Rutter Avenue.

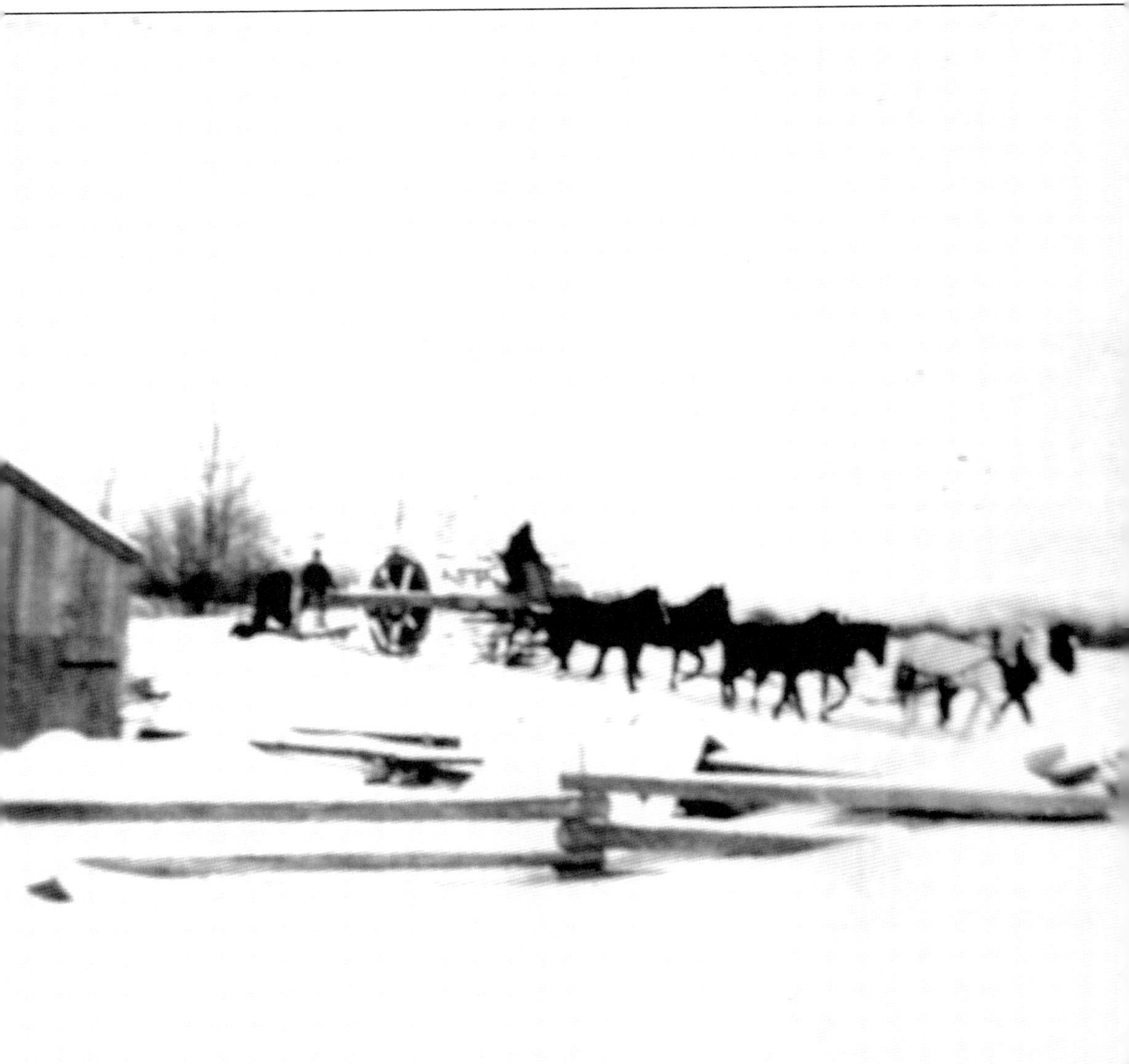

Before *c*. 1922, roads were not plowed; instead, the snow was packed down for sleighs. This unusual photograph is the only one known that shows Oakland's snow roller with three pairs of horses.

Seven

WATER

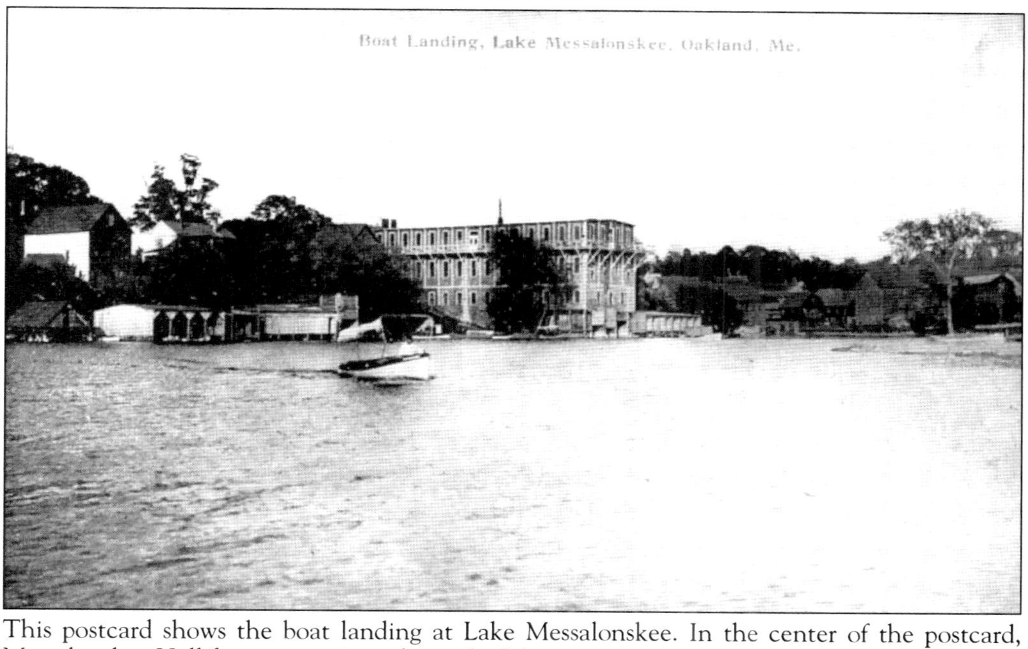

This postcard shows the boat landing at Lake Messalonskee. In the center of the postcard, Messalonskee Hall figures prominently on the lake.

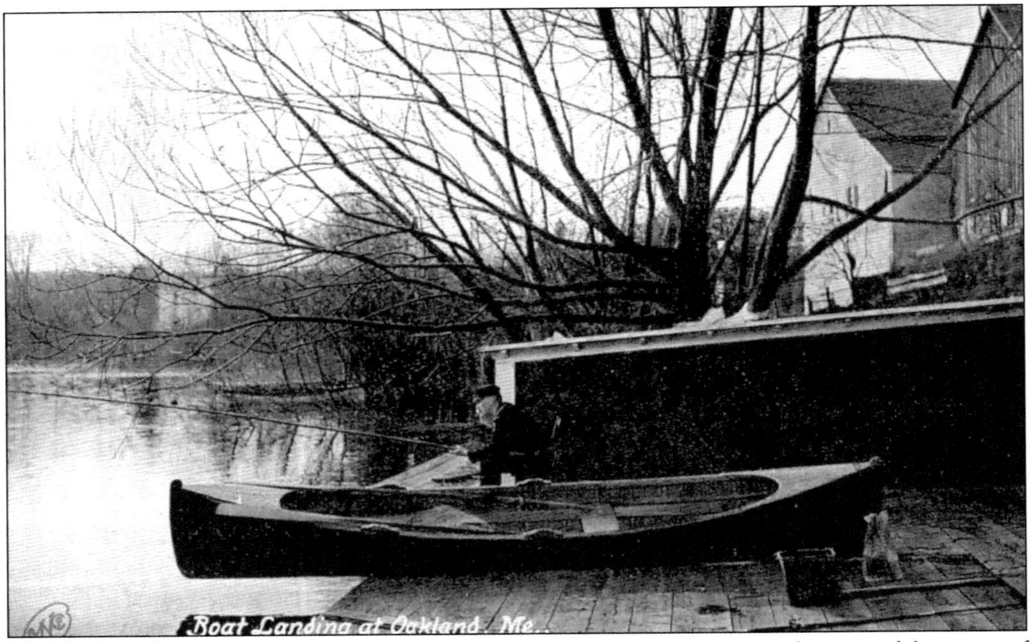

This classic postcard, frequently seen in auctions and shows, indicates the peaceful nature of Messalonskee Lake and some of the uses to which the lake is put.

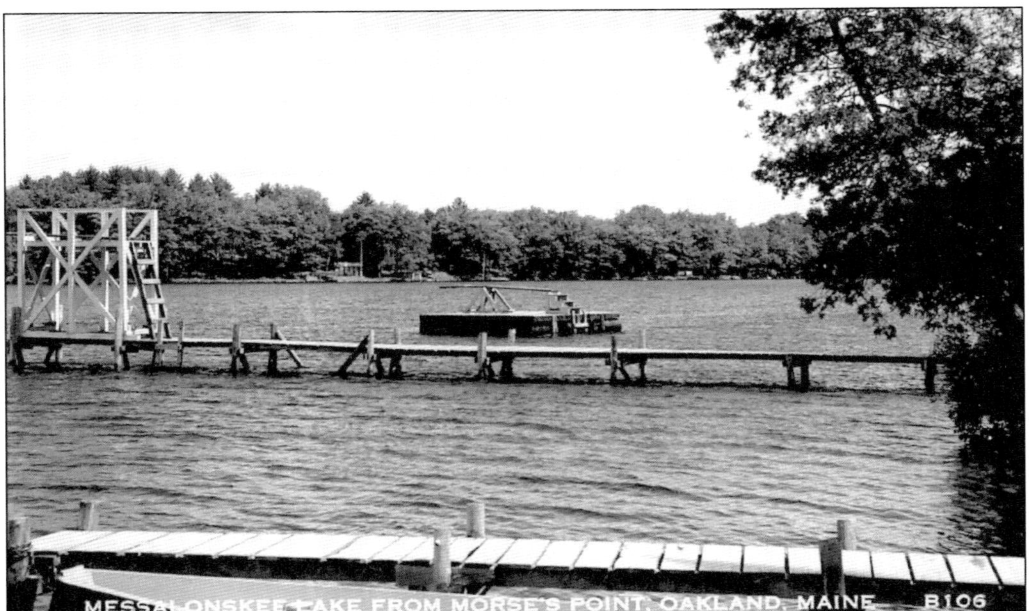

This is a view of Messalonskee Lake from Morse's Point c. 1950. Much of the shore land of Messalonskee Lake is taken up with summer and year-round homes today. Use of the lake for rest and recreation began in Oakland late in the 19th century.

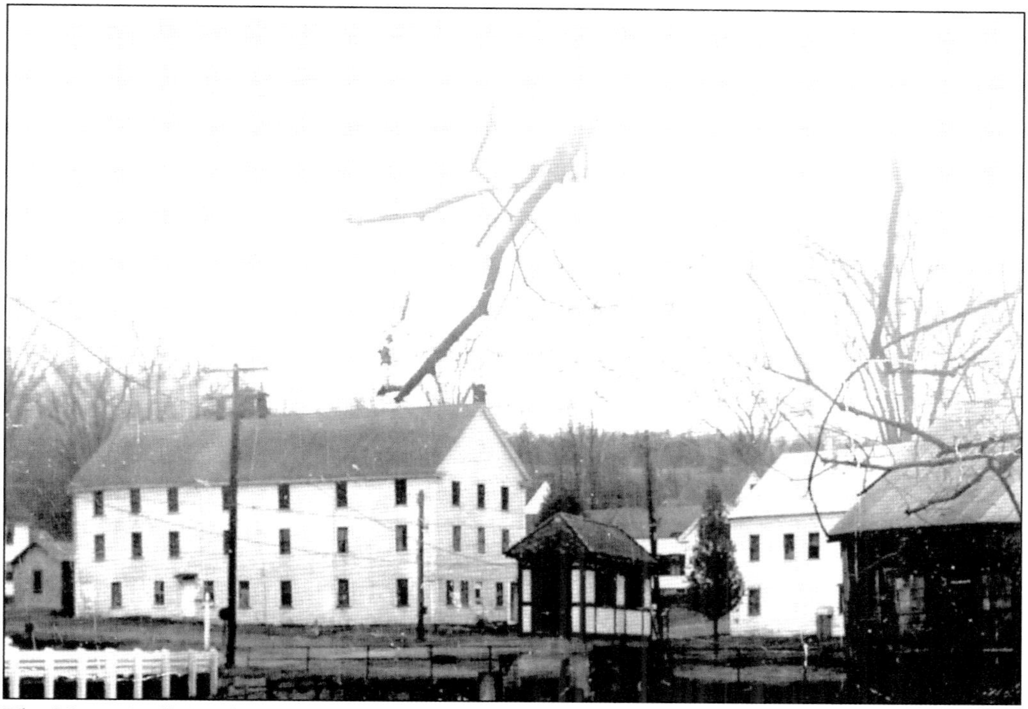

The Upper Mills Bridge is located at the intersection of Alpine and Summer Streets. The large white building on the left was first called Liberty Hall, built *c.* 1850 as an abolitionist's meeting place. By 1875, it housed the Cascade Grange and farmer's store, and by *c.* 1890 it was a shirt factory.

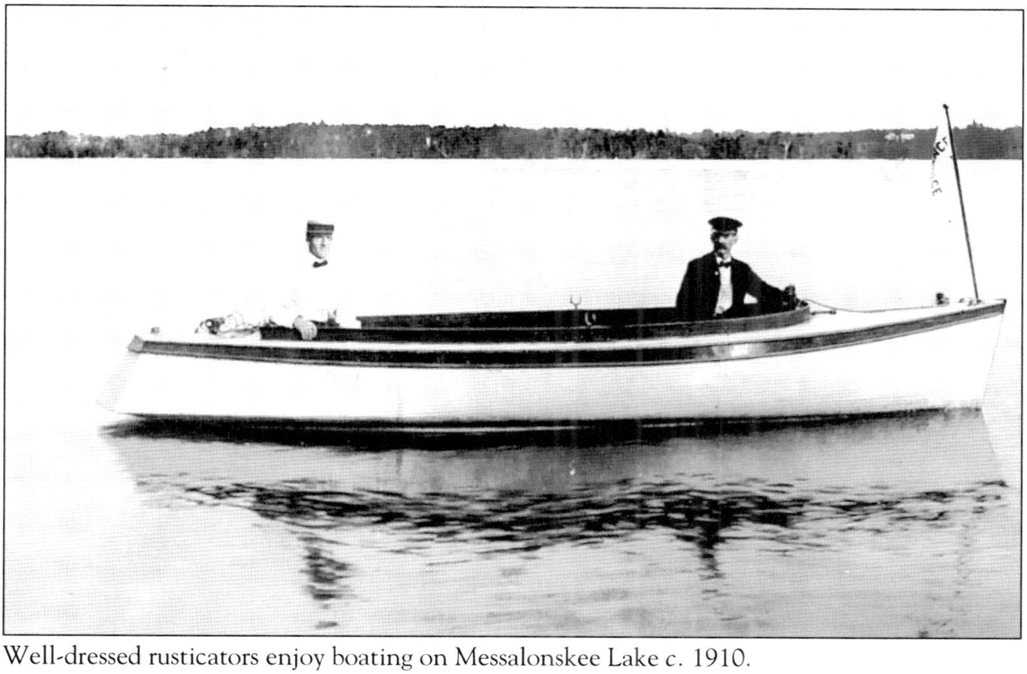

Well-dressed rusticators enjoy boating on Messalonskee Lake *c.* 1910.

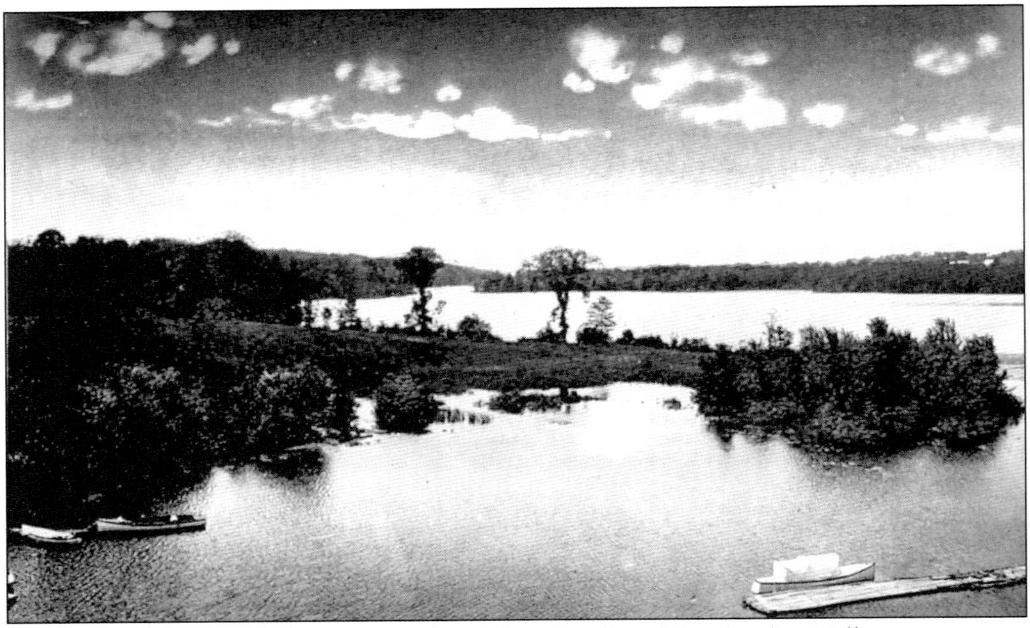

This postcard shows a bird's-eye view of the lake taken from Messalonskee Hall.

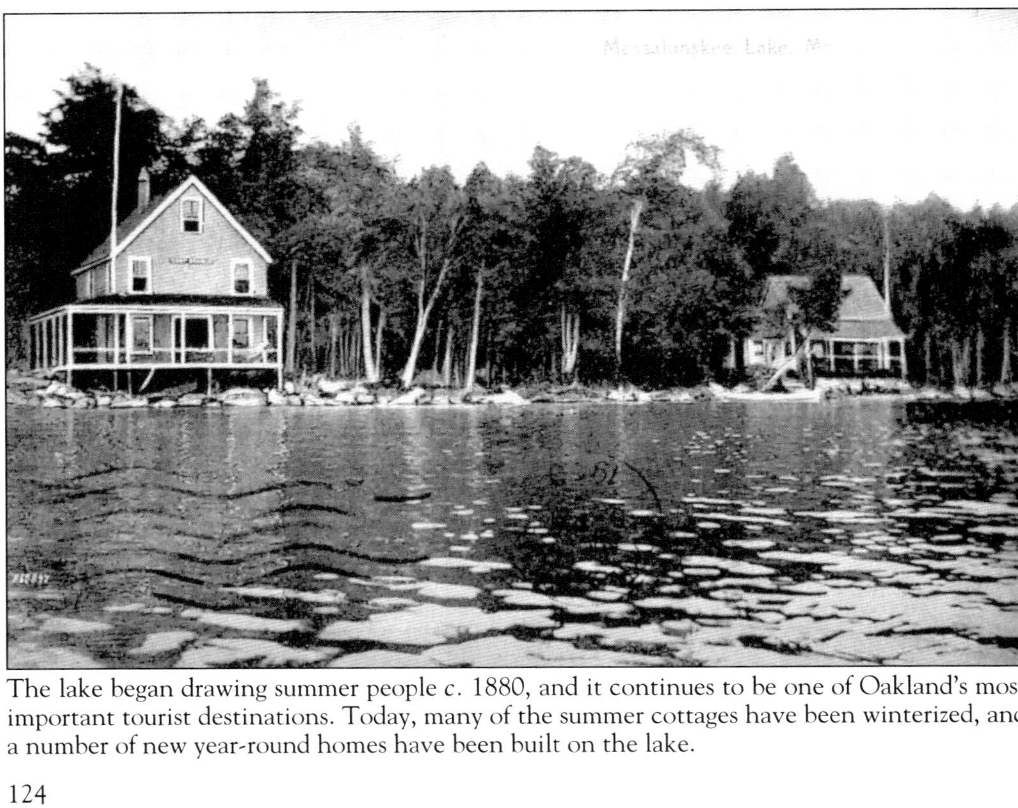

The lake began drawing summer people *c.* 1880, and it continues to be one of Oakland's most important tourist destinations. Today, many of the summer cottages have been winterized, and a number of new year-round homes have been built on the lake.

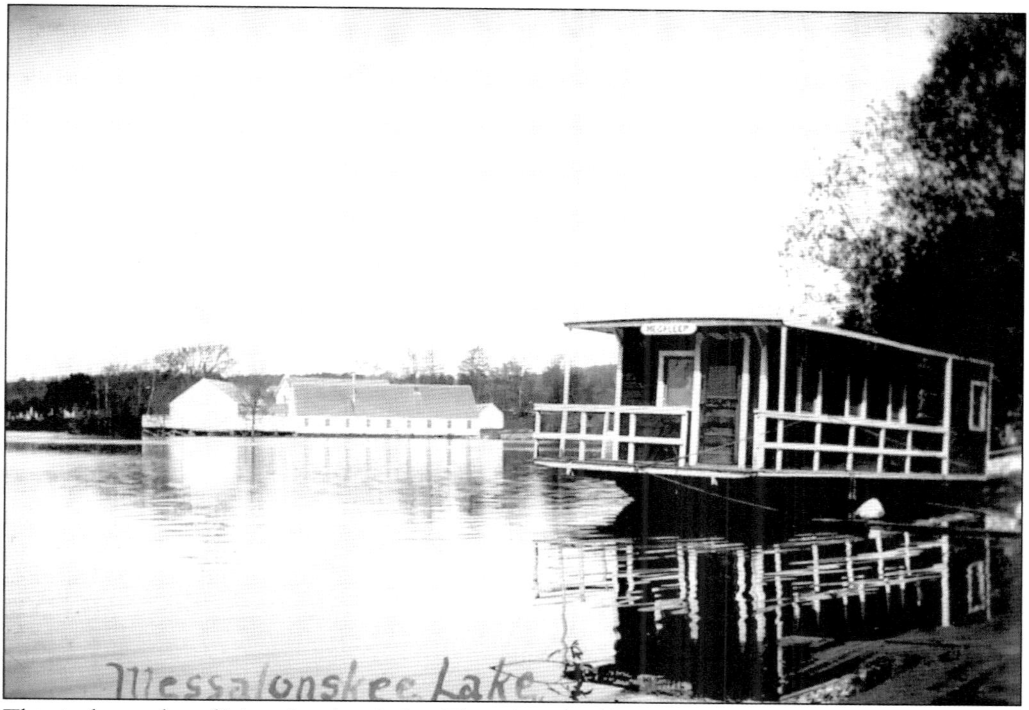

This is the outlet of Messalonskee Lake. The white buildings in the distance were those of the Portland Packing Company.

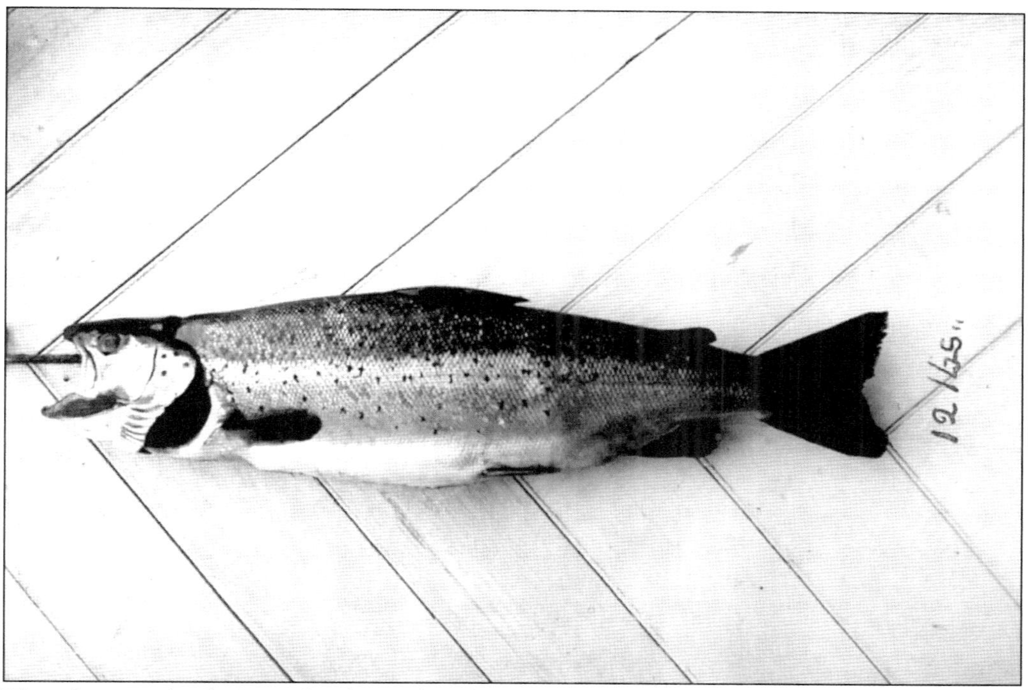

This photograph of a Messalonskee Lake salmon was copyrighted in 1908 by Alice A. Manter. Manter noted that the fish in the photograph weighed 12 pounds.

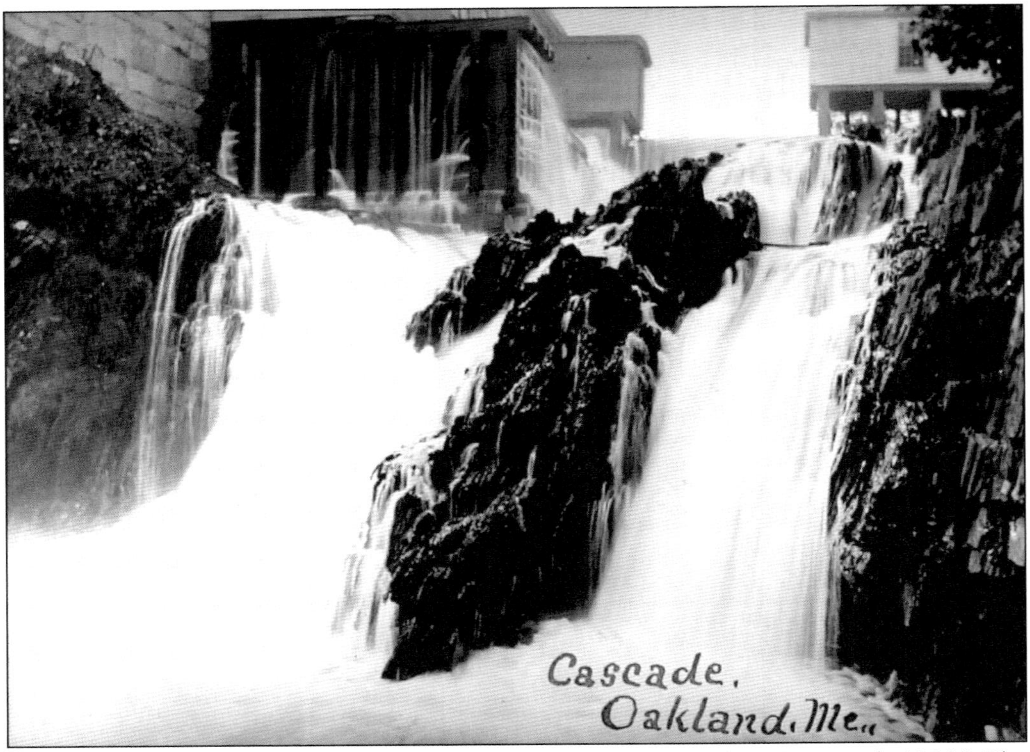

The caption on this postcard reads, "Birthday Greeting from Alice, Dec. 11th 1906." The Cascade was Oakland's main source of waterpower. With a fall of about 100 feet, it produced nearly as much waterpower as the Kennebec River did at the falls in Waterville.

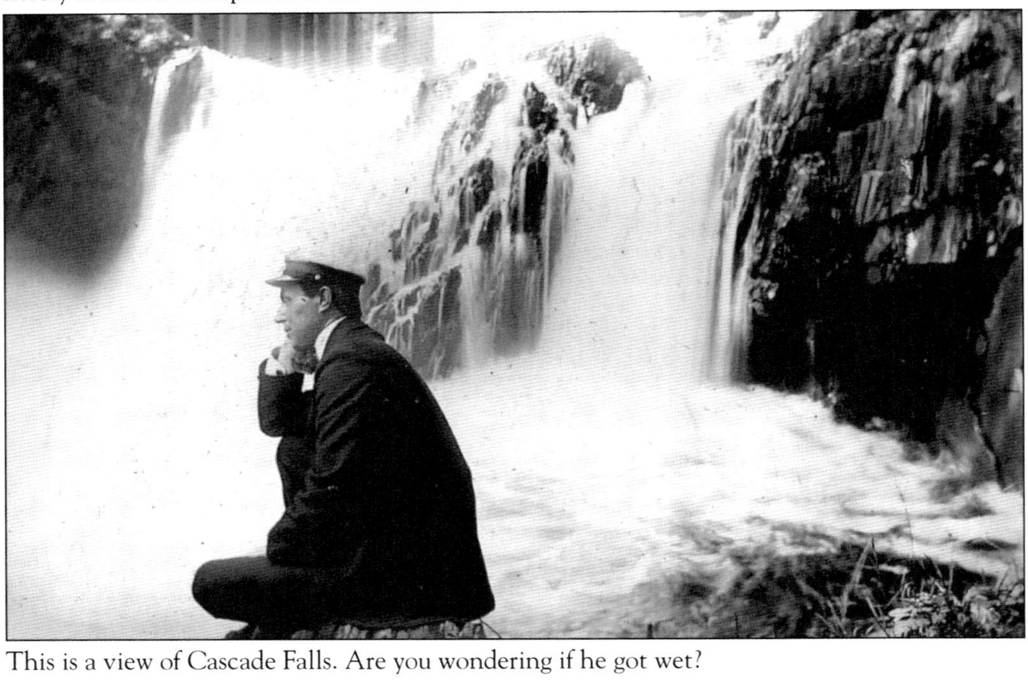

This is a view of Cascade Falls. Are you wondering if he got wet?

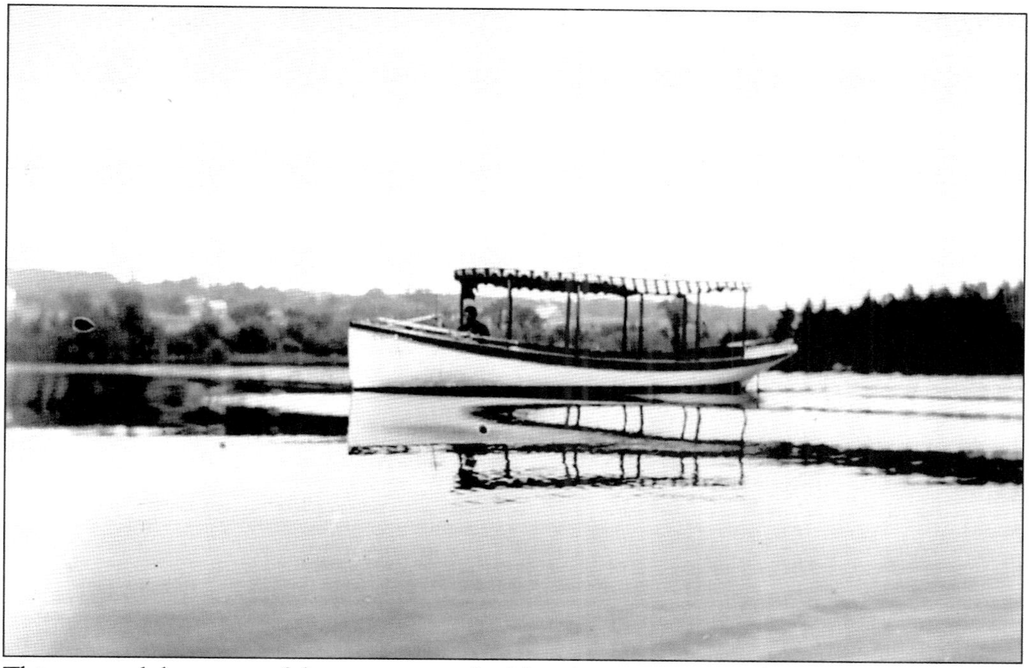

This postcard shows one of the steamers on the lake. At one time, state law said that any body of water large enough to support a steamboat could use the designation of lake rather than pond.

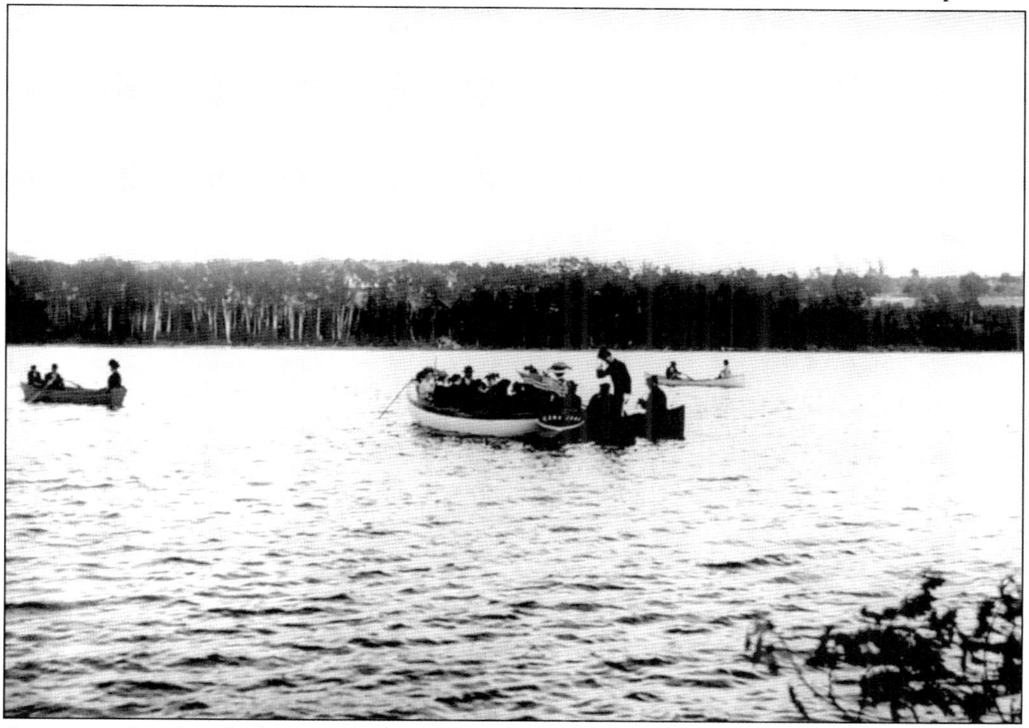

A note enclosed with this postcard in the Oakland Area Historical Society's collection says, "Same card of Alice Manter's at Oakland Library is dated 1910 (Memorial Day)."

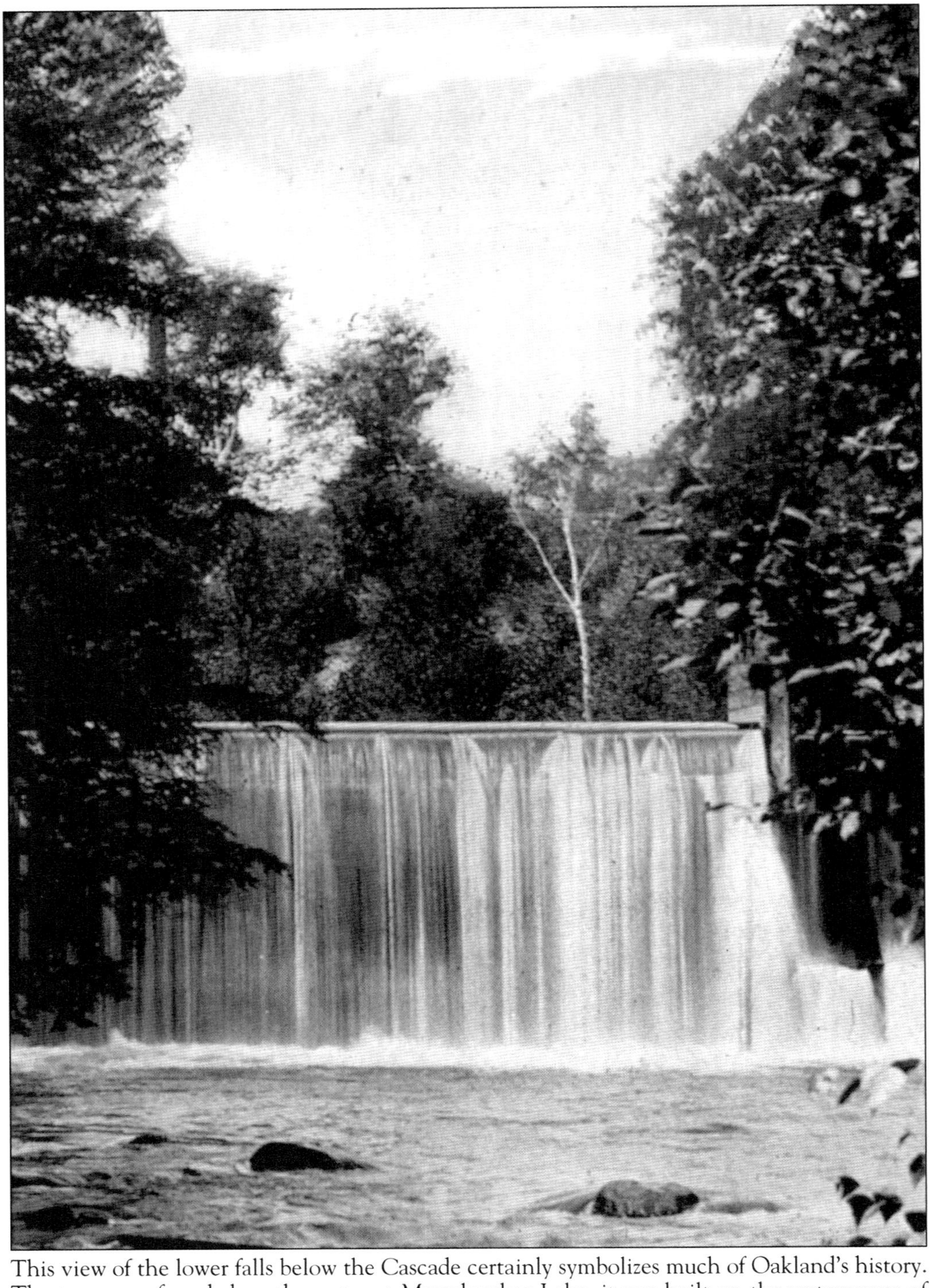

This view of the lower falls below the Cascade certainly symbolizes much of Oakland's history. The town was founded on the water at Messalonskee Lake, it was built on the waterpower of Messalonskee Stream, and water continues to nourish the financial and emotional health of the town.